# Working with
# Community Groups

INTERNATIONAL LIBRARY OF SOCIOLOGY
AND SOCIAL RECONSTRUCTION

Founded by Karl Mannheim
Editor W. J. H. Sprott

A catologue of books available in the INTERNATIONAL
LIBRARY OF SOCIOLOGY AND SOCIAL RECONSTRUCTION and
new books in preparation for the Library will be found at
the end of this volume

# Working with Community Groups

Using Community Development as a
Method of Social Work

BY

GEORGE W. GOETSCHIUS

A report of the development of a service
to housing estate community groups by the
London Council of Social Service, based on 15 years of field work
experience using the community development
approach and method.

LONDON

## ROUTLEDGE & KEGAN PAUL

NEW YORK: HUMANITIES PRESS

# CONTENTS

Preface                                        *page* xi

Introduction and Acknowledgments              xiii

CHAPTER 1          THE NECESSARY INFORMATION

THE GROUPS                                          1

*Characteristics*                                   1
*Work*                                              2
*Resources*                                         2
*Structure*                                         2
*Difficulties*                                      3
*Needs*                                             3
*Origin*                                            4
*Size and Numbers*                                  4
THE SERVICE                                         4
*Contacting the Groups*                             5
*Nature of the Service*                             5
*Role of the Worker and the Agency*                 6
*Approach and Method*                               7
DEVELOPMENT OF THE SERVICE                          7
*Phase 1*                                           7
*Phase 2*                                           8
*Phase 3*                                           8
*Summary of Phases*                                 8
THE WORKING DEFINITIONS                             9
*'Community'*                                       9
*'Community Group'*                                10
*'The Field-Work Process' in Community*
*Development*                                      10
SOURCES OF INFORMATION                             12

CHAPTER 2          THE FACTORS AFFECTING THE
                   DEVELOPMENT OF THE SERVICE

BEGINNING WORK IN THE FIELD                        13

*Problems of Settling In*                          13
*Starting the Work*                                14
*A Basic Policy*                                   15

THE NEEDS OF THE GROUPS 16
*Autonomy* 16
*Identity* 17
*Individuality* 19
*The Basic Need* 20
THE PROBLEMS OF THE GROUPS 20
*Committee Work* 20
*Finance* 21
*Public Relations* 23
*Sharing the Work* 23
*Involving Residents* 24
*Establishing Procedures* 25
CONCLUSION 25

CHAPTER 3    THE FURTHER DEVELOPMENT
OF THE SERVICE

INTER-GROUP WORK 26
*Week-end Conferences* 27
*Inter-estate Discussions* 29
*Reasons for Failure* 31
THE GROUPS BEGIN TO SERVICE
THEMSELVES 32
*The Association of London Housing*
*Estates* 32
*Club-room Courses* 34
*Working out a Common Problem* 38
*Conference on Work with Old People* 38
*Two Results of the Conference* 44
ATTEMPTS IN OTHER SETTINGS 44
*A Deteriorating Neighbourhood* 44
*Comment* 47
*Work with Immigrant Groups* 48
*Comment* 52

CHAPTER 4    EXAMPLES OF FIELD-WORK
PRACTICE: PAISLEY COMMON AS
A REPRESENTATIVE COMMUNITY
GROUP

*The Tenants' Association* 53

*Programme of Activities*    54
*A Chronological Account*    58
*Summary*    69

SIX TYPICAL EXAMPLES OF
HELPING A GROUP    71

(1) *Identifying a Social Welfare Need*    71
(2) *Establishing Priorities*    74
(3) *Working out a Crisis*    77
(4) *Self-evaluation*    80
(5) *Finding and Using Resources*    83
(6) *Encouraging Co-operation*    85

CHAPTER 5    THE ROLE OF THE WORKER:
SKILLS AND TECHNIQUES

THE ROLE OF THE WORKER    90

*Giving Information*    90
*Passing on Skills*    91
*Acting as Go-Between*    92
*Direct Aid*    95
*Encouragement and Support*    95

THE FUNDAMENTALS OF THE
FIELD-WORK PROCESS    98

*Communication*    98
*Interpretation*    101
*Evaluation*    106

RECORDING    111

*Observation, Awareness and Recording*    111
*A System of Recording*    116

CHAPTER 6    CONDITIONS OF FIELD-WORK
PRACTICE

FACTORS AFFECTING THE DEVELOP-
MENT OF THE GROUPS    129

*Location, Size and Age of Estate*    129
*Amenities*    130
*Club-room or Meeting Place*    131
*Social Origins and Social Attitudes*    131
*Leadership*    132
*The Wider Context*    134

THE STAGES OF GROUP DEVELOPMENT  135

(1) *The Starting Point*  135
(2) *Exploration*  136
(3) *Formation*  136
(4) *Development of Programme*  137
(5) *The Established Association*  138
(6) *Integration with the Wider Community*  139

DIFFICULTIES OF THE WORKER
AND THE AGENCY  143

*The Worker*  143
*The Agency*  145
*Values and Standards*  149

CHAPTER 7    FURTHER CONSIDERATIONS
AND CONCLUSIONS

CONTINUED WORK RELATING TO HOUSING
ESTATES  151

*Services to Problem Families*  151
*Services to Autonomous Groups
    in the Wider Community*  152
*Possibility of Working with more than
    One Organisation on the Same Estate*  153
*Need to Extend and Enrich the Pro-
    gramme Offered by the Groups to
    their Members*  154
*Provision of Trained Indigenous Leaders
    for Work Outside their own Immediate
    Locality*  154
*Possibility of Sharing In-service Training
    with Staff Members of Statutory and
    Voluntary Bodies*  155
*Relations with the Wider Community*  155

SPECIAL FIELD-WORK ENQUIRIES
IN OTHER SETTINGS  156

*Community Care for Mental Health*  156

COMPARATIVE STUDIES  157

*Community Groups not on Housing
    Estates*  157
*Social Work on Adult Education: the
    most Appropriate Sponsoring Body*  159
*Experience in New Towns and Overseas*  160

THEORETICAL STUDY 160

PROFESSIONAL TRAINING 161

*New Perspectives* 161
*Students* 163
*A Suggested Training Course in*
    *Community Work* 164

COMMUNITY DEVELOPMENT
AS A METHOD OF SOCIAL WORK 168

*The Helping Process* 170
*The Role of the Worker* 173
*A Working Description* 176
*Community Development and*
    *Other Methods of Social Work* 178
*Comparison of Community Organisation*
    *and Community Development* 182

CONCLUSION 184

APPENDICES 187
ANNOTATED BIBLIOGRAPHY 227
SELECTED BIBLIOGRAPHY 236
INDEX 245

# PREFACE

Nothing is static about the social services. In some fields the need for social action is diminishing, in others it is increasing. Overall, there has been a vast development in the past twenty years, although pockets of resistance persist. New problems arise every year. No sooner do we begin to perfect our techniques in one direction than the need arises for us to apply greater pressure on another front.

It is not surprising, therefore, to find at the present time a noticeable change in emphasis in the methods of social work away from the casework approach with its great concern for the individual to the community work approach with its concern for adjusting the physical and social environment to satisfy the needs of the individual who lives in it.

This report by Mr. Goetschius for the London Council of Social Service is a valuable contribution to present thinking because it is soundly based on study of practical work in the field. Indeed the examples of field-work practice are so interesting and so realistic that one might be forgiven for overlooking the warning he gives that for reasons of confidentiality names have been disguised and field-work situations merged into single representative records.

The report will be invaluable to students of social work and all who work with adults and young people in the community. Indeed, its timely arrival will be welcomed by all who are concerned with the social problems of our contemporary society.

J. K. OWENS

*Director, National Council of Social Service*
April 1968

# INTRODUCTION AND
# ACKNOWLEDGMENTS

In 1950 there were 185,000 families on the then London County Council housing waiting list. Some came from a settled environment with a tightly knit network of street and neighbourhood life; others had been in the Forces, had been moved for the period of the war, or had lived with relatives, and as a result had not had a home of their own before. They all had housing need, and the local authorities operated a points scheme to ensure that those in the greatest need were given priority. As a result it was families with young children who went to live in the new L.C.C. flats which were being built all over London with a sense of urgency.

The London Council of Social Service, through a fairly comprehensive network of committees, acted as a link between voluntary organisations in London, and regarded it as one of its functions to attempt to meet new social needs as they arose. This was sometimes done through the voluntary organisations who were members of their Council, and sometimes by new experimental work of their own, or by reference to the local authority.

The Community Centres Department had always had a special concern for the social needs of people living in newly developed housing areas. This took the form in the pre-war years of promoting Community Associations[1] and centres on the L.C.C. cottage estates at places on the periphery of Greater London such as Downham and St. Helier. From 1946 to 1949 the emphasis was on social provision on the new 'out-county' estates being built by the L.C.C. farther afield at places such as Oxhey, Harold Hill and St. Pauls Cray.

In 1949 the Housing and Education Departments of the L.C.C. made a grant to the London Council of Social Service to enable it to employ two workers instead of one in their small Community Centres Department. The work which is the subject of this enquiry began then and still continues today. Mrs. Muriel Smith, whose training was in social work and youth work, became responsible for the Community Centres Department and was later joined by Mrs. Jill Wiltshire, whose special skills were in working with children and the planning of community centre activities. With the new grants from the L.C.C., interest was focused on inner London, although for some years work still continued on the out-county estates. This was gradually replaced either by the help given to associations through the National Federation of Community Associations or by the Education Authority in the county in which the estate was situated.

[1] See Appendix II.

At this stage the objectives of the Department might still have been stated as 'to promote and help community associations and persuade local authorities to build community centres under the Education Act 1944 or the Physical Training and Recreation Act 1937.'

The promotional work proved very difficult in inner London. The Education Authority regarded provision of evening institutes, with an excellent range of formal classes and at least some informal social activities, as their primary contribution to adult education. The Ministry of Education operated a stop-go policy of grant aid. Land was expensive and difficult to acquire, and building materials in short supply. Nor was there any spontaneous demand for Community Centres, as there had been, for example, on some of the large cottage estates referred to previously. Community Centres as envisaged in the Ministry of Education redbook were not promoted in central London.[1] There were one or two exceptions, such as the provision by the Westminster City Council of the Abbey Community Centre, after the appointment of a full-time worker to make a survey, and the rebuilding of a centre by a voluntary committee in North Kensington.

The grant to the London Council of Social Service from the L.C.C. Housing Department coincided with a new L.C.C. policy of providing tenants' club-rooms, or common rooms as they were sometimes called, under the 1936 Housing Act. These small buildings consisted of a single communal room, a kitchen, cloakrooms and storage space. They were regarded as a necessary amenity for people living in flats. There were tenants' associations or social clubs functioning in some of the new developments, which were anxious to have a meeting place of their own. While the Housing Department had developed reasonably good relationships with some of these bodies, established voluntary organisations in the neighbourhood tended to regard them either as militant anti-landlord organisations 'out to make trouble', or 'merely' social clubs running children's parties and outings in the summer.

Three of the first community group meetings in post-war blocks of flats with which the workers came into contact were in Finsbury, Lewisham and Westminster, and eighteen years later all three are still in existence. It became the practice, when the L.C.C. completed a club-room at the same time as the estate was being built, to inform the London Council of Social Service. The workers then made some enquiry as to whether a tenants' association was already being formed. This was often the case, but if not, the worker took some initiative in finding out whether the residents wished to have the use of the building for their social and other activities.

[1] *Community Centres* (H.M.S.O., 1946).

Residents were under no compulsion to take responsibility for the building: it was explained that it could easily be used for other purposes by the authority, but that it was often easier to build the club-room at the same time as the estate. In fact in fifteen years there was only one estate known to the London Council of Social Service which did not wish to form an association: this was partly due to the design of the club-room, which was incorporated in a block of flats in such a way that the residents were apprehensive that there would be too much noise.

In fact many associations were formed which did not have accommodation of their own. On the older estates they often had to wait for several years before getting a club-room. On new estates it depended on current Government policy whether the authority could get loan sanction to build. It was found that some of the smaller club-rooms were not easily maintained and proved too expensive for the users, and eventually it became accepted practice not to provide one unless there were some 400 or more dwellings (the figure changed from time to time) or unless the estate was very isolated.

The tenants were expected to sign a tenancy agreement to pay rent and all their own running expenses, and they were then free to use the hall as they wished. Gambling and the sale of intoxicants were not allowed, however. They could let the club-room for weddings and parties to residents on the estate and to non-profit-making organisations, although the Housing Authority retained some minor controls over letting of this kind. The rents charged were originally on a sliding scale beginning at something like 10s. or £1 a week, depending on the size of the estate, and rising to half the economic rent. Over the years, as building became more expensive, rents of £5 and £6 a week, plus heating, lighting and rates, became too heavy for many associations, and for this and other reasons the L.C.C. changed its policy and asked each association to pay a token rent including rates of 10s. a week. The association still had to pay all other costs. Some of the then Metropolitan Borough Councils also provided club-rooms for their tenants, and in Hackney the authority employed its own welfare worker to assist associations.

If there was little spontaneous demand for social activities and overt neighbourhood co-operation in some of the old-established districts of London, there was in the new blocks of flats abundant and sometimes chaotic activity. Resources in personnel and finance in the then Community Centres Department of the London Council of Social Service were small. The need seemed greatest in these community groups, and so the Council began to offer their services to help newly formed committees, which lacked professional or experienced leadership of any kind, to achieve the objectives they had set themselves. For the most part these objectives seemed admirable: the improvement of physical conditions on the estate, the encouragement of friendly relationships between neighbours, the provision of social and other activities for people of all ages, the management of their own club-room where there was one (the search for rooms and halls for hire where there was not), and some consideration of special problems such as the needs of old people or young mothers. Most of the residents were families with young children, and it seemed to the London Council of Social Service more important to provide the type of services which would help these young families to meet their own needs most effectively, than to use their limited resources in any other way. In these early days groups were not known to one another, and yet it was surprising to find how far spontaneous development took an almost identical form on the different estates.

The workers soon discovered that if they were to be of real help it had to be on the group's terms and not on theirs. It was no good offering the model constitution for a Community Association if this required the tenants' association to ask the well established voluntary organisations in the district outside the estate to affiliate to them. The tenants were newcomers, and their organisation represented people with common interests. They were tenants of the same landlord and they had problems in common. They needed to feel more at home and secure in their new environment before they went outside. They had quite enough to do within their own community.

The flats were built at net residential densities of anything between 100 and 200 persons to the acre, so that a large population was housed in a small geographic area. For this reason, unlike the cottage estates, which were much more spread out, local branches of national voluntary organisations were not usually formed within the boundaries of the estate. In many instances it was easy to go off the estate to join the local branch of a political party, a church activity or the evening institute if people already had well developed interests; or to take membership in some voluntary organisation such as the British Red Cross, the Townswomen's Guild or the local history society. However, relatively few people had ever been members of such organisations before. Thus the particular circumstances of living in flats were a determining factor in the need for a structure of organisation based on family membership, which was in some ways different from that of a Community Association.

In 1955 Miss Ilys Booker, a Canadian, joined the staff. Her experience had been in adult education. A year later, at a conference held at Wansfell Adult Education College in Essex, some of the community groups suggested that they should have an organisation of their own, and she was quick to see the opportunities this would offer for training and inter-estate activity.

xvi

In 1957 a new stage of development was reached when the Standing Conference of Housing Estate Community Groups came into being. The London Council of Social Service provided the secretariat and Miss Ilys Booker became the first Organising Secretary. This organisation is now known as the Association of London Housing Estates and is generally referred to by that name throughout the book. The Association has a separate office, makes its own policy and is in the process of becoming financially independent of the L.C.S.S.

Since Miss Booker it has had three Organising Secretaries: Mrs. Powell (née Susan Whetman), who had studied history and had gained administrative experience with the National Council of Social Service; Mr. Graham Riches, who was an anthropologist with training in social administration and community development; and the present Organising Secretary, Mr. Nicholas Derricourt, who took the Community Development course at Manchester University after studying history and social administration. There is now an office manager, Mr. Michael Robson.

At one time the organisation itself was able to employ two youth advisers on special grants, Miss L. Montford and Mr. G. Williams. Miss Montford subsequently became a permanent member of the staff as a community development field worker with special reference to youth, and was succeeded by Miss Elizabeth Cohen.

The work was financed from the voluntary funds of the London Council of Social Service and by generous grants from the London County Council. With the reorganisation of local government, grant aid continued and the work was supported by the Housing Committee of the Greater London Council and the Inner London Education Authority. The Association of London Housing Estates also has its own voluntary funds.

As the work of the Community Development Department (ex Community Centres Department) of the London Council of Social Service developed and the Association of London Housing Estates offered more help to its members, colleagues in other fields of social work and students in training began to ask for detailed information. In consequence through the generosity of the Gulbenkian Foundation the London Council of Social Service was able to employ Mr. Goetschius, already acting in a voluntary capacity as consultant, to write a report on the field work. Members of the Association of London Housing Estates who read this report may wonder why there has been more emphasis on the difficulties encountered than the success achieved. This is because, presented in this way, the material may be of more use to students of social work.

*Acknowledgments*

The consultant would like to acknowledge the help given to him by many colleagues and friends. Because of the obligation to maintain confidentiality about people and groups, the names of the field workers will not be used in the main body of the report. The same applies to officers of local statutory and voluntary bodies. Unfortunately, and for the same reason, the officers and other volunteers in the community groups, whose work this report describes, must also remain anonymous. References to housing estates include those of London Boroughs and the Greater London Council, and also housing developments sponsored by private trusts.

The present members of the Committee of the Community Development Department are as follows:

| | |
|---|---|
| Dr. J. H. Nicholson, C.B.E. (Chairman) | Formerly Vice-Chancellor, University of Hull. |
| Dr. T. R. Batten | Reader in Community Development Studies, University of London Institute of Education. |
| Miss I. Booker | North Kensington Family Project Study. |
| Mr. John Hayes | Representative of the Association of London Housing Estates. |
| Mr. Peter Hodge | Lecturer in Social Administration, London School of Economics. |
| Mr. George Mitchell, C.B.E. | A Vice-President of the London Council of Social Service. |
| Mr. K. M. Reinold | Secretary, National Federation of Community Associations. |
| Prof. E. Wedell | Professor of Adult Education, Manchester University. |
| Mr. Peter Willmott | Institute of Community Studies. |
| Mr. P. Winterforde-Young | Chairman Inner London Standing Committee of Voluntary Youth Organisations. |
| Administration:— | |
| Miss K. Proud | General Secretary, London Council of Social Service. |
| Mrs. M. Smith, M.B.E. | Secretary to the Committee. |

When the work on the report started in 1960, the Chairman of the Committee was the late Mr. A. Sanderson, at the time Secretary of the Gulbenkian Foundation in the United Kingdom. Other members of the Committee included the late Mr. Frank Milligan, at that time Secretary of the National Federation of Community Associations, and Mr. Peter Kuenstler, now working with UNESCO in Geneva.

The present form of this report owes much to the editing and in some places extensive re-writing by Mrs. Frances Glendenning, part-time tutor in the Department of Extra-mural Studies of the University of London. The consultant would like to thank Mrs. B. Evans, of the London Area Office, Y.W.C.A., Mrs. Monica Hamilton, of the London Council of Social Service, Mrs. Sheila Llewellyn, of the London Area Office, Y.W.C.A., and Mrs. M. Saunders, of the London Council of Social Service for help with the manuscript. Also Mr. R. Johannes, J.P., for App. Ic.

The consultant would also like to acknowledge the help, before and during his work with the London Council of Social Service, of the members of the Committee and:

Miss Anne Bailey, London and South East Area of the Y.W.C.A.

Dr. Gerald Breece, Bureau of Urban Research, Princeton University.

Dr. Ensminger, of the Ford Foundation, Delhi.

Mr. Robin Guthrie, of Cambridge House, London.

Mr. Donald Howarth, playwright.

Mrs. Elizabeth Irvine, Reader in Social Work, York University.

Mr. David Jones, O.B.E., of the National Institute of Social Work Training, London.

Miss Sheila Lever, Assistant Secretary, London Council of Social Service.

Miss Elisabeth Littlejohn, J.P., of the National Council of Social Service.

Dr. James Mallon (deceased), of Toynbee Hall, London.

Mr. Richard Mills, Gulbenkian Foundation (U.K.)

Mr. Michael Power, Social Medicine Research Unit of the Medical Research Council, The London Hospital.

Although the field staff and the Committee participated in the enquiry, the form and content of this report are the responsibility of the consultant, and the views expressed are not necessarily those of the London Council of Social Service.

1968

# 1 The Necessary Information

Chapter One is an outline of the information necessary as a basis for the discussion that follows. It will give the relevant facts about the groups, about the service and its development, and the definitions of 'community', 'community group' and 'community development or field-work process' that will be used in the rest of the report. It will also say something about the intention of the London Council of Social Service in carrying out the enquiry into the work of the Community Development Department and in publishing it.

## THE GROUPS

The groups which we describe are organisations calling themselves 'Tenants' Associations', 'Social Clubs' and occasionally using the term 'Community Association'. They have come into existence in both London Borough and G.L.C. housing developments and in both pre-war and post-war flats. The work of the Department is a response to the needs and problems of these housing estate community groups so that something must be said at the outset about the latter's characteristics, structure and work, as a background for the discussion to follow.

### Characteristics

The members of the groups are residents on the estates. The groups are autonomous, plan their own programmes and manage their own financial affairs. In short, they make their own policy, They are democratically organised and administered and entirely staffed by volunteers. Committee members and officers, programme and activity leaders are all unpaid workers who reside on the estate.

## Work

The work of the groups is of three kinds. They provide a direct recreation and social welfare service to their members, including activities for children, youth work, services for the elderly and adult social events. Secondly, the groups represent the membership and the estate in discussion with statutory and voluntary bodies and in particular with the housing management department. Thirdly, their work involves the development of social life on the estates through the interaction between individuals, families and groups which is occasioned by the coming together of neighbours to participate in and provide these services. Many associations have their own club-room to manage.

## Resources

There are several factors which are favourable to the formation of a group and to its continuing role in the social life of the estate. These can all be regarded as part of the resources of the group.

Many residents of new estates want to know one another. All are anxious to have adequate social amenities and services. There are residents capable of taking various leadership roles. They are able to raise enough money from their members by subscription and fund raising activities to support their own organisation. They are assisted by the provision of a club-room and other physical facilities and equipment. While they sometimes become more cohesive when they are not well accepted or helped by authorities, it is equally true that they are encouraged by the acceptance and recognition of their work by authorities. There are traditions and social and cultural attitudes conducive to co-operative participation and common social action.

## Structure

The groups have constitutions and are organised as associations or clubs. This constitution sets out the aims of the group and regulates its administrative procedure. Most groups have family membership, each family paying a small subscription, usually between 6d and 1s weekly, which entitles the whole family to share in the activities, services and work of the association. The committee, which is the executive of the association, is formally constituted, with a chairman, secretary and treasurer, and includes members responsible for publicity, collection of subscriptions, the youth section and old people's work. The committee is responsible to the membership for the management of the affairs of the association and is elected at an annual general meeting. Some executive committees now have sub-

2

committees. Membership is open to every person on the estate, and associate membership is offered to a certain number of people living nearby. Some activities are restricted to members, but even so, the association often plays a significant part in the social life of the whole estate, especially in representing its needs and problems to the authorities. The characteristics, work resources and structures of the groups are discussed in detail in Chapters Two, Three and Four.

## *Difficulties*

The nature of the groups affects their work and structure. They are autonomous, plan their own programmes, raise their own funds and are staffed by volunteers. The difficulties they face in offering a service to their members and to the estate usually arise from one or more of the following:

Lack of knowledge of simple committee procedure.

Unfamiliarity with the duties of a chairman, secretary or treasurer.

Attempting to do too many things at once, so that the committee becomes overworked and discouraged.

Too much control of the organisation centred in a small 'friendship group'.

Inability to resolve tensions in the committee or on the estate.

Lack of specific skills, for example in working with children.

Inability to spread out the work among the committee and to involve the members.

The nature of the employment of many of the committee members —shift workers, long-distance drivers, workers in public transport and the post office, which makes it difficult for them to have regular commitments.

Lack of information about where to go for advice.

Aggressive attitudes towards authority.

Lack of co-operation from authorities.

Inability to learn from other organisations of a different nature from their own.

Leadership (sociopathic) which brings personal problems to the fore in the group, blocking the accomplishment of its tasks.

## *Needs*

The primary need of this type of group is for a consultative service which will help them to use the resources which are available to them, including resources in the wider community. The consultative service must be offered in such a way as to help groups achieve their self-chosen aims without endangering their independence or identity. This service has to be provided unconditionally without insisting on

3

certain standards of work or on particular processes or procedures in the organisation. The agency or worker, however, is not bound to work with a group whose objects are unacceptable.

## Origin

The community groups described here came into being in two ways, either spontaneously or with some assistance from outside. The residents may come together to put pressure on the authorities because something is wrong or to procure amenities, or they may be primarily concerned with social activities and the needs of the children. Most groups are concerned with both, although the emphasis varies from time to time.

Where a club-room is built with the blocks of flats, the community development workers sometimes take the initiative in bringing the new residents together.

## Size and Numbers

The groups affiliated to the Association of London Housing Estates vary in the size of membership, the scope of the activities and the services they offer. The largest estate has approximately 2,000 dwellings, and the smallest approximately 300.

There are seventy-five housing estate community groups affiliated to the Association, and the workers are in touch with others. Some groups have been in existence for nearly twenty years, some have only just formed, a few existed before the war. It is the work of these groups and of the Association of London Housing Estates that will be discussed in this book.

The difficulties, needs and origins of the groups are discussed further in Chapters Two, Three and Four, and the factors affecting the development of the groups in Section 1 of Chapter Four.

### THE SERVICE

The services which the groups receive come to them very largely through their own organisation, the Association of London Housing Estates. These include information and advice on simple technical and social skills; direct aid with typing, duplicating and auditing books; legal advice and a special insurance scheme. They can also look for support and encouragement from the workers where needed. These services developed in direct response to the needs and problems of the groups.

The field workers visit the estates, take part in committee meetings and discussions or watch activities. They may arrange for further

4

talks about a problem to take place either on the estate or at their office. They put groups in touch with one another if they have experienced similar problems, and they always try to be available when needed. They are often in a good position to bring about a better understanding between the local authority and the local group, and to make links between the group and the various statutory and voluntary services in the area. So far the field workers have visited the groups from a central office, either the headquarters of the London Council of Social Service or of the Association of London Housing Estates. These offices are close together. The London Council of Social Service provided the secretariat for the Association of London Housing Estates until the spring of 1968.

## Contacting the Groups

As has been pointed out in the introduction, the London Council of Social Service came into contact with the groups in different ways. At first, the Council tried to promote Community Associations in inner London, and then as the service developed, local housing officers and others told groups of the help available. Some groups 'referred' themselves, for example, small informal groups just starting up on estates heard on the 'grape-vine' about the service and made use of it. It also became known through the publications and work of the Association of London Housing Estates.

## Nature of the Service

A summary of the services offered through field work in order to help the groups to help themselves includes:

Opening and defining channels of communication.

Suggesting appropriate organisational forms.

Advising on the methods of setting up an organisation and formalising its procedures.

Helping to identify recreation and welfare needs.

Advice in exploring ways of meeting these needs.

Collecting, clarifying and passing on relevant information.

Helping associations to learn to set priorities.

Helping committees to see alternative courses of action and pointing out their implications.

Showing how conflict can be resolved and co-operation achieved.

Clarifying the process of decision-making.

Helping the association to learn how to present its case to the estate, the wider community or a statutory or voluntary body.

The nature of the service is developed in Chapters Two, Three and Four, and discussed in Section 3 of Chapter Seven.

## Role of the Worker and the Agency

The role of the worker is related to:

The legitimate needs of the groups.

The mandate and policy of the agency employing the worker.

The resources available to the groups, the agency and the worker.

The workers' own abilities, knowledge, understanding and skill.

The role of the worker is characterised by:

His work in *facilitating the participation* of the members in the work of the association, and of the association in the affairs of the estate and in the adjacent community.

His work in *engendering consensus* within the committee; and between the committee, the volunteers responsible for various activities and the members. This is related particularly to aims and objectives, methods of work, and the interpretation and evaluation of the work.

His work in *recognising and building up autonomy*. One of his objectives is to help the group to develop and maintain its independence.

The mode of participation of the worker is:

As an *objective observer*, in that he comes from outside the group and represents possibilities for understanding and action that do not originate in the group.

As a *controlled participant*, in that although he does at times participate in the affairs of the group, he does so consciously and not as a 'natural' member.

As a *resource person*, in that he is expected to be able to indicate, and on occasions provide, the resources (other than finance) necessary to the group to carry on its work.

As a *go-between*, in that he is a bridge between various elements in the situation, in attempting to bring about consensus, sometimes helping get consensus within the group, sometimes between the group and outside bodies.

The responsibilities of the worker in this role include:

Responsibility to the agency and its policy.

Respecting the confidential nature of some of the work of the groups.

Non-judgmental behaviour over differences in social attitudes.

The responsibility to bear witness by his own behaviour to the possibility of minimal exploitation in personal and group relations, and to the value of the democratic process. It should be noted that the worker is not responsible for the policy or activities of the group.

The role of the agency in providing the service is:

To create a framework and an atmosphere which will enable the worker and the service to offer help to groups at their different levels of development, on conditions and in circumstances they can accept and understand.

To give the worker maximum freedom of action and to accept that if the worker is successful the credit will go not to the agency, but to the group he has helped.

To make and state policy decisions about the aims, methods of work, and service available, with sufficient clarity to enable both groups and the relevant statutory and voluntary bodies to understand the nature of the service offered.

To provide the understanding, in-service training and supervision necessary for the field-work staff.

To take responsibility without taking, or wanting, control of the groups served.

To interpret the work on behalf of the groups (collectively) to the relevant bodies and to the general public.

To collect, interpret and formulate the information from the field work in terms relevant to social planning and policy, and to make representations to authorities when necessary.

The role of the worker and the agency is developed in Chapter Five and discussed in Section 3 of Chapter Six and in Section 3 of Chapter Seven.

## *Approach and Method*

The approach used in helping these groups is community development as a method of social work. Until fairly recently this approach was used mainly in rural areas overseas. This method clearly has affinities with social case work, social group work and community organisation in that it seeks to intervene in the social process in order to realise the values inherent in the basic concept of social welfare: in this case to help community groups to learn how best to set priorities, choose among alternatives, encourage participation, find resources and manage their own affairs, in such a way as to provide a better social welfare and recreation service to their members and the estate as a whole.

The approach and method are discussed in Chapters Two, Three and Six, and described in Chapter Seven.

### THE DEVELOPMENT OF THE SERVICE

The service has developed in three phases:

### *Phase 1*

Early attempts to create Community Associations and to use professional leadership.

As pointed out in the introduction, the first attempts to help new residents on the estates took the form of trying to create the formal structure of a Community Association, and this for various reasons was not successful. But it helped in two ways: it put the workers in contact with a number of small informal groups on estates who wanted and needed help; and it suggested the kind of help needed. It then became possible to offer a service on the terms set down by the groups themselves.

During this phase, the workers offered the help of professionals to assist in running activities on estates, but again, for various reasons, as a method of training this was not successful. The nature of the service then became one of support for individual groups, helping them to achieve identity, protect their autonomy, recruit members, and to carry on, however inadequately, the activities which could be run by their own volunteer members.

### Phase 2

(which historically overlapped with Phase 1). Development of service to individual groups and the training of indigenous leaders.

This phase of the work can be seen as concentrating on the attempt to help the groups to come together, to recognise their common problems, and to help one another by exchanging experience about common difficulties and various ways of working them out. There was a system of joint consultation in the field between the officers of the various associations, and week-end conferences that brought the groups together for the exchange of information and advice. This eventually led to the establishment of the Association of London Housing Estates, eight years after the work started.

### Phase 3

Service through, and to, the Association of London Housing Estates.

The third phase was to promote the Association of London Housing Estates and to provide the secretariat. The Association brought groups together for discussion and training as well as inter-estate activities. It represented the interests of its members in negotiating with the authorities and in the public and professional interpretation of the work.

### Summary of Phases

This summary of the development of the service shows the move away from the attempt to impose, with the best intentions, a preconceived idea of the pattern of community participation on the estate.

The small, spontaneous, informal groups showed themselves

capable, with professional help and support, of providing the necessary basis for common action to improve the quality of social life on housing estates.

The professional service of the field workers was offered, first to the informal, unorganised group on the estate, then to the organised but autonomous housing estate community group, then to the groups through the Association of London Housing Estates, and finally to the Association of London Housing Estates as a voluntary body representing the groups on the estates.

At each stage in the development of the work, the aim was always to offer a service from the outside which did not impinge on the independence of the group, but which attempted to support the group and to broaden rather than diminish the opportunities for participation it offered its members and residents on the estate.

The community development approach enabled the workers to formulate the type of service which the housing estate groups required.

It enabled the groups to receive their knowledge and skill so that they could provide better social welfare and recreation services for their members. It helped to gain them recognition and status.

It eventually led to a new structure being created, the Association of London Housing Estates, which would be able to support and carry on the work of the individual groups without the direct assistance of the parent body, the London Council of Social Service, which originally promoted it.

## THE WORKING DEFINITIONS

In what has been said so far, several words and phrases have been used in a particular way. These are: 'community', 'community group', and 'field-work process in community development', each of which must be defined *for the purposes of this discussion* before proceeding.

### 'Community'

'Community' (the word and the concept) as used in this report is a convenient term to refer to a group of people gathered together in any geographical area (in this case on a housing estate), with common interests, actual or potential, in the social welfare and recreational field. This includes the services of the relevant statutory and voluntary bodies.

This limits the use of the word community to a particular setting (in this case the housing estate) and to the factors relevant to the needs and resources of the groups. The term community can then be

9

said to refer to those specific physical, social and psychological elements which the groups and workers need to take into account if both are to perform their task successfully. The particular use made here of the concept of the community is discussed in Appendix II.

### *'Community Groups'*

The second term used in a particular way is 'community group'. This is used to describe a group of people within a community as defined above, who have come together for the specific purpose of providing a recreation and social welfare service to their members.

They have formed within a well-defined geographical area.

Their origins were in part a concern about social welfare, recreation and social amenities.

Their work is to provide these services or to see that they are provided.

Their identity and autonomy, which are conditions of their existence and their work, are defined and secured in relation to other statutory and voluntary social welfare bodies in their environment.

It can be seen that this definition of 'community group' is social-work-orientated, in the widest sense of the term. Throughout the report the terms 'social work' and 'social welfare' include recreation. This description emphasises the role of the group in providing social welfare services to its members, and so makes the 'community group' the unit to which the worker and the agency offer a service.

And lastly, they are termed groups in that the level of association on which they operate (give service and manage their affairs) is not the institutional level of a full scale social agency but the group level. From the point of view of the work, they are community groups whose needs, problems and behaviour can best be seen by the worker and themselves in terms of the dynamics of small or medium-sized task-centred autonomous groups.

The thinking that led us to designate the groups we worked with as community groups is explored in Appendix II.

### *'The Field-Work Process'* in Community Development

(a) The Elements of Field-Work are:

The estate: the physical and social content of the needs and potentials of social life on a particular housing estate.

The tenants' association through which the residents attempt, on a voluntary basis, to meet local social welfare needs, and in the process encourage neighbourliness.

The committee, which is the formalised instrument of the association, designed to work out the ways and means of meeting needs and providing service.

10

Related statutory and voluntary bodies—services available to be worked with, accepted or rejected, in meeting agreed needs.

The worker and the agency: the outsider with the knowledge, understanding and skills, who is invited in to help and advise.

The social, economic, political and cultural forces, factors or trends that influence the needs and problems of the groups and the service they require.

## (b) The Content of the Field-Work Situation

The elements listed above are not clearly separate or isolated factors in the field-work situation, but are constantly inter-relating parts of the whole picture. The field worker, then, in observing, advising, informing and participating in this social action—by offering and giving a service—is concerned with:

People: what they do and why; what roles they play; the effect of the various roles on the elements listed above, from the point of view of the work of the association.

Leadership potential of individuals: the effect of the behaviour of individuals on the work of committee and association.

Procedures: how was the committee organised, how is it organised now, how does it carry on its business, how are the voluntary and statutory bodies organised, how do they carry on their business (flexibility versus rigidity, authority versus co-operation and self-determination.)

Channels of communication: where they fail, how and why, where they succeed; decision-making, how it is done; policy-making, how it is done.

Movement: change; integration versus disorganisation; movement towards goals, away from goals; why, how.

The role of the worker: attitudes towards what the worker does; when, how, for what reason; success or failure in particular situations; why.

Relationships: committee to association; association to estate; estate to adjacent community; how established; how maintained; what services taken, what services rejected; what services given.

Social attitudes: attitudes towards authority; self-determination; money; identification; in-group/out-group feeling; ideas, ideals and values as they affect co-operation.

Used in this way, then, the term 'community development' (in the field-work process) suggests the aims of the work and the material available to the groups, worker and agency in attempting to provide social welfare services.

We take community development, described here as the field-work process, to be a method of social work because:

11

It is concerned with the provision of a social welfare service by the group to its members and by the agency to the group.

It requires an agent (e.g. a social worker) in order to help to do this.

In this way community development is obviously related to, but different from, other methods of social work in that the agent and the process in case work is concerned with intra- or inter-personal relationships.

The agent and the process in social group work is concerned with the interaction between members of the group in relation to the growth and development of each member.

The agent and the process in Community Organisation are concerned with the relations within and between already existing social welfare agencies.

## SOURCES OF INFORMATION

The information for this report was collected from field work, supervision and training records. In addition, notes of committee meetings, meetings or interviews with community agencies and colleagues in the field of social work were used. Perhaps the most difficult problem facing anyone attempting to document field work in the area of human relations is that of confidentiality. At no time, and for no reason, can the confidence of an individual group or community be exploited; yet, if the material presented is to lend itself to meaningful discussion and be used for teaching material, it must be factual, detailed and systematic.

In an attempt to reconcile these two imperatives in this report, we have used only portions of any one record at any single point of presentation in order to make identification impossible. The names of persons and places, and the names of field workers, have been disguised. The order of events has been rearranged where this does not affect the accuracy of the report.

In the circumstances, in order to prevent identification, no single record is that of an actual field-work situation. Each has been constructed from records describing a number of different field-work situations, and assembled into a representative record. When taken together, we see these records as an accurate portrayal of field-work events and the field-work process.

The interpretation of these records in this report is always the commentary of the consultant.

# 2 The Factors Affecting the Development of the Service

Chapter Two is an outline of some of the factors that affected the development of the service during the first phase of field work. It discusses in outline the needs and problems of the groups and describes attempts to meet them.

## Problems of Settling In

While most people were delighted with their new home on the housing estates under discussion it was found that the problems of settling in fell into three main categories.

First, problems caused by a change of environment; getting to know neighbours; distance from the old neighbourhood, relatives, friends and acquaintances; the necessity to accept the new social situation as the material from which the individual or family must build a new network of relationships. Sometimes there is an absence of amenities: shops, play space, church, public house, library, and other social facilities. The family may also experience economic difficulties because of higher rent, travelling expenses and new furnishings required for the home.

Second, problems of moving from a house to a flat. For example, more consideration has to be given to the amount of noise made by the children and the radio. At first there may seem little privacy, and there is no back yard or garden in which to keep a pet, erect a shed or clean a motor bike, although sometimes there may seem too much privacy when neighbours are out at work all day and the housewife is too high up even to see what is happening below.

Third, the difficulties of special groups. Mothers in high flats cannot get down to let the young children play out of doors, or they worry about the children wandering off the estate or climbing over the balcony. Young people feel cut off on the estate, may have nowhere even to kick a ball, and are constantly told not to go on the grass. They complain of having nowhere to meet and nothing to do. Old people have special problems: they have to adjust to using lifts and not being able to see what is going on outside. Unless they are given special consideration they may be very lonely—for example, they should not live at the end of a block where no one ever has to pass their door.

Not all the problems are necessarily the result of rehousing. Yet these problems are significant here because they are concentrated in one situation, the housing estate, and many people experience them simultaneously. This tends to create a feeling, at least in the early days, of taking time to settle down. On the other hand it also leads to a realisation that residents have some problems in common and therefore common concerns.

### *Starting the Work*

The field workers of the London Council of Social Service faced almost as many problems as the residents on the estates. Their terms of reference were clear: to investigate the kind of service necessary to improve the social life on the estate and to find ways of offering such a service. At first it was thought that the development of a Community Association might be the right approach, bringing together statutory and voluntary bodies in co-operation with residents, but inevitably buildings had to be small and the residents wanted a meeting place of their own. They were not yet ready to co-operate with organisations and individuals on any large scale outside the estate. Nor was there much attempt on the part of the settled community to promote new organisations of this kind.

Another approach was to employ a professional leader to assist the residents in planning and organising activities, especially for children, and then to withdraw when local leadership could carry on. The majority of the estates could not have this service; it was impossible for one person to cover the ground, and the very competent leader was only able to pass on her skills to a limited number of residents to enable them to take over the work themselves. To a large extent the tenants' associations and social clubs of these early days had to struggle on alone. An attempt to build a team of advisers with the help of other agencies was not altogether successful.

These groups were in fact a natural response of the residents to their own needs and were seen by them as potentially adequate for the job. It was therefore crucial to recognise the validity of these groups and not try to impose, in however kindly and unassuming a

14

way, what might to a professional worker be 'a better organisational form.' This does not seem to be an extraordinary insight, yet social workers tend to carry with them preconceived ideas about 'good organisation', 'suitable activities', and 'proper administrative procedures'.

Service could only be offered to the residents by first recognising the validity of what they were already doing, and by trying to help them to do it. It was also necessary to recognise why they could seldom get help from established social work agencies in the locality. These groups were not readily accepted for the following reasons:

They were thought to be party political and an anti-landlord type of organisation.

It was said that it was socially undesirable for them to isolate themselves in their own groups and that they ought to join established organisations.

They did not fit into any organisation's terms of reference; they were not 'boys'' clubs or 'women's' clubs but family clubs, and there were no social agencies concerned with them.

They were dismissed as 'only social clubs' and therefore not very important.

They were regarded by some of the churches as purely secular organisations, and therefore not very desirable.

They represented a threat to some of the existing social agencies.

They were regarded as unsatisfactory because they did not have experienced leadership.

They were regarded as unstable.

### A Basic Policy

The field workers had to have an agreed 'policy' to interpret to the groups and to the statutory and voluntary bodies, about the terms of reference within which their services could be offered. Four points emerged:

Advice should only be given on the invitation of the tenants' committee or of a member or members acting on behalf of the committee. The membership of the organisation had to be open to everybody living on the estate.

A worker could only act for the group at its request. For example a worker would not directly approach the statutory and voluntary bodies on their behalf but would help the group prepare their case, state it, and follow it up. He might then support their case or comment on it to the authority independently.

A worker would offer service to a 'protest' group only if it was willing to discuss its problems.

Workers could not join groups as regular members or serve as officers (chairman, secretary, treasurer), but could offer help in whatever problems they were having with committee work. They could advise on the drafting of letters, duplicating of publicity material, and so on, and help the treasurer to keep the accounts correctly and to prepare his books for audit.

The policy set out in these four points was not without its difficulties when it came to interpretation. Some of the statutory and voluntary bodies felt the workers' usefulness to them was lessened if they were not available as extra partners. There was even a feeling that they would be more likely to support the groups than the authorities. On the other hand some of the groups saw the workers as identified with the authorities. For the most part however it depended on the worker to establish a relationship in which he had the confidence of the group and also of the statutory authority: this took time.

Most of the groups felt that there were three aspects to their work: community service, recreation, and taking up problems of tenancy. It became generally accepted that an association would not take up individual complaints, which were matters between landlord and tenant (unless for very good reasons). The association, however, represented the estate on matters that concerned all, or a large section of the residents. Some groups maintained that they only dealt with tenants' problems, and others that they were only concerned to be a social club. The workers regarded both as important.

### THE NEEDS OF THE GROUPS

The development of the service was influenced by the needs of the groups—to be autonomous; to have an identity; to be allowed to make their own mistakes; and to be recognised, supported and, where necessary, encouraged.

### Autonomy

A useful word to describe the general characteristics of these groups is *autonomous*. An autonomous group is formed on a housing estate by residents themselves, often without any help or encouragement from outside; it determines its own aims and activities; it is informal with no preconceived form of organisation imposed on it; it is made up of residents who provide their own leaders and activity; it is self-supporting financially. It is worth setting out this definition of an autonomous group because the whole pattern of service to the groups is determined by, and dependent upon, it.

Because of their autonomous character the groups, as groups, had little or no contact with traditional procedure of any kind apart from

16

their general inheritance of a British democratic way of doing things. Nor had they any relationship with a larger regional or national body which might have passed on accepted structures and procedures. Therefore the groups were in great need of simple social skills, of a go-between, and of information.

Skills were needed for everything from how to handle intricate human relations to writing an agenda. A go-between was needed to help the groups in negotiations with outside bodies and to see both sides of a problem, either within the group or between the group and those outside. Information of all kinds was needed from the beginning, e.g. how to open a bank account, draw up a constitution or write to the Town Clerk.

The groups were quick to frame direct requests for help. But the most pressing need, though not put into words, was for encouragement and support, especially in the early days of an association.

### *Identity*

Survival for an autonomous group depended on the ability of the group to establish its identity, especially in its own eyes. The small, self-contained group without any reflected status from membership in a larger federation or parent body has a greater need to find a definite identity than a group that has the backing of an already established organisation.

The freedom of the 'unattached' autonomous group was jealously and anxiously guarded. The search for identity was urgent because this peculiar freedom had to be justified in the eyes of the group itself and of the outside world. The group was sometimes prickly, until it felt that its existence was accepted. It was quick to resent any outside attempt to say what should be done.

The field workers soon realised that they should be careful how they offered advice or appeared to be critical; most groups learnt by experience, or later from one another. It was often better for a treasurer to keep to his own method of book-keeping than to follow a more complicated system which he did not understand.

The worker might foresee difficulties in organising a Christmas party to include children under five as well as teenagers, when large numbers were involved, but no one agreed with the worker until after the party. Then they remarked that perhaps next year they would organise it differently.

Another reason for not appearing critical was that the committee often had to face criticism from the members. There were often questions about the money and whether they were accounting for it properly, or discontent following an outing or social event at which something had gone wrong. Sometimes they were accused of not taking a strong enough line with the authorities, or taking too strong a line and making the association unpopular. The workers, at first surprised by apparently uncalled-for attacks on other people's motives, competence, even honesty, later came to see this as a measure of the group's need to find its identity, justify its existence and preserve its autonomy.

To describe a group is to describe a collection of individuals who by no means always behaved or felt as one body. While the groups were struggling for their identity, so were individual members, and especially the officers.

It is not unusual for a committee to be formed on an estate and officers to be elected, who say they have not served on a committee before but they are willing to learn. Members then have to find out what their role is as chairman, secretary or treasurer.

How they interpret this will have a considerable effect on the smooth running of the committee and the quality of relationships in the group. The chairman who sees himself as the 'boss' will have a different relationship with the committee from the man who sees himself as only helping the secretary to run the meeting. The treasurer may see himself as guide and friend of those who collect the subscriptions, and adviser on all money matters, or as appointed to catch out people who make mistakes in their books.

Some of the obstacles to good committee work disappear as members settle down generally and lose the need to use their committee roles to voice private grievances. Also, a more realistic understanding of the committee's job helps individuals to take their turn in speaking and to try to cut the length of the meetings. Difficulties are sometimes created by a resident who brings his personal problems to a meeting and 'plays them out' in the guise of normal participation.

Committee meetings and larger residents' meetings also satisfy, in a very positive way, the basic human need to be accepted by others, to speak and be listened to, and to feel part of something larger than oneself or one's family. Individuals have opportunities to contribute skills and talents, and to see them used and appreciated, in ways not otherwise possible on the estate. People may discover that they have abilities and capacities which they were unaware of before.

Members who play a special role in the affairs of the association must be free to make their own mistakes and to learn by experience. Advice can be given, but the field worker must accept that it is unlikely it will be taken until the person concerned sees it as relevant. The worker may urge a group not to undertake a programme that is too ambitious, as for example arranging an activity every night of the week, when they are a new association with a new clubroom: the committee members will become overworked and some will have to resign. It is only a year later, when this begins to happen, that someone remembers the point and appreciates that it made sense.

## *Individuality*

The groups had much in common, but it was also important to recognise their individuality.

So far, the stress has been on the autonomy of the groups and their resistance to interference. But some groups looked for more support than they really needed, and some local authorities took a paternal view that encouraged this. Others only got in touch when there was a crisis.

Each group had its own way of getting co-operation and dealing with conflict. Each had special interests and placed different emphases on various activities. The rates of growth were different. When the field worker first made contact with the groups, some were well developed, others still at the stage of informally discussing what they might do. Some grew rapidly without any help from outside; others seized every chance of help offered. Some organisations disappeared after a time but reformed later; others broke up completely. After a few years some evolved a very complicated structure and a stable organisation to meet a wide variety of needs. Others only just survived.

The rate of growth that distinguishes them is partly accounted for by the degree of difficulty in the social life on the estate. The way in which the groups develop will be influenced by many factors, including:

The physical and social conditions on the estate. Lack of shops, play space, pubs or places to meet, and hostility, real or imagined, from the established community, contribute to the individuality of a group. One group will react vigorously, another hardly at all.

The quality of the indigenous leadership and the number of potential leaders also affect the character of the group. There may not be much difference in the quality of potential leadership in each group, but in some it gets to work more quickly than in others. This may be where some residents have brought with them traditions of organisation and participation, and are quick to see their application in a new situation.

The attitude of the statutory and voluntary bodies, the local press and outside agencies can help or hinder the development. First impressions, for example, made by the housing manager and his staff may affect the work of the group. If the group feels welcome and is regarded as a responsible organisation, progress is more likely to be satisfactory than if they are regarded as potential trouble makers.

## The Basic Need

The autonomous group is very dependent upon acceptance and support, especially from those with authority outside the estate. The field workers and the staff who answered the telephone in the London office and provided a variety of service from consultation to copy typing, were the representatives of an impartial and accepting body which did not try to impose its values and standards on the group, or to infringe its autonomy. Basically it was this attitude of acceptance and support which helped the groups to grow and the service to develop.

### THE PROBLEMS OF THE GROUPS

The third set of factors that affected the development of the service was the problems of the groups—the need to work together as a committee, to agree on matters of finance and accounting, to learn to interpret the work to members and others, to involve the residents, and to establish agreed processes and procedures.

## Committee Work

Committee work seems simple to those who have long experience of it, or to those who have little or no experience. Learning to run a committee was an art which many of the groups found difficult and which some never achieved at all.

Striking a balance between excessive formality and absolute informality did not come easily at first. If the committee was conducted rigidly to rule, with those who knew the rules taking it upon themselves to correct those who were apparently defaulting, offence could easily be taken, and procedure could become more important than the items on the agenda. Extreme informality could also prolong a meeting interminably, and result in no decisions being reached. Both extremes had the same effect of loss of interest of the more able members of the committee and ultimately of the whole association. The delicate balance between friendly consideration and a business-like discipline was difficult to develop and maintain.

New committee members also had to learn how to use their authority and not be overawed by it. The novel experience of officialdom prevented some members from seeing beyond their role to the job in hand. Learning to abide by a majority decision did not always come easily. There were personality conflicts as in any other committee.

It is a long time before a new committee can begin to see all the ramifications of its responsibility. First it has to learn that com-

20

mittee work is not an end in itself, but that the committee is acting on behalf of a wider membership and is responsible to them. The wider membership or association is not the end of the committee's responsibility, but together they have to try to serve the needs of the whole estate. The process of accepting such wide responsibility is accompanied by incomprehension, misunderstanding and sometimes open conflict. If some committees after several years glimpse the full range of their responsibilities, few can carry them out with any consistency. Too much or too little continuity can be an obstacle to consistent growth and development. Too much continuity comes when committee members who know the work well are deferred to by others, and just keep things going in the same old way. They are thought to be indispensable, but unwittingly they exclude new life and vision by not making way for a change in leadership. Too many changes and a lack of continuity are equally hampering if the work has continually to be held up while new members find their feet.

These problems tend to be intensified for an autonomous group which is not guided or controlled by any outside body. The management committee of a local youth club, for example, has to keep half an eye on the Borough Youth Committee because of the grants involved, and half an eye on its own regional or national committees to see that local policy does not go too far off the rails. The autonomous group has no outside reference, nor does it stand in any kind of hierarchy where those below can complain and those above can call to order. It has to determine its own goals and develop its own methods, or cease to function. This is the price of the group's freedom.

The problems of learning to be a committee cannot be by-passed. They provide the material out of which the committee can learn to define its roles and its functions, and out of which committee members can strengthen and deepen their relations with each other.

### Finance

For a newly established community group, fund raising, budgeting and accounting for money are difficult and complicated matters. The handling of money gives status to an individual or to a group, and even in a settled community questions about the use of money can provoke heated debate or excited and extreme behaviour.

A new group, reluctant to press people for money, may persuade itself that not much is needed. As a result, the club-room rent gets in arrears and there is no money for equipment or activities of any kind. This can cause a vicious circle—too few subscriptions collected, therefore not enough money for activities, therefore members lose interest and are unwilling to subscribe to an association which does nothing.

21

A committee can find itself with more money than it really knows how to handle if the membership responds well to an appeal for funds. The committee, anxious to be seen to give value for money, may hastily plan parties, outings and dances. If these are poorly publicised, poorly run and poorly attended, the membership may feel that their money is being wasted by a committee trying to make a splash, and the next appeal will not have such a good response. If donations or other gifts are not wisely spent in the eyes of the membership, income may drop or even dry up. In the early days, residents were very willing to support the committee and to give them a chance. If the committees were over-anxious to prove themselves worthy of this support, they might have too many events for which no charge was made, and then have people complaining when a charge was made. Inexperience might also lead them to put all the money enthusiastically into one side of the work—perhaps the old people's programme—and leave everything else at a standstill. If a relatively small amount of money was equally divided between all the activities, the members might complain that nothing really worth while was being done.

This kind of financial ineptitude might give rise to complaint and criticism, but the flashpoint may well be the need to account for money spent. Money would not only have to be accounted for properly, but people would have to see that this had been done. A half-jesting remark that the treasurer was 'doing very well' out of the situation might cause his immediate resignation, and an item not clearly understood in the statement of accounts might give rise to unfounded rumours. If money was raised at a youth club dance, the young people might assume that all the profits would go to the club, while the committee might expect the money to go into general funds. Other potentially explosive situations would arise when a treasurer used an entirely personal book-keeping system, which no one else in the association could follow. A volunteer leader might get a loan from association funds, or he might subsidise expenditure out of his own pocket and then find that such unauthorised payments could not be reimbursed.

As with other committee problems, they were often the starting point of a determination to learn more about committee procedure and the problems of budgeting for a voluntary programme of social service. The status and responsibility attached to money matters often helped a group to establish its identity as an independent organisation.

All these problems of handling money had to be seen by the worker in the context of the traditional attitudes of the residents to money, and of the personalities of people directly involved.

## Public Relations

'Public relations' is a rather grandiose title to describe such action as the first efforts of two or three neighbours to get a pedestrian crossing. The basic function of public relations is to open channels of communication, and from the first days on the estate, individuals and small groups needed to inform a larger audience of their needs and plans. When a small group had developed, it was essential for the committee to pass information to the membership, to non-members and to the rest of the community.

If the committee set out utopian aims for the association, exaggerated the benefits that membership would bring, and promised big and expensive events in the programme, disappointment was certain. Such an overestimation of the group's contribution to the social life of the estate could also produce disbelief among the residents and even hostility from statutory and voluntary bodies in the area. A committee which seriously underestimated the capacity of an association to improve the quality of social life also ran the risk of damaging public relations. If the membership was led to believe that there was so much to be done and so few resources, either of money or of voluntary help, they might feel that the odds were too great and that any offer of help would be a wasted effort.

Other obstacles to communication appeared if the committee found it difficult to gain support from the residents. At a general meeting, a nagging, accusatory tone might be heard in the chairman's voice: 'If we can't get more people to act as collectors we shall have to close down. We need more people on the committee. If only you few are interested, it's not worth it. . . .' These domestic problems were difficult to work through but, when misunderstandings or feuds were given wide publicity in the local press, negotiation or compromise was even more difficult. Committees had to wrestle with the problems of keeping in contact with the membership, giving information that would catch their imagination, convincing them that the committee was doing a good job, and so obtaining for the association the support it needed.

## Sharing the Work

A division of labour satisfactory to committee and membership is difficult to achieve. At first the committee, anxious to get things going, does all the work itself. The rest of the association comes to feel that its subscriptions entitle it to the service offered, or that the committee is so competent there is no need to help. Or it may be the other way round, the committee sitting back with the idea that having 'founded the association' it is now for the membership to do

23

the work. If the association has begun life with a great rush of parties, trips and social gatherings, some residents begin to contract out, feeling that they have got to know enough people to make a 'private' social life of their own; this, of course, is not necessarily a bad thing. It takes a long time to develop the kind of co-operative atmosphere where committee and membership can share responsibilities equitably and easily.

A co-operative atmosphere grows fairly quickly within the smaller group of the committee itself as they work together. Some of them lose patience on finding that co-operation with the membership takes so much longer. Some find that the petty conflicts, which are inevitable in the growth of a small working group, are not to their liking. Some have not realised how much is involved in committee work, or their husbands or wives have not realised and protest at the amount of time spent away from home. Some are bored by not having enough to do. A single-minded enthusiast who fails to carry the rest of the committee with him may feel personally frustrated and compelled to leave. When there is a quick turnover of committee members this adds to the difficulties of establishing a good working relationship within the association.

The nature of volunteer leadership can also be a centre of dissension within the committee and the association. A keen youth leader may carve out a little empire and accept help from no one, perhaps not even from the young people themselves. A less efficient leader may equally alienate the membership by being unreliable about time and place and careless with equipment. The committee may be advised by the worker to start in a small way with a minimum of publicity, while expert help is sought.

### Involving Residents

A keen committee, anxious to get the full co-operation of members, may not be aware that in the early days many residents are still, as it were, living in the old neighbourhood. If the new estate is near the old neighbourhood, some of them may continue to patronise familiar shops as well as visit friends and relatives. Residents who keep up the old neighbourhood life may resent being pressed to join in activities on the new estate.

It also takes time for new residents to learn to budget their time economically. They have to discover how long it takes to get to work, to the shops, to take the children to school, to attend the clinic, to go to the launderette. Women may start to go out to work for the first time. The new flat needs a good deal of time spent on it. As a result they are not always prepared to spend time on the association.

Residents who come from a settled neighbourhood with working-class traditions may regard the whole idea of a community group for getting to know the neighbours as unnecessary. Back at home, the neighbours were there; friends were made without the help of any artificial organisation. It was hard for a struggling committee to convert this attitude into one of willing co-operation. Sometimes conflict, real or imagined, within the association or with an outside body could stimulate new residents to take a part in the affairs of the estate. Sometimes it was the desire to have a social environment that was of benefit to themselves and their children that called forth the necessary effort.

## Establishing Procedures

Most of the problems listed above are concerned in one way or another with establishing agreed processes and procedures for carrying on the work with the group. After consultation with several of the groups, a model set of rules or constitution was worked out. It covers the objectives of the group, the nature of membership, subscriptions, management, the annual general meeting, committee procedure and finance. (A copy of a constitution is included in Appendix IA.)

## CONCLUSION

After five years in the field, the workers understood something of the nature of the groups they were attempting to help, their needs and problems, and the difficulties involved in offering them a service.

In a later phase the groups came together to discuss and work out common problems and to found an association of their own.

A discussion of the factors affecting the development of the groups themselves (size, location and age of the estate, presence or absence of amenities, a place to meet, and indigenous leadership) is included in Chapter Six, 'Conditions of Field Work'.

# 3 The Further Development of the Service

Chapter Three is an account of the further development of the service. It covers the inter-group work both before and after the founding of the Association of London Housing Estates. It also describes two proposals to use this method in a different type of situation.

The work began in the field with a handful of groups. By the end of the first phase there were more than 100 groups known to the workers, but they were able to work with less than half. During this phase, which was discussed in Chapter Two, the emphasis was on service to the individual group, and the relationship was between the worker and each committee with its officers. During the second phase groups came together to discuss common problems and began to offer each other a service of advice, based on experience. During this phase of field work the emphasis was on service to the groups in their relationship to one another: the residential conferences, the discussion of common problems and the planning of joint activities led to the formation of the Association of London Housing Estates. These two phases represent the first stage of development of the service. The second stage began when the Association of London Housing Estates came into existence.

### INTER-GROUP WORK

Some of the earliest meetings for committee members and officers were held in the office of the London Council of Social Service. Meetings were held to discuss activities, publicity, and a model constitution. Groups began to advise and help one another. Out of this came the idea of a residential week-end conference, when there would be more time to talk over problems.

## Week-end Conferences

The first of many conferences was held at Wansfell Adult Education College in Essex. It was easy to reach by train, and representatives were met at the station and made to feel welcome. The house was comfortable and the atmosphere friendly. For the first conference, even with staff and speakers, it was difficult to fill the minimum of twenty places: to many it was a new idea, and it was not easy for people with young families to get away. Numbers at subsequent residential conferences never exceeded forty, though sometimes two were held in one year.

The following is a summary of the consultant's record of a residential conference held just before the formation of the Association of London Housing Estates.

*Conference held at Beatrice Webb House.* The conference was held from Friday evening to late Sunday afternoon. The programme included discussion groups (referred to in the record as workshops), an outside speaker, a discussion with a panel of experts, and various social activities. The four workshops dealt with committee procedure, publicity, ways of involving more members in the work of the association, and work with young people on the estates. Each was led by a field worker, and the chair was taken by a representative from one of the estates. An outside expert (referred to in the report as a resource person) was also present.

The panel discussion took place on the Saturday evening. Questions from the floor were put to a panel made up of the chairmen of the workshops (estate volunteer workers), the resource persons from each workshop, and the field worker. The success of the volunteer chairmen as members of the panel was one of the best features of the conference and was a useful pointer to ways of developing the field-work service. They showed great willingness and ability in dealing with questions, sharing their experience, giving information and advice, and handling the difficult problems of social attitudes. In answer to one woman who asked what she could do about her committee, which constantly ignored her good advice, a voluntary chairman on the panel said, 'No one likes good advice, least of all a full committee trying to get a job done. Take on a job yourself, do it well, and try to show by what you have done what might be done in other cases.' It was obvious that the panel members could be used as resource persons in the field, and would often be able to give assistance in ways not open to the field workers.

The conference produced a general and complex concern about youth work. 'They' (the young people) were said 'never to have had it so good,' and therefore they should not behave as they did. 'They'

27

were at fault and needed more discipline. Complaints varied about the noise they made on the estates, about their dress, about their behaviour to one another and especially to the girls, to their parents and to adults in general. This concern and the way it was expressed was particularly interesting because most of those present were parents of the young people under discussion. The willingness and the decisiveness with which they aired their views suggested that the matter was a good deal more complex than a simple concern for youth on the estate, and included elements of real feeling about being a parent in contemporary society.

The actual nature and content of youth work were also vigorously discussed. If it were all football, what was there for the girls to do? What sort of activities should there be? It seemed generally agreed that none of the young people showed the slightest interest in anything except getting together to talk and dance and listen to records. 'Should we just give in and let them do what they want?' This expressed a deep perplexity felt by many at the conference. There was first-hand experience of broken equipment and raids by rival groups on the club-rooms. Some felt this was the result of a 'let them do what they want' policy. Some were groping after a positive aspect of this policy and beginning to recognise that if it could be achieved this type of informal club would be immensely valuable, although even more difficult to run than a regular youth club, and so the discussion came back to the problems of leadership.

The conference brought to light several aspects of youth work on the estates. The field workers had been aware of the difficulties of the groups in attempting to provide some kind of youth service, but the mixed feeling and the real division of opinion had never been expressed so clearly. Opinion was divided between those who thought that youth work was of prime importance and those who thought it could not and should not be done. The field workers were also made aware of the amount of time and thought given to youth work at the committee level end of a great variety of practical attempts, successful and unsuccessful, to work with young people on the estates. The community groups were not alone in their perplexity, but the fact that it was shared by even the long-established professional youth work agencies neither lessened the problem nor suggested how to solve it.

At the conference there was an extraordinary contrast in tone between the discussions on youth and youth work and those about work with the aged. There was complete unanimity about the need for work with the old and confidence in the ability to do it. The groups and their voluntary workers were alert to their needs and generous in time, money and effort. There were a number of examples of good co-operation with local authorities and voluntary bodies

28

resulting in a comprehensive service to old people on the estates. The question raised here for the field workers was whether any elements in the confident work with the aged could be related to the more hesitant work with young people.

The final question raised at the conference was about the planning and organisation of an annual general meeting. Field workers had frequently been asked to help with such meetings, but usually at the last minute, either to grace the occasion or to deal with difficulties. At this conference the groups considered a model agenda for an annual general meeting. The aim of these meetings was to tell the members the story of the association's work, to recruit new members, to give some account of how the money was raised and how it had been spent, to find new committee members and volunteer leaders for the various activities, and to discover new ideas for activities and services. Obviously all these things could not be done at a moment's notice, and it was clear that the groups felt the need to plan their meetings in a more orderly way and to begin thinking well in advance.

The conference amply fulfilled the planners' hopes that ideas for future programmes and training schemes might emerge. The success in getting the chairmen to answer questions was noted for future reference. The marked contrast in attitude to work among the young and the old was particularly noted in the hope that some of the confidence from the one sphere could, with help, be carried over to the other. More written information about how to organise an annual general meeting might be made available, perhaps a special information leaflet. The conference expressed its wish to have another conference the following year.

The idea of an organisation to link all the community groups had originated at a previous conference at Wansfell. This conference confirmed the need for an organisation of this kind, and one was set up two months later.

*For a list of other weekend conferences, their content and dates, see Appendix IC.*

### Inter-Estate Discussions

When youth work was discussed at the week-end conference some very vigorous and divergent views were expressed on what could, or should, be done in this field. As a result of that conference the most vocal participants continued an intensive exchange of ideas and opinions. Some concluded that youth work in the club-rooms on the estates was too difficult for most voluntary workers from the associations to attempt without special training and some form of support on the job.

D

The appointment of a paid, professional worker was discussed, but was ruled out because he would be seen as responsible to an outside body and would want to run a regular youth club, which the young people did not want.

The next suggestion was the possibility of voluntary workers from outside the estate, who had some experience of youth work, coming to help the local leader, sharing responsibility with him and having the same responsibility to the committee. It was hoped that the local leader would get some training through working with a more experienced leader, who would at the same time provide help and support on the job. One voluntary agency (the Y.W.C.A.) had provided a worker who had come in on this basis and had been successful.

As a result of these discussions attempts were made to find opportunities for training for any of the association volunteer leaders who felt they wanted it, and also to interest experienced youth leaders from the voluntary bodies, or students reading social studies, in helping with youth work on the estates. Opportunities for training were explored first of all through local youth committees in the area where the association leaders lived and worked. Places were obtained for them in local youth leadership courses. This was not a success. The association leaders felt out of their depth, ill at ease in the mixed social and intellectual setting, and more important, they felt that what was being offered as training was quite irrelevant to their work in an informal youth setting.

The emphasis on informal activities in youth work, self-programming and work with the unattached, is much more evident in leadership training courses today, so that local association leaders would probably fare better now than they did then. At that time they felt that their situation was so diffierent from that assumed in the training that everything was almost totally inapplicable. This was particularly true of the concept of leader. On the estates, the voluntary leader was seen by the young people, and by himself, not so much as someone 'in charge', but rather as an adult helper who could provide opportunities for young people to come together informally to do what they wanted. He had no authority to say what should be done. His greatest need was to know how to stop fights, what to do when the club-room was attacked by an outside gang, what to do when a room meant to hold 50 had to take 150 packed too closely even to dance. Even if it was too much to expect a quick answer to these questions from a training course, the absence of any recognition of such questions meant that the existing training schemes were not satisfactory.

The attempt to bring in voluntary youth leaders from outside to work with the association youth leaders was beset with similar problems. Outside leaders were recruited from those already in youth work and from university students reading social studies. Small groups met to discuss the peculiar difficulties of this kind of work, but after six months or so this attempt to provide help and support for the local leaders was abandoned.

## Reasons for Failure

In spite of the initial exposition and discussion of the nature of youth work on an estate, the outside leaders could not abandon the idea of 'club work' and could not see the usefulness of an interested adult just being present, or being on tap in case of emergency. They complained of the unorganised nature of the work. There was no real discipline or order: 'everyone did what they wanted when they wanted'. 'There never seemed to be anything happening.' 'I don't see what I'm supposed to do.' 'I'm of no real use in these circumstances.' 'I'm not really interested in just standing around and talking all the time.' 'All we do is dance.' These comments made it clear that the youth workers could not see that their very presence was a help to the local leader as well as to the young people.

Some of the outside helpers felt compelled to 'push rather hard', as one committee member put it, for a more organised, regular kind of club programme. The outside helper found it difficult to accept the conditions under which the committee, the local leader and the young people expected the work to be done. He could not as an outsider attempt to influence the situation until he had been given authority to do so by virtue of his acceptance by all those concerned. The experienced youth worker, even more than the student, tended to want to get things started, to reorganise everything, to put things on their feet, almost from the first session. The student, on the other hand, took longer to settle in but having done so he too would want to introduce traditional club activities. These were unacceptable to the young people and made it almost certain that the outside leader would remain on the outside, perhaps even be resented, and eventually lose interest. The outside leaders, even when they proved helpful to the local leader and to the young people, often tended to resent having to account to the committee. There were exceptions to this tale of failure, and some students in particular were able to see what was required and to offer help in just the right way.

The difficulties were not only made by the outside leaders. The local leader, even when he had asked for help and support, resented his need of it, and so resented the presence of the helper and felt particularly threatened if he 'got on better with the kids than I do'. Committees also found it difficult to use the outside leader properly. They might play him off against their association leader, favour him in order to play down their worker for reasons of internal policy, or themselves be touchy about their prerogatives in dealing with an outsider. The crux of the difficulty was the inability of the field workers to provide the right kind of constant help and mutual interpretation between the association, the committee and the outside leader.

In retrospect of course it is possible to see that the failure to work in this way could have been foreseen. The difficulty experienced at the beginning of the field work in developing the insight and skill necessary to help the groups should have been a pointer to the much greater difficulties that would confront workers without any field work experience. The most positive result of this failure was a deeper understanding of the needs of the situation, from which a new approach could be developed. Later, when the groups had formed an Association of their own, the Association decided to employ on an experimental basis two youth work consultants, whose services would be available to the groups on the estates—a point to which we shall return shortly.

## THE GROUPS BEGIN TO SERVICE THEMSELVES

It is not proposed to go into detail about the history, structure and activities of the Association of London Housing Estates. This would require a separate book. The Association is important here because it was the organisation set up by the groups which enabled them to carry on their own field work and to service themselves. Subsequently it was the Association of London Housing Estates and not the London Council of Social Service that planned the conferences and training programmes and worked out the programme of the inter-estate activity.

### The Association of London Housing Estates

The Standing Conference of Housing Estate Community Groups was founded in 1957. Subsequently it changed its name to the Association of London Housing Estates, and this name is used in what follows.

At the request of the groups meeting at Wansfell Residential Conference in 1956 the London Council of Social Service agreed to help them set up an organisation of their own. Invitations were sent to the groups known to the Community Development Department in May 1957, to attend an inaugural meeting. This was held in the Abbey Community Centre, Westminster. About 100 people were present. A constitution was presented to the meeting and agreed, with some minor amendments. This had been prepared by the London Council of Social Service in consultation with their legal adviser, the National Federation of Community Associations, and representatives of the groups. (See Appendix IA.)

The Association of London Housing Estates has an Executive Committee of twenty people elected at an annual general meeting and representing different estates. It has six sub-committees: Conferences and Training, Inter-Estate Activities, Old People's Work, Youth Work, Finance and Policy, and Publicity. The Executive Committee meets once a month, on a Saturday afternoon. The subcommittees meet as and when necessary, six or eight times a year. These sub-committees are responsible for planning all the activities.

It was unlikely that the Association would have come into being without the residential conferences and inter-estate activities which preceded it. These created the friendly, informal, but 'work-centred' atmosphere in which the idea of an association of groups seemed both desirable and profitable. The experience of coming together in the work-shops and conferences was valuable not only for learning more about the job but of sharing success stories with other people. The smaller, struggling groups did not seem to resent this but rather to take encouragement from others' achievements. The more successful groups were equally encouraged by their ability to help others and by the approval they received—an approval not always available to them from the meetings with statutory and voluntary bodies in their own communities.

The growth of solidarity among the groups was based partly on their common aims and problems and partly on shared memories of a 'hostile' social environment or of misunderstandings with the statutory and voluntary bodies. Also they talked in the same way about the same things.

When the Association had been established for some time, it could be seen that it offered a wider field of operation for those leaders who could take more responsibility. It also enabled the different estates to join together for purely social activities. Visiting other estates was very popular.

The work of the Association was divided into three main areas: (a) field work; (b) policy, planning and administration; (c) relationships with outside bodies, both statutory and voluntary. Field work was concerned with the work of individual associations. The main work of the Association itself was concerned with training, interestate activities, old people's welfare, youth work, and the general provision of social welfare and recreational programmes. This work was carried out through committees, conferences and work-shops. The Association tried to establish good relations with, for example, the London County Council, the Borough Councils and the London Council of Social Service, with a view to influencing social policy.

33

The formation of the Association was a declaration of identity and independence. The setting up of a federal organisation was a sign for all to see that even the most informal relationships between individuals and groups had grown to a visible point of stability. It was a sign to the members themselves as well as to the outside world. The field workers and consultant believed that it could not have come into existence without the help given to the groups in the early days, and saw it partly as a vindication of their method of working. The Association was also an indication of the willingness and ability of this kind of informal group to come to terms with its social environment and to attempt what they felt to be necessary modifications.

The Association did not please everybody at first. Some of the groups feared for their independence and did not join. They felt that the Association might start telling them what to do. Others feared that the organisation might become party political. But by the end of its first year it had won recognition from its own members and from outside bodies, and the number of member-groups steadily increased. It was seen as a federation of independent community groups, banded together to help one another and to offer service to the wider community.

One of the first activities of the Association was to hold a series of workshops that came to be called club-room courses. These club-room courses were to provide local opportunities for discussions similar to those held at residential conferences. They were planned and sponsored by the Conferences and Training sub-committees.

The course usually consisted of a meeting one evening a week for four weeks, and was held by invitation of one of the member associations in their own clubroom. The community groups in that district of London were given a special invitation to attend. The host association provided refreshments.

## Club-room Courses

At first recruiting for these courses was a little slow. Some committees felt that their representatives might come home from the work-shop with 'new-fangled ideas that would make matters worse'. Sometimes reluctance was based on feelings of diffidence or inadequacy, expressed in such words as, 'Even if I did come, I wouldn't know how to tell the other committee members about it when I got back.'

In the course of several special visits to estates it was stressed that club-room courses were not like going back to school. It was not a question of knowing what to say or of knowing the right answers, but of being prepared to listen both to people with long experience of this kind of work as well as to people with similar difficulties. Eventually the courses became very popular. One had 100 per cent attendance. For some committee members it was the first time they had visited another estate, and for some associations it was the first time they had met their opposite numbers doing similar voluntary work on other estates.

A typical programme of one session a week for four weeks might include: a mock committee meeting; a session entitled 'Have you tried this?', in which a discussion could be based on a new activity launched by a group; a session devoted to one aspect of youth work; and, in the final week, a programme entitled 'Any Questions?'

An example is given below of two different ways of starting a discussion on committee procedure and the duties of the chairman, secretary and treasurer.

*Workshop Agenda.* The evening opened with a speech of welcome from the chairman of the host estate group. A field worker then gave a short introduction, and outlined the programme for the evening. The first mock speech, 'What committees do', was a kind of prize-day speech that praised committees to the skies. They were efficient, devoted, self-sacrificing, business-like and community spirited. They never argued, there was no rivalry between officers or factions, they were the cream of local democracy and of all community effort. The speech ended by suggesting that association committees had so far managed very well as they were. There did not appear to be any need for workshop training or the like. What was needed was more support for the committee in its 'truly marvellous efforts'.

The speaker was serious and convincing, and the speech was delivered like a memorial sermon at an Old Boys' Reunion. The audience was taken aback, although they had been told that the speech was simply a lead-in to discussion. The speaker was warmly applauded, and only when this died down did some of his listeners dare to remark that it was 'a bit much' or 'a bit overdone'. The second speaker's script put exactly the opposite case—that committees were unorganised in their approach to the work, inefficient in getting the work done, they behaved rudely to each other, played power politics in the association and on the estate, were irresponsible with other people's money and made scandalously exaggerated claims about what they were doing. The speaker was convincing. He concluded by suggesting that a good deal more thinking, planning and training would have to be undertaken before the committees could begin to carry out their responsibilities.

During coffee the whole assembly was busy agreeing or disagreeing with the speakers, comparing their own experiences with those described in the speeches and discussing them with the people sitting

35

nearby. They also formulated questions to be put to the chair later in the evening.

On another occasion a mock committee was held. An agenda was carefully prepared beforehand, with items that were directly applicable to the interests of the groups. Some of the field workers and some members of the Conferences and Training sub-committee took part. They had one 'rehearsal', but no one had a script. They agreed in broad outline on the characters they were to represent, and the line they were to take at the mock committee meeting. They put on a very good show indeed. One item on the agenda was about purchasing equipment and sports kit. It began very quietly, the committee agreeing that the expenditure was necessary, but when one woman proposed to make the shirts for half the price, things began to go off the rails. The treasurer thought this was a good idea; the youth leader said it was 'mad', no one would play in clothes like that, they had to be 'professional' in order to compete with other teams. Mrs. Jenkins, who had made the offer, was offended. The treasurer complained that it was the same old story, the youth worker persuading the committee to spend more and more on equipment—'endless, endless money'. Mr. Stanton, a former volunteer youth worker, agreed that 'all they seem to want to do nowadays is spend money', implying that things were different and better when he was in charge.

The chairman trying to restore order was told off by Mrs. Jenkins, who said that she had never been insulted when the 'old' chairman was in charge, he was able to keep the committee in order. One member suggested that the committee agree on the amount to be spent, then consider the items most necessary for the activity, and authorise the expenditure. He was getting this good point across when the secretary said he felt it was all a waste of time, since Bill, the youth leader, had already listed the equipment needed and priced it. The secretary felt that Bill should not be pushed around by 'us on the committee, as he is doing so good a job'. Charges and counter charges were made, and finally the youth leader admitted that he had already ordered the uniforms at wholesale prices, 'as cheap as they could be got'. The treasurer ruled that the order was unauthorised and invalid, and the youth leader said he would resign. The chairman accepted the resignation; the youth leader withdrew it. Mrs. Flowson, who had not yet spoken, said she really needed to have the advice of the committee on the old people's work, as she desperately needed help, and wanted them to publicise the need for volunteers in the estate News. Mr. Jones, the publicity secretary, said 'Of course'.

Finally the treasurer had to leave because the meeting had overrun by half an hour and he did not want to get home too late. The chairman said the committee had to continue in order to get all the work done. Mrs. Flowson and Mr. Jones started a meeting on their own on publicity for the old folks' work, planning what they would say in the next edition of the estate News. The youth worker and the chairman started arguing again about the sports kit and the meeting ended in disorder and ill-feeling, having accomplished nothing.

The members of the mock committee stayed on the stage, while the field worker picked out some of the things that had gone wrong with the meeting and asked the committee to account for some of their actions as committee members. The chairman thanked the speakers on the stage and opened the meeting for general discussion.

At once it was apparent that many of the points from the first speeches and from the staged committee meeting had gone home. Speakers from the audience reinforced much of what had been said and made similar points about committee behaviour. Gradually the emphasis passed from their own failings and inadequacies to questions of why things had gone wrong and what could be done to improve the conduct of committee meetings. The audience became very much aware that their own problems were not unique and began to take some responsibility for their situations instead of putting all the blame on their 'ineffective' chairman or 'obstinate' treasurer. This relieved the apparent hopelessness of some situations, especially when some members described how an even worse situation had been improved. It was obvious, if not explicit, in the general discussion that the ability to talk about these problems and to share experiences was extremely valuable. There was plenty of encouragement for the idea of future workshops.

As the evening progressed, some members were really beginning to learn how to use a workshop. There were fewer prolonged recountings of personal reminiscences or experiences, less accusation of their committee, fewer disguised questions intending to conceal the fact that it was the questioner who was facing the problem, and a readiness to consult others present—the experts, the field worker, the speakers and other members. By the end of the evening, instead of a few speakers from the floor, nearly everyone was taking part in the discussion. The workshop had in fact become a working group with the chairman playing less and less part in regulating the meeting and with members addressing questions to each other, elaborating or re-interpreting what had been said, and spontaneously offering information or advice.

Before the meeting closed the field-worker began to sum up and invited one of the experts to make some comments about groups. The expert began to describe the difference between a spontaneous friendship group and a task-centred group such as a committee. Both the summing up and the expert's comments fell on deaf ears:

there was a feeling that the group had done its work and did not want to go on. The chairman therefore brought the meeting to a close.

*Follow-up.* The club-room courses whenever possible were followed by a series of informal visits by the worker to the estates where there were committee members who had been present. They were asked whether the course had proved helpful in the work they were now doing, and whether there should be more of them.

Great satisfaction was found in the mock committee meeting and in the general discussion afterwards. 'Just what the doctor ordered', and 'Really to the point', were two of the comments. As might be expected, most of the members found the greatest satisfaction in the opportunity to meet others from similar groups, seeing 'what they had to put up with' and 'learning how they got on with the same problems'.

The club-room courses gave rise to a certain amount of practical activity. Some of the members visited other community groups and several telephoned members on other estates to ask for information and advice. The consensus of opinion indicated that the courses should continue.

## Working out a Common Problem

Most of the groups belonging to the Association of London Housing Estates were doing some kind of work with old people. Some had elaborate and well-run programmes, some engaged in sporadic bursts of intensive activity, some still found it all very difficult. The concentrated and sustained effort needed to keep a well balanced programme going was no easy task for any of the groups. A special feature of the conference they held on work with old people was the fact that the delegates were the actual members of the old people's clubs, not only the leaders.

## Conference on Work with Old People

In the preparation for the conference the Association of London Housing Estates sent out to all groups a notice outlining their proposals for a conference. They asked for information about particular problems encountered in work with old people on each estate, for suggestions for discussion at the conference, and for the number of members who would be willing to attend. The replies to the questionnaire showed that groups with a well developed programme of old people's work had much to tell other groups that would be both helpful and appropriate to their needs. These stronger

38

groups were also willing to organise detailed presentations of their work and method for discussion at the conference. The questionnaire showed too that groups who found the work difficult tended to feel so discouraged that they could not believe a conference could be of any help to them. These groups were visited several times and encouraged to give it a chance. Another result shown by the questionnaire was that the largest number of groups provided a middle range of service for old people and had five problems in common.

The first problem was that the old people who apparently needed the most frequent visits were sometimes said to resent the intrusion of a visitor. Secondly, volunteer visitors on the estates could never make the full round in time and many old people were omitted from the weekly schedule or were visited at random. Thirdly, relations between estate workers and Borough Old People's workers were often confused, intermittent or non-existent. Fourthly, a programme of varied activity, weekly visiting, and club-room meetings tended to develop, reach a climax and sometimes fall off again. Fifthly, some volunteer workers tended to monopolise old people's work, and even when unable to do the job properly themselves, would resent offers of help.

Information about these common problems was very helpful to the Planning Committee of the Association as they came to draw up the conference programme. An important decision was to make this a conference to give 'the consumer's point of view'. Transport was provided. The programme included outside speakers, experts on the problems of old people, and reports from estate committees and volunteer workers, as well as a series of workshops for the participants.

The conference was planned to last for a whole day and to take place at Oxford House settlement which had accommodation for general meetings, small study groups, morning coffee, lunch and tea, and was easily accessible by bus and tube. It was felt to be very important that several Borough Old People's Welfare Workers should be present, both to speak to the conference and to be available in the study groups, in order to stress the need for co-operation between workers of the local authority and of the associations. Much of the study and discussion at the conference centred on the five common problems brought out by the questionnaire. Some of the comments and points are summarised here.

*Resenting Intrusion.* On the subject of old people who did not want to be visited, the following suggestions were made:

'If you say you come from the association to do something for them, they may take it amiss, as they often do not want to be given things or to be helped. It is often better not to mention the association

39

at all, but simply to say you dropped in as a neighbour to say hello.'

'If a person does not want a visit from a stranger, even from one on the estate, why not simply ask the family on either side to drop in occasionally? Then you can visit the family to see if anything is needed, and give them any help that can be passed to the old folk.'

'If some of the old people are already visited by a priest, minister, relative or friend, try to find out when these visits take place and say that you are ready to step in if need be and certainly in any emergency.'

'Some people are just no good at visiting old folks and unfortunately they are often the very people who want to do it.'

'Visiting is not always needed, some old folks like to be independent and this should be respected.'

'We mustn't always take their grumbling too seriously. I visit an old lady who runs to the window to make sure that it's me, rushes back to put on the kettle and then comes to the door. She opens it and every time says in a very sharp way indeed, "Oh, it's you again. Well, come in. I suppose you want some tea as usual. That's all you come for." I'd be very foolish indeed to be discouraged by this, since it is obviously her way of getting on with people.'

*Failing to Fulfil the Schedule.* One reason why some volunteer workers failed to complete the full round of weekly visiting was because they tried to combine the visiting with their work as subscription collectors. This was generally felt to be too much for one person. While she was sitting talking with the old people, she would be nagged by the need to get on with the collecting, and if she was kept talking while collecting she would feel she ought to be with the next old person on the schedule. A separate worker for each job was far preferable.

Some visitors failed to plan their visiting to fit in with their own housework and domestic itinerary. They tended to try to do it all in one afternoon or evening the same day each week. One visitor described how she planned her visits throughout the week, one on the way to the shops on Monday morning, one on the way home where she could be sure of a cup of tea, a short visit on Wednesday while the washing was whirling at the launderette, one to an early riser on Friday morning after taking the children to school, and one on the way back from taking a toddler to the playground. Not everyone felt that they could cope with this rather intricate interweaving, but the idea commended itself to some rather than trying to make a single span of time outside the ordinary household schedule.

On the whole it was felt that the best method was to have a team of visitors who planned complete coverage of all the old people on the estate and who agreed to visit the same people week by week. It was felt that the team idea fell short if it involved too many changes in visitors or if there were any doubts about who was responsible each week. The old people who needed and enjoyed visits usually preferred to see the same face at the same time each week and it was agreed that this expectation should be met whenever possible.

*Co-operation with Local Authority Workers.* The conference was able to bring some apprehensions and misunderstandings out into the open. There was a general feeling among the delegates from one association that their plans and their work were not approved of by the authorities. The origin of this was found to be in some advice given by a worker, which was taken as criticism. The association had organised two outings, one to the sea, where the buses were over-crowded, and one to Canterbury, which was too long a trip without enough stops. The advice from the worker, which would have prevented this, had not been accepted at the time, and this had rankled ever since. The associations also felt that some workers disapproved of their giving things away, especially Christmas baskets and hampers. This turned out to be a misunderstanding of advice given by a few professional workers on the contents of some hampers. They advised more substantial food but the associations liked to put in things which old people would not ordinarily get.

The conference was an excellent opportunity for stating frankly and simply that the work of the associations and their groups was seen to be very important indeed by most local authorities and professional social workers. Difficulties arose when the groups took on regular visiting and then let it lapse without notifying anybody. Sometimes work seemed to be duplicated. If, for example, an association organised a club for old people it could well be that those attending club-room activities were those most able to get out and make use of existing social amenities in the neighbourhood; the association workers could have better spent their time visiting those who could not, or did not want to, leave their homes. The conference clearly showed the need for closer relations between the associations and the local authorities, and also the need for more open appreciation by the authority of the part played by the associations in the service of old people, and for their recognition, support and encouragement. Even the most problem-prone estates, usually the first to resent the idea of 'integration' with other services, glimpsed the wisdom of closer, although not formal, co-operation with those already at work with the old people in their communities. Not every borough was able to offer the same recognition or help, especially as some boroughs themselves were not very far advanced in their provisions. But wherever possible, local associations should make use of the help and experience of the authorities.

*Rise and Fall.* When old people's programmes built up to a climax and then fell into a decline, the reason was said to be more likely poor budgeting on the part of the committee than poor planning on the part of the volunteer workers. If a committee had done some successful fund-raising, it might almost forcibly expand the old people's programme, saying, 'This is our first concern. We have the money now, let's spend it on something worth while before it's all gone.' Another version of a committee's wish for quick expansion was given by a worker who had been told, 'You are always asking for more money for the old people's work. Now that you have it you're slow off the mark.' The recommendation arising from this discussion was that a half-yearly or if possible a yearly budget should be planned in order to keep the programme on an even keel throughout the year. This was felt to be an acceptable suggestion for groups with a moderate programme already in action, but groups in more difficult situations could not see how their workers could educate the committees to this way of thinking. The decline that often seemed to follow expansion was thought to be partly due to the old people themselves, who at first were pleased to have something to do and somewhere to go, but as the activities multiplied found that it all became too much. It was also noted that the fuller the programme, the more planning was done by the volunteer workers and the smaller part played by the old people themselves. Examples were given of complete lack of consultation and there was a good deal of discussion of self-programming in old people's work.

*Lone Workers.* The volunteer worker who insisted on doing everything herself was seen to be a real problem. While she did a very good job and was often very well liked by the old people, it was clear that her methods prevented the work from developing. She could not do all the visits, so on her own authority she would leave out a number of old people. She often did club-room work as well as visiting and there were times when one or other had to go by the board. She was rarely 'under the control' of the committee and was more like a lone wolf or a one-man show.

Two suggestions to improve the situation were made. First, that a lone worker might be invited and encouraged to visit a number of associations with a varied programme of work, in the hope that she might see what could be done on her estate with more help from the membership. Second, that a professional worker might get to know her informally, encourage her to visit other work for old people and make a special point of recognising the value of her work on the estate. It was said that a lone worker will often take advice from a 'professional' who approved of her efforts but not from another volunteer worker or association member on the estate. (After the

42

conference, it was established that this last suggestion had been successful with one lone worker, who after helping with some old people's work nearby, came back to the estate to work with other members of the association.)

The crucial question, 'Whom are we doing this for?' was raised at the conference, both in the discussion groups and in the open discussion. For many present, it was the first time that the implications of such a question had been explored, and they saw the possible confusion and negative attitudes that could affect the work if this question were not looked at seriously. It was recognised that one of the reasons for doing this work was to build up the local association, so that it should be seen as a 'Housing Estate Community Group that is doing things for its members'. The volunteer workers, too, naturally wanted to do the work in order to be seen to be helpful or because they liked to organise and get things done. But simply to see old people as an opportunity for service could lead to their exploitation for the sake of the association's reputation for good works. To see the need for the work to be done and to enjoy doing it came second to the old people's understanding of what was necessary. Ideally the programme of service and activities should grow out of good contacts with the old people themselves, with the workers showing themselves willing and able to provide a service to meet their needs.

The conference brought out the point that once an association becomes established it tends to have the same expectations of its members as the statutory and voluntary bodies seemed to have of the association in its early days. Just as a professional youth leader expected the association to share his definition of a 'youth club' so the association now expected its members to share its definition of service. The field workers were delighted to have this point made by the conference, as their own relationship to the groups made it difficult for them to draw attention to it as often as circumstances warranted. The delegates themselves were quite clear that 'we should not be forcing things on them; we should help them to see what they need and stand by ready to help; we should help them to say what they want and let them help us to provide it'. It was possible in the workshops and in the open discussion to remind the groups how much they had resented in the early days any idea of service being laid on without their active assistance and co-operation. Simply to discuss this with delegates at a conference on a single aspect of the work did little to change the attitude in the field. Yet once the point had been made it could always be referred to and this proved to be very valuable in the future.

## *Two Results of the Conference*

First, the problem-prone groups were readily able to admit their discouragement. But even the most discouraged saw the possibility of giving more attention to old people's work on their estates because it could be started without too much internal controversy. The conference had given many examples of associations where members and residents were willing to 'forget old scores' or to sink differences in order to get on with work for old people. This was in clear contrast to some other kinds of work which were more difficult. The conference enabled the field workers to arrange to visit the groups in difficulties and, even more important, to arrange for volunteer workers from estates where the work was going well to visit and share some of their experience and know-how.

The second result was a strengthening of the Association of London Housing Estates itself. Delegates returning to committees and associations reported on the Old People's Conference as the work of the Association of London Housing Estates and not of the field workers of the London Council of Social Service.

## ATTEMPTS IN OTHER SETTINGS

During the course of the field work, the question was raised many times, both within the Community Development Department of the London Council of Social Service and by colleagues outside, of the possibility of using this method of work in other settings.

This section gives two illustrations of attempts by the Department to translate the approach and method of working with housing estate groups into other situations, and suggests some of the factors that need to be taken into account by those who would like to work in the same way. The first project did not get beyond the discussion stage; in the second, one of the workers became involved but was not able to continue.

## *A Deteriorating Neighbourhood*

The problem was presented by social workers, clergy and councillors in different ways. There was general agreement however that the neighbourhood under discussion was physically and socially deteriorating. There was a wide variety of social problems ranging from shortage of housing and resulting overcrowding to incipient racial tension. The scheme was for working with autonomous groups, but at the same time for trying to fit into the pattern of existing statutory and voluntary services. The neighbourhood was already somewhat familiar through the presence of some West

Indian residents, with whom contact had previously been established. After further reconnaissance of the area the following observations were made:

It was an area of great social disorganisation—families on National Assistance, children in care, broken families, juvenile delinquency, young people on probation, and a fairly high adult crime rate, mostly in petty crime.

The residents were from many places of origin, with many families from the north and from Ireland, a sizeable West Indian and African population, and a good number of families from clearance areas in other parts of London.

There was a serious housing problem. Most of the Victorian and Edwardian houses, built at the beginning of the century, were divided up haphazardly without adequate kitchen and toilet facilities, and in a very bad state of repair. There was often severe overcrowding, and some exploitation by landlords.

There was a great lack of recreational facilities for the whole area, especially of the kind that could be expected to meet the needs of different ethnic groups. There were no small formal meeting places.

The population was not as transient as had been expected. Most families had been resident for five years or more, but the coming and going of unattached males, and to a lesser extent of un-attached females, gave a first impression of excessively high turn-over of residents. Sometimes the males were father, uncles or brothers from another part of the country, who would bring their families as soon as they settled. Sometimes the father simply left his family, or returned after a long absence. On the whole, however, it seemed that the area did have a stable resident population which could be offered an informal neighbourhood service.

Most of this information came from colleagues in the voluntary and statutory bodies—school care committee members, landlords (or more accurately, landladies),—and some from former contacts in the West Indian groups in the community.

Based on the experience with housing estate community groups, a scheme was outlined which could best be implemented by workers with different skills, according to need. It might consist of a case worker who would help people to make contact with the existing social services, a group worker whose main contribution would be to help organise and service already existing groups or those which might form, and a community development worker as their team leader. Ideally, all the workers should have some understanding of community development as a method of social work. The success of any scheme would depend on the workers getting to know, and becoming accepted, by the residents.

E

A starting point for a scheme for work in the neighbourhood was suggested by the existence of several informal groups. Some of the mothers with whom the social workers were in contact were anxious to improve conditions in the neighbourhood because they were worried about their children. A start might be made with an attempt to bring these mothers together to say what they thought needed to be done. The scheme outlined the following points:

The workers would try to get to know the autonomous groups in the neighbourhood, encourage and support them, advise and help them, without attempting to superimpose what they or the agency saw as a suitable programme, and with no preconceived ideas about the structure of autonomous groups or the processes of group management most appropriate to the task. They should not be planning activities that they thought best for the individual members, the group or the community, but helping the group to do what emerged from its own experience. The method of work would be similar to the work on the estates. The objective would be the social development of the area.

Some small part of the area, preferably a part in which three or four autonomous groups were already known to exist, should be made the focus for further inquiry. The work, at least in the early stages, could then be seen to take place within discernible geographical boundaries, which would help make the task manageable for the worker, and later comprehensible to the groups and their members. This geographical area would doubtless change its shape several times, along social lines, patterns of association and social interaction, as the work developed, but the work could at least begin within some definite, even if tentative, boundaries.

A meeting place that could accommodate small and medium-sized groups would be necessary eventually. This was important because overcrowding in the home and the need to get out from time to time was something of which the mothers in several of the groups were very much aware. It would be necessary for the workers to have some base in the neighbourhood to work from, but this should not be an office.

The first efforts to get in touch with residents would be through families who had already established some roots in the neighbourhood, in spite of the fact that it was probably the newer residents who were in most need. The older residents had already formed small house and street groups. They met in the ordinary way when out shopping or at the launderette. These established patterns of association might be broadened to include coming together on a slightly more formal basis to discuss matters of common concern. This view was supported by the fact that the older residents seemed to do most of the complaining about the lack of amenities, the behaviour of the newcomers, and the absence of neighbour-liness, all of which they claimed rightly or wrongly was different from 'the old days'. The complaints were probably aimed at the changing patterns of neighbourliness in the area.

At first the statutory and voluntary bodies should be kept well in the background. This would encourage the residents to feel that they must get on with the work themselves and not leave it to others. Also the residents might be unable or unwilling to state their case, discuss their needs, and suggest ways of beginning the work in the presence of 'professionals'. This way of working would help the residents make better use of the existing services of the statutory and voluntary bodies. The work would also aim to help the agencies to move out into the neighbourhood and offer the service in a less formal way in a less formal setting.

It was hoped that the sponsoring committee would accept, and that it would be made clear by the worker, that the service being offered was not individual guidance or counselling or family case-work. This would not prevent a person with casework skills helping individuals to use the appropriate casework services. The work from the beginning should be seen in its widest perspective and based on local self-help in a variety of situations, avoiding when possible too early a definition of any one aspect of the service. No publicity, either city-wide, or in the local press, should be permitted in advance of the work. This could prejudice the issue in the neighbourhood before the work had a chance to get established.

It would be necessary that the sponsoring or management com-mittee should understand this method of work, and that the nature of the service should be deduced from the actual local situation and not from preconceived ideas of the committee or of the agency. The committee should see that its main task in the early stages would be to support and encourage the workers in the unavoidable slow start of the work and the many discouragements that they would

have. The object of the work would be to encourage a number of autonomous groups to work towards providing for themselves whatever activities or amenities they needed, and to press the authorities to provide the relevant amenities and to improve the services.

The general verdict at the time was that this particular scheme was impracticable. There are other schemes along similar lines, which have started since.

## *Comment*

After much discussion and consideration the main reasons why it was not undertaken appeared to the consultant to be:

It was not possible to say exactly how the scheme fitted into the already existing pattern of social welfare services and so it would not be seen as the job of any particular agency. It was felt that to set up a new agency to do this work was unwise and would only complicate the existing pattern of social welfare provision.

The scheme as outlined did not seem to be designed to fulfil any specific existing need. 'Wouldn't traditional mothers' clubs organised by a worker be a better and easier way of starting?' asked one of the professionals.

The analogy to housing estate community groups was not developed sufficiently by the field workers to be convincing. The groups on housing estates were seen as special groups with special difficulties in a recognisable local area, and very different from the informal groups in the neighbourhood in question. It was not agreed that the autonomous neighbourhood group in most urban settings faced the same kind of problems or required the same kind of approach from the worker and the agency as the housing estate community group.

But perhaps the greatest difficulty was seen as finding the money and the workers for such a scheme.

Although in this instance the scheme could not be put into practice, the approach and method described has some relevance to the problems of the rapidly deteriorating neighbourhoods in large urban centres. In such a neighbourhood there will be existing social agencies. These have long traditions of work, but their own understanding of what is needed might not tally with that of the local people or of community development workers. The formal agencies might find this method of approach difficult to accept.

Part of the work involved would mean offering a service to the agencies that would help them to understand the special needs of autonomous groups. As a result these agencies would then be able to offer more effective services to the neighbourhood.

### Work with Immigrant Groups

In the early days of immigration from the West Indies the newcomers made their own informal arrangements for supporting and helping one another. They were assisted in various ways by individuals and organisations in the existing community.

The West Indian groups were, for the most part, scattered, unorganised and difficult to identify. Neighbours and friends met together to celebrate the arrival of a relative, a wedding, a christening, or some religious festival. They also discussed amongst themselves major problems such as housing and employment, where to go for information and how to use the social services. People from the same island or town met together, and West Indians living in the same street or district tended to use the same pub, cafe or other informal meeting place. A few inter-racial clubs were formed.

In 1958 evidence of racial tension in some parts of the country caused alarm and concern in the West Indies and in the United Kingdom. Immediately it became important to consult with representatives of West Indian opinion at the local level. But these indigenous leaders were unknown: they had to be found, and this could only be done by identifying local autonomous groups. The same year the Federal Government in the West Indies decided to send two community development advisers to assist the Migrant Services Division of the High Commissioner in this country. As part of the normal work of the Division, their aim was to encourage good relations between the immigrants and the settled community. In particular the community development workers tended to identify and make contact with informal groups. They offered help and advice to clubs and inter-racial organisations, and encouraged and tried to develop West Indian leadership.

At the invitation of the head of the Migrants Division, West Indian leaders met once a month in London to discuss various problems. The two community development workers took an active part in these meetings. The groups represented gave a report of their activities, discussed news from home, met visiting politicians, and invited speakers who could discuss subjects of importance to West Indians living in this country.

Social events were planned and information exchanged on a wide range of topics. There was always a sprinkling of English people present. Among these was a representative of the London Council of Social Service who was especially concerned with the problems of immigrants. The L.C.S.S. had previously set up an Immigrants' Advisory Committee with representatives of Government departments, local authorities and welfare organisations in London.

The genuine desire for integration, and anxiety about recent events, created an ambivalent attitude towards the development of West Indian leadership among those responsible in this country. It was hoped that West Indian leadership, when it emerged, would do so through existing organisations and that immigrants would join church, social welfare, Trade Union, political and recreational organisations.

But to the newly arrived immigrant, membership often meant that even in his leisure time he had to fit in and conform to an unfamiliar way of behaving and a different type of programme. There were relatively few who could do this easily. Those who could, had either lived in this country for some time, or had been in more privileged positions at home.

49

Any type of organisation sponsored by West Indians, though obviously contributing to the development of West Indian leadership, was vaguely felt by the social agencies as a possible threat to integration itself, and therefore not to be encouraged.

It was against this background that eventually the Standing Conference of West Indian leaders was formed. It arose directly out of the monthly meetings. It was guided in the early days by the two community development officers from the West Indies and was well supported by some English representatives.

*Autonomous Groups.* By 1960 the number of individual groups known to the community development workers had greatly increased. These groups met locally. They enjoyed one another's company and the opportunity to share experiences. They did not resent the presence of non-West Indians; indeed they invited representatives of the majority group to address them and to discuss particular problems. But, at the beginning, they were not completely at ease or entirely happy with this situation. They wanted to voice common grievances, and explore common difficulties in their own way, and the presence of someone who might misunderstand their interpretation of the situation or resent the emphasis put upon certain aspects of their difficulties, particularly of colour, would not be helpful. On the whole the groups seemed to want to meet on their own, argue matters out, state their grievances as strongly as they felt them, and then trim the grievances down to size for discussion in a 'mixed' setting.

Sometimes these groups had difficulties in running the business part of their gatherings—difficulties in working out the role of the person chosen to chair a meeting in the same way as any other new organisation might have. Although they saw the need for linking up with other immigrant groups to discuss common difficulties, they did not want to lose their independence. They were on the whole anxious to do something on their own and to solve their own difficulties. They needed an identity in their own eyes, in the eyes of the communities in which they existed, and in the eyes of other groups of the same kind. As autonomous community groups in the early stages of development they clearly had much in common with the housing estate community groups, but had come into being in response to different social pressures and in different social circumstances.

On the whole the situation with the groups in London appeared to be an encouraging one. It was possible to consider the actions of the groups as entirely normal in the early stages of development as autonomous groups. They needed time to achieve common agreement about their own difficulties, and to develop common processes and procedures in individual groups and among the various groups, before any move could be made towards integration. It was extremely important that the groups should be free to work on their own and to develop at their own pace, so that in their own time they would be willing and able to make fruitful contact with the larger community and to face the difficulties entailed.

*Indigenous Leaders.* The emergence of indigenous leaders is crucial to working successfully with autonomous groups. It is necessary to progress from finding and helping indigenous leaders in the separate groups to the emergence of indigenous leadership arising from the whole complex of groups. Such leadership helps meet the needs of individual groups and of groups in association, and gradually it can learn to interpret the problems of immigrant or housing estate or other autonomous groups to the outside community. It can also interpret the feelings, attitudes and behaviour of the outside community to the groups. The importance of this new leadership is that it represents the groups, their needs and aspirations, and is seen to do so by the larger community as well as by the groups themselves.

The self-appointed leader, as distinct from the indigenous leader, bases his leadership, not on the groups he represents, but on his recognition by the statutory and voluntary bodies, the 'authorities', and the outside world. Although he is a member of a minority group and knows something of its needs and aspirations, his own values and standards and the exercise of his leadership belong more to the outside world, and he is not seen by the section of the community he is supposed to represent as 'really one of them'. This is especially so of the middle-class professional worker, who may by his training have already identified himself with the majority culture. This is not, of course, in any way to underestimate the need for this kind of leader or to doubt his usefulness and sincerity, but simply to point out some of the difficulties that need to be faced in establishing minority group leadership as truly representative.

*Social Integration.* This method of offering help to immigrant groups does not imply that efforts should not be made at the same time to encourage the groups and their members to make contacts outside the immigrant community. But such efforts must take account of the needs of groups to husband their social resources for self-development in the early stages of their existence. The point comes at which the groups and the whole immigrant community are encouraged to move out and join in the life of the larger society, but the timing of this move must be of their own choosing. In the same way the housing estate groups are now much more ready to take responsibility in the wider community.

51

## Comment

Although the Immigration Act has restricted the number of immigrants coming into this country, there are large groups of immigrants in many cities who are still in the early stages of adjusting to urban British society. The need for development work along these lines is still pressing.

Important considerations to be taken into account in using this approach are:

That it should be made clear to the statutory and voluntary bodies and to the immigrant groups that the isolation of the immigrant group in the early stages is not the ultimate objective of the work, but a necessary starting point for future integration into the larger community.

That the field work programme, especially the preliminary contact with the groups, should be based on the natural divisions existing within the immigrant community, e.g. place of origin, class, etc. Any attempt to help create points of contact and lines of communication between the natural divisions should come later.

That the programmes should have three main emphases:

(a) The development of solidarity within the various subgroups. (b) The later development of contact and communication between the individual groups, the complex of groups, and the larger community. (c) The development from within the different groups of indigenous leadership whose experience of helping to build solidarity within a particular group will probably enable them to take on the work of developing communication between the groups and the community.

Taking into consideration all the difficulties of this method, it would seem to be the most appropriate in the *first phase* of work with immigrant groups.

Because of the similarity of the housing estate groups to the immigrant groups, when the community development workers from the West Indies returned home, the community development workers at the London Council of Social Service would have liked to continue some of their work. At that time, however, it was not generally accepted that there are two levels of community work, one at the formal and organisational level, and the other concerned with informal or autonomous groups (community organisation and community development). For this and other internal reasons it was not possible to experiment in this way.

# 4 Examples of Field-work Practice

Chapters One to Three have outlined the needs and problems of the groups and the development of the service. This chapter is an attempt to give a picture of field-work practice by presenting a typical association, and six separate examples of the kind of field-work situation that may be met.

PAISLEY COMMON AS A REPRESENTATIVE COMMUNITY GROUP

The new Paisley Common housing estate is in south London. It has 700 dwellings, let and managed by the local authority. The population is 2,000–2,500. The estate was constructed in two parts, 550 dwellings in 1954 and a further 150 seven years later. The latter consist of a 16-storey tower block of flats, and some small houses. The early development was in eight-storey blocks of flats of uniform design. Most of the families in the new part of the estate had transferred from other local authority property or had been re-housed from a redevelopment area. Thirty of the new houses were of the bungalow type, specially designed for elderly people. The housing authority had provided a club-room consisting of a small hall, kitchen with hatch into the hall, cloakrooms, a committee room, and storage space.

### The Tenants' Association

The Paisley Common tenants' association was founded in 1955 to encourage a friendly atmosphere on the estate, to take an interest in the amenities of the estate, to manage the club-room and to sponsor activities. The first initiative came from three residents who wanted a pedestrian crossing and a playground. They joined with several others to make an approach to the local authority, as a result of which they stayed together as a committee, and a tenants' association was started.

The association has a constitution providing for democratic procedures, and its work is organised through an executive committee of twelve members and a chairman, secretary and treasurer. Its meetings are usually attended by nine or ten people. There is a sports section and a social committee, and special activity groups. The association has a family membership subscription of 6d. a week, collected every two weeks from each flat. Elderly residents are not asked for subscriptions.

An annual general meeting is held to report to the membership and to elect a new committee. The activities of the association are open to all the members. Children's outings are open to all children on the estate, whether their parents are members or not. Through its committee the association keeps in touch with the Housing Manager, the Borough Youth Organiser, the Old People's Welfare officer, the Citizens' Advice Bureau, and one of the local churches, whose hall it uses for large socials. It also has the use of the school playground some evenings in the week. The association is affiliated to the Association of London Housing Estates.

The largest items of expenditure are the rent, lighting and heating of the club-room, and the hire of the church hall. Other items include adult socials and outings, parties and outings for the children, the youth club, and other clubroom activities. There is a welfare fund which enables the association to give small presents to people who are ill or in hospital. The association has a turnover of about £1,500 a year. Its income comes from subscriptions, raffles, Bingo, the canteen and special events.

## Programme of Activities

The association has a programme of social activities for the residents on the estate. Besides those mentioned above, it runs a youth club in the club-room with two meetings a week; it sponsors a football club for teenagers; it has a Golden Age club for older residents, meeting two afternoons a week; it joins with other housing estates for an annual sports day, and takes part in a swimming gala. It offers opportunities for residents to participate in its work either on the committee as officers or members, or on special committees for particular activities or events. They can also give service by visiting old people who may live alone, or families temporarily needing help or support, or collecting association subscriptions. There are also opportunities for special responsibility in one of the activities, for example, as a youth work leader, doorman, canteen supervisor, or editing the news sheet. The association has organised special outings to the bulb fields in Lincolnshire and the hop fields in Kent. Once for a women's outing, about 30 husbands cooked the dinner and looked after the children on a Sunday.

For a while the mothers ran a nursery group and a children's club. A Bingo session is held once a week, as the subscriptions alone will not finance the activities, and this has become an important social occasion, providing a regular opportunity for a large number of people to get together. Old-time dancing is very popular. The association has a small film discussion group and a fishing club, and has organised several theatre parties. Recently it lent money to a family in difficulty, and helped a child care officer to find a foster home for a child in court. Several of those now working with old people are discussing a luncheon club, to be held in the club-room, with meals provided through the meals-on-wheels service, once or twice a week. The association acts on behalf of its members, and sometimes on behalf of all the residents on the estate, in dealings with the Housing Department and various statutory and voluntary bodies.

*Notes on Some of the Personalities.* Mr. Ormond, the present chairman of the tenants' association, works with London Transport. He is good at running meetings, is fair and not easily roused, is a stickler for procedure, and makes the committee meetings a little too formal. Kind and considerate as a person, he is inclined to expect too much from committee members, and he is disturbed if his standards are not met. He has a much needed stabilising effect on the committee and on the association's work.

Mr. O'Leary, the secretary, is a tall Irishman, who works in a brewery. He has a ready wit and a rather erratic attitude to his secretarial duties, which upsets the chairman from time to time. He is a likeable man with a warm personality, though apt to flare up at committee meetings, usually when he is taken to task for forgetting to do something. But, as even the chairman admits, 'the committee wouldn't be the same without him'.

Mr. Johnson, the treasurer, is a book-keeper. He is a thin and cantankerous man, not very happy at home, with a rather domineering wife. He is usually the main opponent of any financial or other help proposed for the youth club. His financial reports are long and complicated, but the association knows they are sound.

Mr. Mortimer works in the docks. He was a founder-member of the association, and regarded it in its early days as a grievance committee to fight the landlord when necessary, and to take up complaints. As the association developed he became interested in meeting social and recreational needs.

Mrs. Miller is a widow with teenage children. She and a friend have run the canteen for the youth club and the adult socials through-out the existence of the association. She is one of the youth club's most valuable allies.

These are perhaps the outstanding members of the committee. Three other members represent various sections such as the old people's work, youth club, and social activities.

One of the people with whom the association has to deal is Mr. Rufus, the Housing Manager, who at first saw the association as a possible threat to his authority but later came to realise that it could be of help to him. The association and the Housing Department now work hand in hand.

*Pattern of Participation.* Of the 700 dwellings on the estate, about 500 families pay a subscription regularly. Many pay a subscription but seldom use the club-room except for special events. They occasionally go on outings. They like to feel that the association is there should any trouble arise, and that it provides recreation for the children and looks after the old people. If asked for special support in money or kind, most of them are willing to give it. They read the monthly news sheet (which is of a high standard.)

About 300 families take part more or less regularly in a number of activities. About 50–60 people undertake the work of the association. They sit on committees, organise sports activities, collect subscriptions, work in the canteen, and carry the weight of the organisation.

New activities are suspect and have to be nurtured for a long time and heavily publicised before they find support. In this way an excellent drama group, a small photographic society, a holiday planning group and a fishing club came into being. It is the familiar programme—adult socials, the youth club, the children's outings and activities, the football teams, welfare activities, and Bingo—that keep the association going.

The pattern of participation is affected by the season of the year, the age groupings among the residents, and the size and location of the club premises. In the summer there are a number of outdoor activities, but in winter the club-room is heavily booked for activities on week nights and for weddings and parties at the weekends.

When the tenants first moved in and the children were young, the emphasis was on play groups and junior clubs; later the play group was dropped and there was much more emphasis on working with teenagers. Since the club-room is small and has no stage, the association has to hire the church or school hall for larger gatherings. As one would expect, the families living nearest the club-room use it most.

*Current Problems.* The association is currently facing four problems:

As more families on the estate come to own cars, the parking problem has become more difficult. The number of official parking spaces is insufficient for the residents, and people from outside also park their cars on the estate. Mothers worry about the children, who have less space for play and are apt to be in danger. The association is negotiating with the Housing Department to see if barrier gates could be erected that could be closed at night except to residents with cars, who would have keys.

The committee is also worried about a number of families who have come to live in one part of the estate, whose standards of behaviour leave something to be desired. They feel that some of these families are giving the estate a bad name, and they are at a loss to know what to do. The chairman and the treasurer are in favour of making some complaint to the families and to the Housing Manager, but the rest of the committee feel they should be given time to settle down.

The association is concerned about the work with young people on the estate. They have had a flourishing youth club, with sometimes more than 100 young people in the club-room twice a week. Recently the numbers have fallen off. Interests seem to have changed in the same age group. Even activities such as football, cricket and camping are not very popular. More young pepole are going off the estate for their social life. While some of them join in the adult activities and are willing to undertake some service for the association, the majority are not so interested. They often go and talk to individual members of the committee who are sympathetic towards them, and occasionally ask for special activities such as the organisation of an all-night walk, a trip to the coast, or a holiday abroad, but the committee feel that they are not doing enough for the young people.

Committee organisation also presents a problem. The range of activities and the number of special events have increased over the years. The size of the committee, however, has remained the same, and young people are not being trained to take over some of the work. The chairman is very much aware that new blood is wanted in the committee, but the annual general meeting re-elects the same people year after year.

The Paisley Common Tenants' Association is not isolated socially, nor is it living in a vacuum. The work of the association is directly affected by national policies for housing and rents, by the transport problems of a big city, and by changes in social attitudes in the community as a whole. Some of these wider issues are beyond the scope of small, autonomous groups, but where possible and appropriate they can be considered by the Association of London Housing Estates, representing many such groups.

It was inevitable that the Paisley Association was slightly isolationist in its attitude during the early years, when it had to create its

57

identity and consolidate its work by differentiating itself from the neighbouring community. Now it is represented on the Road Safety Committee and the local Council of Social Service, and takes a more active part in borough affairs. More could be done, however, to strengthen its links with organisations in the immediate neighbourhood, particularly with reference to facilities for young people.

## A Chronological Account

The following chronological account of field work on the Paisley Common estate, by Miss Paget, covers a number of years and provides enough information to show the representative nature of the estate and of the situations encountered there.

### 1954

*June.* Paisley Common had been open and occupied for about five months when Miss Paget, the field worker, received a telephone call from Mr. Rufus, the Housing Manager. He said he had given her name to a Mr. Mortimer, who was a resident on the Paisley Common estate, as he thought she might be able to help him and some of the residents who had got together to form a committee.

Phone call from Mr. Mortimer: they had several problems on their new estate, and he understood that she might be able to help them. Miss Paget made an appointment to visit and to meet some of the residents at his flat.

The main item discussed was the need for a pedestrian crossing. Miss Paget explained that this was not the responsibility of the Housing Department, and she suggested that they write to the Road Safety Officer for the Borough asking if they could go and see him, or inviting him to the estate. There was then a general discussion about the need for a playground. Miss Paget found out that there was to be a club-room on the estate, but that it was not yet finished, and that the committee had some general intention of forming a tenants' association. The worker walked round the estate and heard about some of the minor problems which had arisen in connection with the lifts and the communal laundry. She said she would be very interested to keep in touch with the group, and perhaps they would phone her if she could do anything to help them. She had previously explained the nature of the agency she worked for and the services which they offered.

*November.* The worker wrote to Mr. Mortimer saying she hoped that they had been able to get a pedestrian crossing and that things were settling down on the estate; she wondered how they were getting on. She enclosed an invitation to a meeting at her office which was to be

58

attended by representatives of some of the other groups. She suggested that he and his wife, and perhaps other members of the committee, might like to attend. She did not get a reply.

## 1955

*January*. When Miss Paget saw the Housing Manager about some other estate, she enquired how Paisley Common was getting on, and he said he thought there had been some changes in the committee and he had not heard from them recently. He had been afraid, to start with, that they were going to come to him with a constant stream of complaints, but after the first few months, when he had managed to deal with some of their problems, he hadn't heard anything.

*March*. Telephone call from Mr. O'Leary, who said he was now chairman of the tenants' group. He reminded Miss Paget that he had formerly lived on the Planetree estate and had met her when he was a member of the association there. He said he had recently taken over from Mr. Mortimer and he wanted the committee to be a properly constituted tenants' association. He understood that the club-room would be ready by the end of the year, and he thought they ought to hold a meeting for all the residents on the estate very shortly.

Miss Paget attended a meeting, which once again was held in Mr. Mortimer's flat. About 10 people were present. There was no agenda. In the course of the evening they discussed the fact that they were a self-elected group, that they were not collecting regular subscriptions, and that they had no formal rules. A raffle had been organised on several occasions to meet their expenses. It was decided that a tenants' meeting should be called to form an association, and that they would try to get the use of the school hall. Miss Paget suggested that if they drew up a notice calling a meeting, she would be pleased to get it duplicated for them, and they could then deliver it personally, talking to the tenants where possible.

*April*. Meeting to decide on the wording of the leaflet to be distributed on the estate and plans for the meeting in the school hall. Miss Paget asked whether they thought it would be a good thing to invite the Housing Manager: as this was the first time that all the residents had had a chance of getting together, they might well bring up questions about the estate which only he could answer. On the other hand the main business of the evening was to discuss the formation of a tenants' association. They decided after some discussion not to invite the Housing Manager on this occasion. They would need to ask him later, when they knew when the club-room was likely to be handed over.

59

*May*. Meeting in the school hall. The worker was invited to take the chair for the election of a committee, and this she did. It was decided that the committee should elect its own officers at its first meeting. All the original group were elected to the committee, and several other representatives from different parts of the estate. The worker was also invited to say a few words about the activities of other tenants' associations, and to explain where she came from. The meeting had at first thought she was a representative of the Housing Authority, and she had to explain that she worked for a voluntary organisation. Under *Any Other Business* many of the tenants raised questions about the amenities on the estate. The acting chairman said that they would make a note of these and would as a committee take them up with the appropriate authorities.

The meeting decided that the association should be called the Paisley Common Tenants' Association, that it should have a subscription of 6d. per week per family, and that the committee should draw up a constitution, which would then be agreed at a meeting to be specially called for the purpose. When the meeting closed the worker tried to get to know some of the people in the body of the hall, while the committee members stayed behind to make a date for their first meeting.

Miss Paget was invited by Mrs. O'Leary to go back for a cup of tea. She congratulated Mr. O'Leary on the way the meeting had been conducted and on the large number (nearly 100 people) who had attended. She offered to send him copies of the model constitution, which would be a guide when they came to decide on their own, and to give him copies of the notes that the London Council of Social Service had prepared of the duties of a chairman, secretary and treasurer. She agreed to attend the first committee meeting.

Miss Paget telephoned the Housing Manager and told him that she had attended the meeting, which she thought had been very successful. She explained why he had not been asked, and said he was to be invited to a later meeting. She thought the association would soon be getting in touch with him.

*June*. Miss Paget attended the first committee meeting. Mr. O'Leary was elected chairman. Before the meeting started she discussed the agenda with him, but she did not say very much during the meeting unless she was asked a question. She left saying that she hoped they would get in touch with her if there was any way in which she could help, but she did not think she would be able to attend their next committee.

*June-July*. The committee went full speed ahead, organising its first children's outing for August. Subscriptions were easy to collect.

*August.* The children's outing went well. Miss Paget had been able to put them in touch with another tenants' association nearby, who advised them on hiring the coaches, the best places to stop on the way, where to get refreshments, and how to book in advance.

*September.* After the children's summer outing things slowed down and did not pick up again until the end of September, when the secretary received a letter from the Housing Manager saying he thought the club-room would be ready by about the first week in November. A committee meeting was called immediately and Miss Paget was invited. Before she went she made a note for her own benefit of all the questions she thought the group would want answered.

*October.* The meeting was not a very orderly affair. Several people talked at the same time. It finished at 11.30 p.m. Some important decisions were made. The officers were to write and ask for an interview with the Housing Manager, and would take with them a list of questions which they wanted answered. This included questions about the rent of the club-room, the heating system, the tenancy agreement, and what furniture and fittings would be supplied. Would they be able to let the hall for weddings and parties? Could they sell drink on the premises? What would happen if they could not pay their way? And so on.

The worker said she would send them information about insurance for club-rooms. She also gave them the name and address of the secretary of another association that had recently had a very successful opening of their club-room. She tried to influence the group not to spend too much time discussing activities until some of the other practical considerations had been settled.

The committee held at least one meeting a week for the next four weeks. The worker attended only one.

Plans were made for a series of parties and socials to be held during December and January. The club-room was to be officially opened early in December. They decided to invite the chairman of the Housing Committee to perform the ceremony, and the Mayor to take the chair. The worker agreed to attend a special committee meeting to discuss the constitution.

Another special meeting was held to go over the programme of activities. The worker was alarmed to find that they had planned at least one activity on every night of the week, and were proposing to run socials every Saturday night unless they had a special booking. She suggested that other groups had found it was better to start with a few activities run really well, and gradually to add to them. If committee members were on duty almost every night, they or their

F                                                                                       61 wives would soon feel that the work entailed was far too much: they would fall down on the programme, and this would lead to discontent among the members.

*November.* A general meeting was held; refreshments were provided and members were able to see the hall for the first time. The chairman made a speech of welcome and hurriedly went through a copy of the constitution, which had been circulated to all the members the previous week. There were a few questions and then the constitution was adopted unanimously. The plans for the old people's work and the proposal to do something for the young people were warmly welcomed. The Housing Manager attended and answered a number of questions and made a note of various complaints.

*December.* The club-room was formally opened. The chairman of the Housing Committee attended and some other councillors. The short speeches were strictly non-party-political. Members welcomed this opportunity to meet their elected representatives and the officers. Miss Paget was treated as an honoured guest, but also helped out when it was discovered that the shop had not delivered the flowers for the lady mayoress. She rushed off to fetch them in her car.

Before Christmas every flat occupied by an elderly person was visited to find out tactfully who would be alone on Christmas day. Since there were about 20, it was decided to cook a special dinner in the club-room. Some of the young people offered to serve and wash up.

## 1956

*January.* Successful children's party and adult social.

Meeting of the committee. The new treasurer, Mr. Banks, was not able to produce a statement of accounts. It looked as though there was not enough money to pay the bills. Some collectors had not handed in their subscriptions since November. Committee members had paid for things out of their own pockets and had had no receipt.

Mrs. Miller said that they hadn't made any proper arrangements for cleaning the hall. She and two other committee members had been doing it, but it was really too much for them and she thought they ought to have some paid help.

There were recriminations all round and the chairman (not the treasurer) resigned.

*February.* Telephone call from the secretary: could he and the treasurer come and see the worker. A meeting was arranged. The treasurer had been able to sort out some of the accounts, but he
62

wasn't sure they were right. There were rumours going round the estate that money was missing. Miss Paget suggested that the voluntary auditor, who often helped associations, should be asked to assist the treasurer in preparing a statement of accounts, that this should be duplicated, and that a general meeting should be called.

A general meeting was held. It was not well attended. The statement of accounts was explained. Only £4 5s. could not be accounted for. The association, however, was about £50 in debt. Mr. Mortimer, who had 'led the opposition' and had caused Mr. O'Leary to resign, spoke up for the committee and tried to rally the meeting in support of them.

It was decided to find out the rules for playing Bingo and to organise a jumble sale. A young journalist living on the estate offered to write a news letter each month, so that the members could always be well informed of what was happening.

*March.* Jumble sale held. This raised £17 10s. The association started to play Bingo. The club for old people was opened to be held twice a week, and the worker put the ladies organising it in touch with the service for old people in the Borough. The new chairman was a Mr. Bentall. Mr. O'Leary agreed to remain on the committee.

*April.* Three representatives from the Paisley Common committee attended a meeting in the worker's office with two other new groups and representatives of three estates that had had a tenants' association for some time. The meeting was informal, with coffee and sandwiches, and there was a free exchange of information. The members from Paisley Common asked a number of questions.

*May.* The first annual general meeting was held. The school hall was not available. With some difficulty they obtained the use of the new church hall.

The meeting was well attended. An account was given of the year's work. The audited accounts were presented, showing a small balance. Someone said he understood that about £45 had been missing at the beginning of the year. This took the treasurer by surprise. Mr. O'Leary, however, remembered that there had been £4 5s. unaccounted for when the crisis had arisen in January. The chairman then explained that the committee had made up this £4 5s. among themselves, and that the speaker had probably mistaken the item of £4 5s. for £45. Everybody appeared satisfied.

There was criticism that nothing was being done for the children and young people, except the football. They needed a club. The Housing Manager answered one or two specific questions. A new committee was elected.

*June.* The new committee got off to a good start. Mr. Bentall was re-elected chairman, Mr. O'Leary became secretary, and Mr. Banks remained treasurer. Mr. Dressler, who was new to the committee, offered to take on the youth work. He said he had himself been a club member and a Scout, and he would be glad to help. His wife was also interested. Mr. Dressler made an appeal in the news sheet for helpers and especially for women to help with the girls' activities. They particularly wanted helpers for the canteen, and several were found. It was decided to open the clubs in September.

*September.* Mr. Dressler visited some of the youth clubs in the neighbourhood but did not get a very warm reception. Most of the clubs said that they could take more members, and was it necessary to start another club. Mr. Dressler explained that it wasn't exactly a club but that the parents and children and young people wanted to have some activities in their own clubroom.

It was decided to have one evening for children of school age, and to have the youth section on a different day. The clubs were well advertised, and Mr. Dressler and the members of his section made their plans carefully. They had not been prepared, however, for the large number of children who came. There were 80 the first evening, including a number of boys of 11–12. There was not enough for them to do, and the helpers were exhausted by the end.

The youth section for the over-15's was well attended: about 30 young people came the first evening. They danced, brought their own records, and sat about talking. Some of the boys played darts. There was a friendly, informal atmosphere.

*November.* By mid-November there were two groups organised for the children. The youth section was so popular that Mr. Dressler was trying to keep them out rather than attract them in. Young people on the estate brought their friends from outside.

Telephone call to the worker from the Housing Manager. Tenants were complaining of the noise made by the youth club on the estate. It was said that a lot of the young people hung about outside afterwards and that they did not live there. Miss Paget said she would be attending a social on the estate in a week or two, and she would try to find out what was happening.

*December.* The worker attended a special social evening arranged by the old people's section, at which the children's club were providing the entertainment. During the evening she was able to talk with the chairman and later with the youth leader, Mr. Dressler. She asked how the youth section was getting on, and was told that they had had complaints from the neighbours about noise. The Housing Manager had also written to the association about this. Mr. Dressler explained that the club had become so popular that there were often 100 or so young people on a Friday night. Recently they had been troubled by a group of boys from outside, who gate-crashed on club evenings. He did not want to call the police and had tried to assimilate them into the club. He thought they were responsible for a lot of the noise outside afterwards.

The chairman said that after Christmas they were going to have a committee meeting to thrash out the problems of the youth club. There were a number of people on the committee who thought there ought to be more specific activities and a lot more discipline. The worker suggested that the youth leader might like to get in touch with some of the workers on an estate in the same district, where they had had difficulties of a similar kind. She subsequently arranged a meeting.

## 1957

*January.* Miss Paget attended the meeting to discuss the youth work. She was asked to say something about their difficulties. She gave support and approval to the job they were already doing, and pointed out that on some other estates community groups had been able to accomplish far less. Some members of the committee wanted to close the youth club; some wanted a drastic cut in numbers; and others felt that if they could discuss the problem with the young people perhaps they could find a solution. Finally it was agreed that Mr. Dressler would try to get a representative group of young people to meet representatives of the adult committee for a discussion. The committee were anxious to deal with this as a domestic problem, and they preferred not to invite anyone from the statutory or voluntary organisations outside. Mr. Dressler was pleased with the meeting, and felt that as a knowledgeable outsider Miss Paget had given him much-needed support.

*March.* Telephone call from the chairman to ask if the worker could attend a committee meeting the following week, and would it be possible for her to arrange for the voluntary auditor to do their books before the annual general meeting in May. The local bank official who had voluntarily audited them the previous year was away on sick leave.

Miss Paget attended the meeting. The committee was dispirited. Several collectors had fallen out and this meant a lot more work for the others. Attendances had fallen off, and even the Bingo was not well supported. The worker said that activities did sometimes slacken after Christmas when the weather was bad, and that no doubt things would pick up again. There was a long discussion about the collection of subscriptions: some people said it would be easier to have an annual subscription, but others pointed out that this would mean less contact with the residents, and that people wouldn't pay as much all at one time. Miss Paget said that she thought a great effort should be made to get more collectors, since those who were doing someone else's work as well as their own were likely to become overburdened and give up too. She asked about the news sheet, as she hadn't received a copy recently, and found that the editor had left the estate and no one had come forward to take his place. She pointed out that this meant less communication between the committee and the residents. They might not be as well aware of the activities that were taking place as previously.

One of the helpers in the old people's club said she thought the hall was not being heated properly. It was then discovered that Mr. O'Leary had failed to write to the Gas Board about two of the radiators which were not functioning. Since he had agreed to do this at a committee meeting held in November, the committee was very annoyed, and Mr. O'Leary flared up and said if that was how they felt they could get a new secretary in May.

*May.* Miss Paget attended the annual general meeting. There were some changes in the committee. Suggestions for new activities included proposals to start a fishing club, and to see if they could get the use of the school playground for ball games.

*June.* The worker received a letter giving the names and addresses of the new officers. Mr. Ormond became chairman, Mr. O'Leary remained secretary, and a Mr. Johnson had taken over as treasurer.

*November.* Mrs. Martin, the leader of the old people's club, telephoned the worker to tell her that she was moving to Dorset to live with her married daughter and would not be able to continue. She said that she had given all the particulars of the work going on for the old people to the chairman. Some of her helpers would carry on, but no one was prepared to take responsibility for co-ordinating all the work. There was the old people's shopping rota, the visiting of the house-bound and handicapped people on the estate, the organisation of the outings, and the weekly meetings in the club-room. In addition there were cards to be sent for birthdays, and the parcels to be organised at Christmas. She described the activities of her co-workers and said she was worried that the general committee would not give them enough support. Would the worker try to see that everything was all right when she left?

Miss Paget phoned the secretary of the Old People's Welfare

Association in the borough and mentioned that Mrs. Martin was moving. The secretary said how good she had been with the old people and that she would be greatly missed. She added that she would write and thank Mrs. Martin for her co-operation and her work for old people in the borough. She would also keep in touch with the main committee of the estate until they found someone to take Mrs. Martin's place.

*1958*

*May.* Miss Paget met some of the representatives of the estate at the annual general meeting of the Association of London Housing Estates, to which they were affiliated. She caught up with their news, and things seemed to be going well. There were still some troubles in the youth club. The old people's work continued: one of the helpers had been persuaded to take over the main responsibility and new helpers had been found.

*1959*

*September.* At the sports day organised by the Association of London Housing Estates the Paisley Common Tenants' Association won two events.

*December.* Miss Paget attended the special Christmas social for old people.

*1960*

*February.* The Association of London Housing Estates asked the committee if they would be willing to lend their club-rooms for four separate evenings for a training course. The committee willingly agreed, said they would provide the refreshments, and would be pleased to welcome members from estates in the same district.

*1961*

*May.* Miss Paget attended the annual general meeting. There had been few changes in the committee. She noticed that the appearance of the estate was very good, and one of the committee members said to her that people were happy there and were sorry if they had to move, unlike some estates he knew. The parking problem was getting worse, and the committee would have to take this up. A new section was being added to the estate: a tall block was being finished and some new houses were already occupied. Some of the newcomers were at the meeting, and the chairman made a special point of getting a representative from the new part of the estate on to the committee. Some of the tenants in the old part were trying to get a transfer to the new. The meeting ran smoothly.

*1962*

One routine visit.

*1963*

*November.* The worker was invited to a committee meeting to discuss parking problems. The secretary said they had written constantly to the local authority to try to improve conditions on the estate. There were cars everywhere. The worker found that they had been negotiating with the Housing Department for some time, and they admitted it was likely that they would get barrier gates erected, and that cars not belonging to residents could then be kept out.

Later in the meeting the worker discovered what she thought was the real reason for their special invitation to her to attend a committee meeting. They were worried about one part of the estate from which several families had recently moved. The new tenants appeared to the old residents to have a much lower standard of behaviour. There were complaints about the children, about the language they used, and the conditions in which the families left the communal facilities. Refuse was left outside the dust chutes, and flower beds were trampled. The committee was not unsympathetic to these families. They realised that many of them had been living in very difficult circumstances, but they didn't want the appearance of the estate ruined. The worker asked how many families were involved; they thought about half-a-dozen. There followed a discussion on ways in which they could be brought into the association and whether this would help. Mrs. Miller volunteered to try to get to know some of the families as a first step to enlisting their co-operation.

The worker asked how the youth club was progressing. Mr. Dressler, who was still a member of the committee, said that the numbers were not so large, but there was quite a lot of activity off the estate. Afterwards he told the worker that he was worried about the youth club and felt that they were not doing enough for the young people.

The Paisley Common committee at the end of this period of field work was affiliated to the Association of London Housing Estates and was using the services of their Youth Advisers. The youth club was meeting two nights a week. The committee was represented on the Executive Committee and on two sub-committees of the Association. The old people's work was as extensive as most groups', and they were able to use some services in the neighbouring community.

### Summary

*Origin.* Paisley Common, like most of the community groups, had its origin in the needs of families in a new social environment to get to know one another and to work for improvement in the amenities. It is also typical in that the field workers were available in the early stages of the group's development, at first as advisers on the improvement of amenities and later as consultants to the group itself on the method of forming an association and the development of a programme of activities.

*Activities.* The Paisley Common programme of activities is typical in its provision for particular groups (e.g. old people, young people, children) and interest groups (sports, social activities, dances), and for service to individuals and families with special problems. It is also typical in offering special activities (outings, theatre visits) which are occasional rather than regular. It is also representative in encountering many problems in its attempt to work with youth.

*Organisation.* The organisation of the Paisley Common group is typical in having a general committee, which takes responsibility for planning, organising and carrying out the work of the association, and in having its membership resident on the estate. Its activities are organised entirely by volunteer workers, and subscriptions are on a family basis. It has a constitution, and elects its officers and committee at an annual general meeting.

*Leadership.* Paisley Common is typical in having indigenous leaders, some with previous experience of committee work from trade union and other organisations, others who had never been on a committee before. The association provides an opportunity for many residents to take an active part in local affairs.

*Pattern of Participation.* The pattern of participation is typical in having a hard core of not more than 50 or 60 residents, who do the work of the whole group and maintain the service for a much larger number. The rest of the members are involved in the association through participation in the activities rather than in the organisation of running them. As in all groups, participation in activities varies. Both committee and membership always show a high level of interest in the work for children and old people.

*Problems and Abilities.* Paisley Common had problems and abilities similar to those of other groups in the middle range of development. For example:

Ability to agree on the aims of the group in the early days, on committee procedure and on what services could be offered, especially to young people.

Problems of finding, using and keeping volunteers for committee work, the collection of subscriptions and the staffing of activities.

Problems of keeping lines of communication open between the committee, the membership of the association, other residents and the activity volunteers.

The ability to interpret the work to the membership in order to retain participation and support, and to the statutory and voluntary bodies whose help was necessary for the work.

Problems of keeping the balance between the committee, the membership and the statutory and voluntary bodies. The Paisley Common group also had the ability to find adequate human and social resources for the task it had set itself, provided they were efficiently and effectively recognised, organised and used.

*Development.* Paisley Common is representative in its stages of development, from the early days when it was an isolated unit, up to the time that it could make some relationship with the wider community.

*The Wider Community.* Paisley Common is typical in its relations with the wider community, as it moved from relative isolation and potential conflict to co-operation with the community and with the statutory and voluntary bodies.

Paisley Common is typical in the use it made of the field-work service in different ways at different stages in its development. For example:

In the early stage for special needs such as a pedestrian crossing and a playground;

Later a more general use of the field-work services during the organisation of a community group;

During the stage of its developing programme, an intensive use of the service for improving committee behaviour, for help with the provision of services and with the organising and running of activities;

When Paisley Common had achieved an identity, developed a programme and joined the Association of London Housing Estates, it ceased to depend on the field-work service and merely kept in touch or sought advice on special problems.

*Reason for Existence.* Paisley Common shared the following reasons for existence:

70

To provide an opportunity for residents to get to know one another;

To provide amenities not already available;

To provide opportunities for indigenous leaders to exercise their skills, especially in committee work and activities;

To help to achieve, on behalf of the membership and the residents, an identity for the association and hence for the estate.

To serve as a link between the estate community and the wider community.

Paisley Common then is representative of the middle ring of groups in touch with the field-work service and equally representative of the housing estate community groups under discussion. It is also a representative autonomous community group because:

It arises naturally from the informal, spontaneous interaction between persons and small groups and is not organised by outsiders to meet the standards of any formal social welfare body.

It attempts to do its work by making its own decisions, using its own resources and its own efforts outside the established network of statutory and voluntary bodies.

It needs help to find and develop the necessary social skills for this work, help to survive and establish itself in order to do its work, and help to demonstrate its independence to the already established statutory and voluntary bodies.

The help needed by a group at this stage is different from that needed by a well established community group. The help must be offered on terms which are acceptable, comprehensible and useful to the group, and which do not threaten its independence.

SIX TYPICAL EXAMPLES OF HELPING A GROUP

The illustration of the Paisley Common Community Group showed some of the helping situations that the workers and the agency met. In this section some typical helping situations are set out in more detail, together with comments to show more clearly the nature of the field-work process.

### (1) Identifying a Social Welfare Need

This example sets out a problem that often arises in the early stages of group development—the necessity to identify a social welfare need in order to provide the appropriate service.

The Abbey Close Community Group had been in existence as an organised community group for about six months, and had been an informal part of the life of the estate for a year before that. It had begun with some old people's work on the estate and was also working with some of the young people. There was a boys' football club run by the father of one of the boys, and a small girls' group supervised by a mother. Saturday night dances were held in the clubroom. The group had organised a series of successful socials for adults. The problem arose when, after a successful Christmas party for the members' younger children, several of the mothers said they wished that more could be done. The party had been run by the mothers themselves, one of whom was a committee member who reported to the committee the request that something more be done for the younger children. Three opinions emerged from the discussion. First, that these children were their mothers' responsibility, too young to be offered a service, and the committee should not take the responsibility for minding other people's children. Second, that Saturday morning film shows should be arranged. One of the committee members offered to bring his own projector, and said it would be possible to show some old Mickey Mouse films quite cheaply, but of course they would have to spend a bit on getting some up-to-date ones sometimes. The mothers would have to work out a rota system, sit with the children, look after the refreshments, and take the money. Third, that nothing be done at the moment as all the time and money available were already committed to other activities.

Mrs. Browning, the mothers' representative on the committee, reported the discussion to some of the mothers, who agreed to organise and pay for several Saturday morning film shows. Only the first of these was a success. At the second, mothers turned up and left their younger children, sometimes with an older sister or brother, and went off shopping. Most of the children were too young to watch the films. They soon became restive, some started crying, others running about the room. With too few adults in attendance the situation became chaotic. The committee member working the projector gave up and said it would have to be better organised next time or he wouldn't come. Everybody went away dissatisfied.

Mrs. Browning spoke to the committee chairman and told him she felt sure something needed to be done, but she had no precise suggestion. With his approval she reported back to the next committee meeting, at which one of the field workers happened to be present, having been invited to talk over a proposal intended to improve the system of collecting subscriptions. After discussing Mrs. Browning's report, the committee divided into those who said, 'We tried and the mothers didn't co-operate; it didn't work out, let's drop the idea,' and another section which was not so anxious to stop the work and felt that a meeting of the mothers should be arranged to persuade them to organise it better.

After the meeting the field worker, who had limited her contribution to the discussion on collecting subscriptions, asked the chairman whether, with Mrs. Browning's agreement, she might attend the proposed meeting of mothers. This was approved, and when she did in fact attend, it emerged that most of the mothers were not really interested in film shows on Saturday mornings, but wanted a children's play group, which would meet regularly two or three times a week. This would give the youngsters a chance to play together and the mothers time to get on with other things, knowing that the children were being properly looked after. The worker described similar situations on other estates where associations had organised supervised play groups in club rooms on a rota system, sometimes with outside help, and said that some of these play groups were very successful. The mothers decided to meet again, to visit some play groups, and to write to the committee asking that a play group be formed. The worker and Mrs. Browning also arranged to meet again to discuss the written request and how best to make their case. After reading the letter the worker felt that it was too demanding and might cause offence, especially a paragraph about the committee being run by men 'who really didn't care'. She suggested that this should be omitted and that a paragraph about outside help should be amended to avoid any idea of outsiders coming in and trying to take over. She also suggested saying that the mothers would need some money for equipment. After talking this over with Mrs. Browning, and with her permission, she telephoned the chairman suggesting it might be helpful if she attended the next committee meeting in order to speak to and interpret the mothers' request. She explained the alternatives to him so that he was prepared beforehand and knew something about it. When the request came up three different opinions emerged.

First it was said that if the film shows were a failure the play group would also fail, since the mothers were far too busy to be reliable in such matters. The second speaker was the youth work volunteer, who said that if much money was needed he thought they ought to consider the sports equipment for the youth section first.

The third opinion, as the worker anticipated, was that the mothers would need outside advice and help. But who would help them? They didn't really want someone to come in and take over. After Mrs. Browning had defended the mothers' request to the best of her ability, the chairman asked for the worker's comments. She said she felt that the mothers' need was a real one, and that they were in fact willing to take some responsibility. She explained to the committee how a rota system might be worked, and suggested that the mothers be asked to make up a definite plan for a children's play group, and that the committee meet the mothers' group to consider the plan. She would herself be willing to suggest ways of getting the initial

73

equipment if, after such a meeting, the committee felt that the work should proceed.

One of the committee members immediately said he could get a lot of toys at wholesale prices. The worker took a little time to explain the kind of equipment that was needed. Some of it could be very simple and cost very little, but other items needed to be especially designed to stand up to use by a large number of children. This meant that it might be better to buy from a firm that made special nursery school and play group equipment. By this time it was clear that the chairman was getting a little impatient and wanting to get on with the meeting. The worker said she would help in any way she could and would keep in touch with Mrs. Browning and the other mothers. After three months of discussion and planning, a children's play group was organised and opened, with the help of a mother on the estate who had had some training as a nursery nurse and who had been discovered for them by the Health Visitor.

This example of helping a group is typical in several ways. It shows a conflict in interest, a lack of adequate information, and a poor estimate of resources. These were typical factors which made difficulties for groups trying to identify a social welfare need.

Conflict in interest is often aroused on a committee when one section, with a special interest in a particular service, will not admit the claims of a new need for fear that time, attention and money will be diverted from their special interest. A lack of adequate information frequently prevents groups from seeing a need clearly and offering an appropriate service. In this example the mothers did not want film shows for their young children but some kind of supervised play group. They were unable without the help of the worker to formulate their request adequately. A poor estimate of resources also means that needs will not be met. Again in this example, the mothers tended to underestimate their ability to make themselves understood by a committee composed mainly of men. The committee tended to underestimate the mothers' readiness to take responsibility, and its own ability to use outside help with advantage. The worker also tried to prevent money being spent on toys that might not be suitable.

The role of the worker in this situation was to help the mothers to collect the right information and to put their case adequately; to re-direct attention from the failure of film shows to the potential success of a children's play group, and to support and encourage both the mothers and the committee to give the scheme a trial.

## (2) Establishing Priorities

A community group is continually involved in establishing priorities —the order in which to perform its tasks and use its resources.

Helping the group to establish priorities is one aspect of the role of the worker.

The worker was attending a social on a large pre-war estate where there were a number of elderly residents. During the interval Mrs. Gilbert and two of her friends, who were responsible for the old people's work, came and sat beside her. Mrs. Gilbert said she had recently been to see Miss Jones, the welfare worker at the Town Hall, to enquire about holidays for old people. Miss Jones had been very helpful, but in the course of conversation had said she wished Mrs. Gilbert could organise a visiting service for old people. She added that this was far more necessary than running an old people's club, since there were plenty of these in the borough and most old people would be able to get to one of them.

Mrs. Gilbert had thought that she should report this conversation to the committee. She explained that the Town Hall hadn't the volunteers or the trained staff to visit elderly people on the estate except in emergency. Unfortunately she had given the committee the impression that the Town Hall wanted to see the old people's club closed, and as a result they had not been sympathetic about a visiting service.

When the secretary of the tenants' association and his wife joined the group a little later, the worker said that Mrs. Gilbert had been discussing the problem of old people's work on the estate and wondering if they could do any more to help the house-bound and those who could only get out occasionally. The secretary said he knew all about this but the club was already running parties, outings and weekly meetings, and that was all they could do. They neither had the money nor could they spare visitors to take on any more.

A few weeks later the secretary telephoned the worker and asked if she would come to a meeting in his flat with Mrs. Gilbert and a few other members of the committee, as they wanted to start a visiting service. When the worker arrived she found that there had recently been an incident on the estate, when one of the members had noticed that quite late in the afternoon the milk was still standing on the doorstep of an elderly lady who lived alone. When she knocked and got no reply, and some of the neighbours had said they were sure the old lady had not gone away, the member fetched the caretaker, who broke in and found her very ill in bed and unable to call for help. This incident had made the committee change their mind.

At the meeting the worker helped the group to work out a plan. She discovered that because the old people did not pay a weekly subscription like the other families on the estate, they did not get a visit from the collector. It was decided that as a first step the collectors should call to keep the old people informed of what was going on in the association, and in this way all of them would be visited once a week. It was then decided to make a special index of the old people who lived alone. The worker suggested that they should ask the caretaker if he knew of any who might have special difficulties. It was decided to invite the welfare worker at the Town Hall to attend a meeting of the committee and to give her advice, as they were anxious that visits should not look like interference.

In this situation it was clear to the worker that the committee's priority in the past had been 'big' events that would make an immediate impact. Therefore Christmas parties and summer outings for old people were seen as very good indeed, but regular visiting was not sufficiently spectacular. Once the committee had seen what could happen in the absence of a visiting service, they were willing to try to do something about it. A visiting service had sounded rather vague and they had not really thought out what it meant.

During the next three months the worker took part in some of the following discussions:

A meeting of the committee with the Old People's Welfare worker, to find out her idea of what a visiting service ought to be and how the workers could keep in touch with the Town Hall about it.

A discussion between the treasurer and other members of the committee, about finance, volunteers, and the confidential nature of the work.

A meeting of the committee with the caretaker, to find out what information he could give them and how they might co-operate with him in the interests of the old people on the estate.

A meeting between Mrs. Gilbert and the Youth Club committee, to ask if the young people would co-operate by shopping and carrying out other services at her request.

In order to work with this situation, the community development worker had to realise:

That the committee was proud of its old people's club activities and afraid of losing them. They felt that the club activities might be sacrificed for a visiting service, which would be difficult to interpret to the membership. They also felt that their own old people's work was not valued enough by the local authority.

The committee had not realised the importance of keeping in touch until the incident of the sick woman.

Communication between the volunteer worker, the committee, the local authority and the caretaker needed to be improved.

In this situation the role of the worker was to help to open channels of communication between the various parties; to support Mrs. Gilbert and her assistants; and to advise the chairman and the committee on what steps they might take once their interest had been aroused. This was done not by direct involvement in the work of the association, but by helping Mrs. Gilbert and the committee to plan a scheme and to mobilise the support needed from outside, as well as inside, the estate. All this helped to clarify the importance of and the need for continued regular work in addition to the big events on the estate.

## (3) *Working Out a Crisis*

A worker is often called upon to help in a crisis within a community group: either within the committee; between the committee, the membership and the residents; or one that affects the whole association and can endanger not only its day-to-day work but its very existence.

One cause of such a crisis is often the growth of one side of the service or the programme, in such a way as to upset the balance of the group and its work.

The Hillview Estate Association had for some years been running a successful family social once a fortnight. During the two years of the group's existence, there was no club-room on the estate, and so the association used a hall nearby. At first the socials were informal gatherings rather than organised adult socials. As they developed they became more formal, with entertainment laid on, refreshments (including beer), and music by fairly big, named bands. Members and residents, including many of the younger married couples and the young people, came to regard the socials as major events in their social calendar. Admission charges rose from 5s. to 10s. for a couple as the entertainment became more professional, and the prizes for the Bingo sessions larger. At first this was thought to be a very good thing indeed by the committee, by most of the membership and by many of the residents. The association was providing an obvious service and as it developed so the status of the association grew.

The power and prestige of those on the social committee increased as the socials developed during the first two years before the club-room opened. The social committee were anxious to plough back into the association, for use in the rest of its work, every penny that could be spared from the running costs. At first the social produced a sum almost equal to the subscriptions from the membership and the weekly raffle, then slightly more, until finally it provided the largest share of the association's income. The work with the children, the youth work, and the work with old people were largely supported by the income from the social. Difficulty began to appear when an association member at an annual meeting suggested that as he and his wife, and often his son and girl friend, spent about £2 a week at the social, the subscriptions should be entirely abandoned and the income from the social should be the sole support of the association and its work.

G

At a previous committee meeting there had been differences of opinion on the finances of the youth group. It had for some time been running a Saturday night programme in the estate club-room, which was now open. (The social continued to be held in the large hall nearby.) The youth leader reported that the youth section needed more money in order to get a really good pop group for the spring dance. They asked for an additional float or an advance on some of next year's activity money. The members of the social section on the committee opposed this request.

The underlying difficulty of the social in relation to other work of the association then began to come to the surface. The committee was divided into two sections—those who were on the social committee, and those doing 'the rest of the work'.

The argument of the social section was that the youth club dances were in competition with the adult social. The older young people generally went to the social, often at a reduced rate. If the Saturday night dance continued, this would inevitably take away custom from the social, which was 'real cheek', since the youth work was subsidised by the social. The job of the youth club was not to give socials of its own; it was supposed to arrange sports, table tennis and the like; if they wanted socials and did not like what was being offered at the hall, they could join the planning group of the adult social and say so.

The second line of reasoning was quite simple: 'those who pay should say'. The social section brought in all the money, therefore those responsible for organising it should make the decisions as to how the money should be spent. It was the largest and best attended activity, the most profitable, the most widely known; and it made a name for the association.

The argument of those supporting the other work of the association was, first, that the social sub-committee 'had got too big for its boots; the same people had been running it for too long, and they now had too much power.' Second, it was well known that a large number of non-members and non-residents attended the socials, and that if the sub-committee really took over, it would no longer be the estate association. Third, the growth of the social had stopped the development of the association. Members were reluctant to pay their subscriptions, thinking that the association was rich because of the socials. The committee constantly 'kow-towed' to the social sub-committee and the voluntary leaders were tired of having to please them instead of the membership and the committee.

After the controversy had shown itself at an annual general meeting and been smoothed over by the chairman, the sequence of events was roughly as follows. After the A.G.M. the chairman asked to see the worker in her office, described the controversy in some detail and asked for advice. His personal opinion was that the social was a good thing, but for it completely to dominate the association would be a bad thing. He hoped conflict could be avoided, but he was doubtful. He said it was an open secret that the social section had decided to take over, or to 'go it alone'. Without a clear decision about the place of the social in the life of the association there might be a long-drawn-out conflict, leading to the ruin of the association.

After some discussion the worker and the chairman agreed that the issue should be fully brought into the open. It was decided that the worker should attend the next committee meeting and make three suggestions. First, that the social section should prepare their case for presentation to the membership; second, that the opposing group on the committee prepare its case; and third, that a committee representing both parties, including a respected member of the association and an impartial outsider, be formed to organise a full discussion of the problem at an emergency meeting of the members.

Before the committee meeting took place, the chairman telephoned the worker to say he thought it was not necessary for her to attend, as he felt he might be able to get agreement on what had been suggested. The committee agreed to the plan outlined above, chose the representatives who would make the case to the meeting of the members, and asked the chairman to invite the worker to serve on the committee.

The committee met several times to prepare the material and to organise the emergency general meeting. The worker met each group separately, and also met the representative of the association and several residents who had been added to the committee. These conclusions were drawn from these meetings:

The socials were no doubt very popular with the members, who felt they provided the only entertainment in the community. At the same time they felt that the other work of the association was valuable and necessary, and should be supported.

It was best for the social committee to become an independent club, which could be represented on the estate committee.

The independent club would be responsible for its own finances. It would pay for the use of premises and also an affiliation fee to the parent body. The estate committee would continue to explore alternative ways of raising funds.

Several important points emerge from this experience of helping to work through a crisis in a group. First, although the association did not recognise it during the crisis, it was providing a community service by helping the social section to become independent. Second, the conflict had not immediately been faced because the social skills necessary to prevent it destroying the parent group were not available. Once these skills were introduced into the situation the conflict could be handled and worked out. Third, the role of the worker was to offer the social skills necessary by suggesting appropriate action for mediating between the various parties, to suggest possible alternatives, and to act as the confidante and counsellor of the chairman.

## (4) Self-evaluation

Community groups often become so absorbed in one aspect of their work that either new needs are not recognised, or they are seen only as obstructions to established routine. In situations where responsibility and privilege are so settled as to be beyond question, the association may find itself in need of self-evaluation.

The Castle Gate estate association had been in existence for four years. It ran a children's play group, a youth work section, old people's work and trips to the seaside in the summer for the children. In addition it had a regular schedule for adult socials and was considered by the worker and the committee to be doing well. The committee was stable, most members having served two or more years. The first signs of unrest came at the annual general meeting. The chairman discussed the agenda with the worker and had invited her to attend the meeting. After reports from the chairman, treasurer and several voluntary leaders, and the presentation of a work plan for next year, the meeting was opened for discussion from the floor. First came the usual congratulations to the committee and voluntary workers, and their appreciative acceptance of the same; then followed some relatively minor discussion about small financial matters, which was handled calmly and with confidence from the platform. The meeting was then opened for other business. 'One could almost feel the atmosphere change,' the worker recorded after the meeting.

First there was a question about the children's playground promised by the local authority: what was the committee doing about this? Then there was a complaint that a previous request to the committee about noise made by the dust chutes had not been dealt with. The temperature of the meeting rose with succeeding questions. What had been done about the constant loss of light bulbs in the indoor corridors? Did the committee not appreciate what it meant to a woman coming home after dark, to have to 'navigate in a pitch-black corridor'? If they did not, the speaker would be only too willing to inform them. What had the committee done about the persistent salesmen who almost forced themselves through the door on mornings when they knew the housewife to be alone? Why had the stair-cleaning rota arranged at the last meeting with the management not been put into operation? What had been done to keep gangs of ruffians from using the lifts and incidentally leaving them in 'really foul shape'?

Question after question came, suggesting that the committee was not adequately doing its job, and implying that matters brought to the committee's attention were ignored. The committee seemed surprised. Most of the questions came from the back of the hall. Committee members attempted to answer the complaints, which were often contradictory. Several members panicked, and pleaded, 'We are working as hard as we can.' They spoke at random, each testifying how hard the others had worked, and finally one suggested that they should all resign. As the next item on the agenda was the election of officers, this got an unintended laugh. In fact, only the chairman resigned, but he admitted that he did not like 'leaving under a cloud'; the meeting re-elected the rest of the committee, one member agreeing to serve as chairman.

The original committee chairman, Mr. Powell, was very distressed about what had happened, and though not now a committee officer, asked to come and see the worker at her office. During the interview it transpired that a new block of flats had been opened just over a year before. In addition there had been a fair turnover in residents, so that some 60 families on an estate of 350 were new. Mr. Powell felt that they were the trouble makers, but was at a loss to explain why. The children and young people of the new tenants took part in the activities. Most of them had joined the association and were paying their subscriptions fairly regularly. He said he was not concerned for himself so much as for the association and the new chairman, but he admitted that he did not like 'leaving under a cloud' or leaving a lot of problems for his successor. The worker asked if Mr. Powell knew of any one person or small group among the new residents who might be contacted to discuss the matter. He said that his wife would be more likely to know than he, and agreed that the worker should telephone her. Mrs. Powell suggested a new tenant who had asked questions at the meeting.

The worker obtained permission from both Mr. Powell and Mr. Single, the new chairman, to get in touch with Mrs. McRae. Through Mr. Powell she offered help, should he need it, to the new chairman as he settled in to his job.

The worker made an appointment with Mrs. McRae. In her opinion Mrs. McRae was easily excited, tended to be over-demanding, and was rather dogmatic in her opinions. However she thought Mrs. McRae and her supporters had some justification for their stand, and that most of the questions thrown at the committee at the general meeting were legitimate.

She telephoned and exchanged views first with Mr. Single, the chairman, and then with Mr. Powell. After some discussion it was suggested that both she and Mr. Powell attend the next committee meeting to consider some of the questions that had been raised at the annual general meeting. From the committee discussion the following points emerged:

That the committee had been so absorbed in its current programme of activities that the tenants' welfare, which had played a dominant part in the early life of the association, had gone by default.

That the new residents had some of the problems that the other residents had had when they first moved in.

That it was too late to organise a special welcome party at this stage: it would look too obvious. (The idea of a party came in response to the worker's suggestion that their absorption in the established programme had prevented their being alert to the needs of the new residents.)

That Mrs. McRae and several of her supporters should be invited to a special meeting of the committee to discuss particular problems and how they might be met.

That because the committee had been re-elected en bloc, the newcomers were not represented on it.

Mr. Single (the chairman) asked the worker to be present at that meeting 'as an old friend of the association'. She agreed and suggested that the committee should have some plans of its own to offer, as proof of its goodwill and in order to begin from a prepared position, which might, she suggested, prevent wrangling.

A meeting was held with several members of the Executive Committee, including Mr. Powell, in order to prepare for the meeting with Mrs. McRae and her supporters. It was agreed that Mr. Powell should admit that the committee had been somewhat lax and that some of the questions raised at the annual meeting were justified. Mr. Single was prepared to follow up and say that the committee now had plans to rectify the situation, including the appointment of one member of the committee whose job it would be to deal with complaints.

At the joint meeting Mrs. McRae took the offensive and accused the committee of being 'stooges of the management' and having no interest in the tenants' welfare. After some wrangling Mr. Powell made his statement and Mr. Single followed with his. Several of Mrs. McRae's group seemed appeased, but after some discussion they thought that the committee member to deal with complaints should be appointed by the membership and not by the committee. After further heated discussion it was agreed that the committee should appoint a man for a period of four months. If things did not improve, a full membership meeting was to be called to elect a Tenants' Welfare Secretary from the floor.

Mrs. McRae then rather surprised the meeting by saying that she agreed to this and would 'keep her eye on the new man'. She also suggested what turned out to be a very useful plan indeed. The subscription collectors were to be given the names of all the new tenants who most needed this service, were to keep a small notebook in which to enter complaints, and were especially to ask if everything was all right, when on their rounds. They were then to report to the committee member acting as Tenants' Welfare Secretary, whose responsibility it would be to visit the family and follow up the complaint. In addition, it was agreed that the officer himself should be available at the club-room one evening every second week at a stated time.

This plan was only a partial success, as it offered no opportunity for leadership from the new residents within the association. But it had the effect of calling the association's attention to this problem of keeping the dissident group interested and of avoiding open conflict.

The importance of this illustration from the Castle Gate association is that it shows how a situation of this kind can arise without any ill intention from anyone. The committee was not deliberately negligent, but so engrossed in the familiar pattern of activities that new needs could only make themselves known through apparent conflict at the annual general meeting. The new residents were entirely justified in making their voice heard and were without malice.

### (5) Finding and Using Resources

Throughout the development of an association the resources needed to initiate and sustain the various activities have to be found and used as effectively and efficiently as possible.

If an association finds itself under pressure, the almost automatic process of finding and using resources may break down and produce a 'programme crisis'.

The Walnut Grove estate association had been in existence for five years, operating a fairly full programme of service. It was exceptional in the spontaneous pleasure the participants seemed to derive from the activities themselves, and from the running of them. The association's work often went for long periods without a committee meeting. There was occasional trouble with book-keeping, not from any intention to defraud, but simply because of ordinary carelessness. The annual general meeting was always chaotic but happy; committee meetings were high-spirited but well-meaning and very enjoyable. In this informal atmosphere the association had done a great deal to make social life on this small estate a more neighbourly and friendly affair. Yet this method of management produced an annual programme crisis. The immediate cause was the crowding of all the main events, which was often disastrous. They were ill-attended, or fell through just before the appointed date or even hour; sometimes they disintegrated as they were taking place; and funds were often squandered on one event. Often this led to ill feeling, accusations of inefficiency, muddle-headedness or even downright incompetence, but these things were usually argued out a little heatedly at first and then resolved. One of the characteristics of this association was that ill feeling was dissipated after a surprisingly short time.

A particular example of this kind of crisis is found in the Christmas programme of the Walnut Grove estate association. Before Christmas, when the programme was fairly slack, the suggestion was made that this Christmas on the estate should be 'the biggest and best ever'. The activity leaders sprang into action, with plans of every conceivable kind. There was to be a special old people's party in addition to the usual Christmas boxes, a visit to the circus followed by tea for the children, an adult social, and a special youth club dance. Christmas planning seemed to have brought the association to full life with a bang, as one association member put it. The committee meetings were hectic. Although much was discussed, little was accomplished, and no co-ordinated schedule of activities was agreed upon. No budget was made to be passed by the committee as a whole. Activity leaders recruited their own assistants, friends and interested acquaintances, and planned their own work without knowing what other groups were doing. Funds were raised and spent without committee approval, and the leaders and their associates sometimes spent their own money, hoping to recoup it at least in part after the events had taken place. Everyone was at work, busy and excited, without the wrangling and personal conflict usually involved in such intensive endeavour in better organised associations.

The inevitable happened about 15th December, at a final meeting of the committee before the holiday. Bills were presented that could not be met, either because the money was not available or because there had been no agreement about the legitimacy of the expenditure. The club-room had been booked twice for the same evening by two groups, and both had their tickets and circulars already printed and distributed. The children's outing had been arranged for the afternoon of the same day as the adults' social. The theory was that the parents taking part would need the social to relax, but in practice the trip would probably get back later than expected, and leave no time for parents to wash and dress, not to mention getting youngsters to bed after the outing. Far too many tickets had been sold, many to non-residents, for the adult social and the youth dance. The club-room could not hold such numbers. Far too much food had been ordered. The youth dance was to have beer, in spite of the committee's ruling against this. Activity leaders had used or pledged some of their own money, which they needed before Christmas.

This was the crisis in the programme which prompted the association to ask for help from the field worker. Mrs. Rose, the chairman's wife, telephoned the worker, saying good humouredly, 'Please come to our meeting tomorrow night if you can. We had a terrible meeting last night.' The worker rearranged another engagement and went.

The committee sat down in a determined way to try to straighten things out. They decided on:

A change of time for the evening social, to accommodate the adults who wanted to go to the circus with the children.

Close consultation with the publican's wife to work out more realistic catering arrangements. Some orders were cancelled, some transferred to the public house so that there could be more effective co-ordination.

The adult social was moved from the club-room to the public house to ease the pressure on the club-room. This also solved the beer problem: the adults would have had beer in the club-room, and the young people were apt to argue, 'If you can have it why not us?'

Arrangements were made with the public house to supply the food for the adult social, the youth dance, and the children's tea after the circus. A catering committee would help with service for all three events.

An agreement was made that the food bill could be paid in instalments over the next four months.

The worker offered to get her agency to supply specially duplicated dated expense sheets to all concerned, including the public house, to allay the anxiety of the treasurer, whose responsibilities meant that he was the only one who was not fully enjoying the whole thing.

This illustration shows an association doing the most important part of the job of a community group—bringing people together, doing things for each other and enjoying it. The point of the illustration is that even such an association needs support and help on certain occasions.

The nature of the field-work service at its best is shown here. There were no recriminations from the worker about inadequate planning and preparation, no demand that rules must be kept for their own sake, only a variety of practical suggestions and direct aid, without strings attached and especially without moralising.

The illustration also shows the need for continuing care and support for community groups at every stage in their development. Readiness to provide this service for as long as it is needed helps the group in its turn to provide its own service to the estate community.

### (6) Encouraging Co-operation

Almost every situation that the worker is asked to help with is one where co-operation needs to be encouraged and conflict to be resolved. The recurring pattern of conflict and co-operation is basic to the work of the group, and so it is of extreme importance that the worker should be able to offer her service in a conflict situation with the hope of encouraging co-operation.

The Northside Estate association had for some years been running a youth club in its own club-room, at first mainly for the 12–14 age group. This example arose from the following incident. A young married couple were brought home by car shortly after the youth club had closed one winter evening. The husband went ahead with the carricot and the baby, and went into his flat opposite the club-room, while his wife stayed behind and chatted for a few minutes with their friends before following. Several of the boys standing outside the club saw the unaccompanied woman and began to sing a slightly risqué parody of a popular song. The boys were from the estate, but said later that they did not recognise the young woman in a coat and hat. The young woman called her husband, and a row took place that involved several passers-by, several residents at their windows, the woman's husband, the boys, and in the end the youth leader.

This brought to a head a situation that had been gathering for some time. At the next committee meeting the woman's father-in-law, who happened to be on the committee, led an attack on the youth work on the estate and on the youth worker. He claimed that noise, bad language and shouting after the club closed were a regular thing, and that equipment was frequently destroyed. By the middle of the committee meeting, his description of the incident had developed into 'an insult to a married woman'. The meeting grew more and more excited, and finally Mr. Howard, the volunteer youth leader, resigned and his resignation was accepted. He left the meeting before it closed.

At the next meeting the youth leader returned to say that he felt he could no longer work with the boys and the club should be closed. At the same meeting Mr. Stanley, a friend of the chairman's, said that he was willing to take the youth work over, and outlined his plans. Mr. Howard interrupted to say he felt that Mr. Stanley had been trying to get him out for a long time, and that he had turned some of the older boys against him. In the ensuing discussion it appeared that Mr. Stanley, the new leader, felt that Mr. Howard was accusing him of 'staging the whole incident between the boys and the married woman'. The committee meeting broke up in a fury of recrimination, with the woman's father-in-law saying that if Mr. Howard returned to youth work he would advise his son to go to the police about the incident the other night. During the weeks before the next committee meeting the youth club remained closed and the association was split down the middle, committee members, members and residents taking sides for or against Stanley and Howard, for or against reopening the club.

At the next meeting it was decided by vote not to reopen the youth club until further notice. During this period of conflict within the association and on the estate, the other activities suffered because neither faction would speak to the other, and a great deal of time and energy were consumed in the conflict. During the time the youth club was closed, a neighbouring youth club was broken into and damaged, and it was established that the older boys from the estate were involved. The club worker from the neighbouring club protested to Mr. Connolly, the chairman, about the damage to his club and the closure of the youth work. In a telephone conversation with the worker the chairman said he thought the club should stay closed until the young people had learned their lesson. He was inclined to agree that Mr. Howard, the former worker, was useless with the older boys, but he was at a loss to know what to do, especially as the whole community was beginning to team up against the committee, and the association was engaged in 'civil war'. Several members had already refused to pay their subscriptions if the club did not open, and on hearing this, several had said they would not pay if it did. The chairman was doubtful if the worker could do anything to help.

(This was before the time that the Association of London Housing Estates had their own Youth Advisers, who might have been expected to know the club well and the people involved.)

The worker asked Mr. Connolly if he knew Mr. Wilson, the chairman of an association not very far away. He said he did, and that his committee had visited the estate. The worker said that Mr. Wilson was a quiet and diplomatic person, who had recently handled a difficult situation on his own estate, when there had been tension between residents and a group of young people. She wondered if Mr. Connolly would like to discuss the situation with him.

A visit to the estate was arranged for Mr. Wilson, who agreed to help and to share his own experience. On his suggestion he investigated the whole situation and then met each faction separately to hear each side of the story. He was able to work with Mr. Stanley and Mr. Howard on the basis of common concern about youth work problems.

After a good deal of discussion on the Northside estate, and some discussion with experienced people on his own estate, he reported back to the worker and to the chairman. It appeared that one root of the difficulty was that Mr. Howard, the former leader, had done a good job with the boys when they were 12–14, but was unable to get on with them when they grew to be 16–18, or to pass them on to anyone who could work with them. In an attempt to hold his own he had lost control and he knew it, but he was determined not to allow

Mr. Stanley, the new leader, to take over. He said he would rather that the club remained closed. Mr. Stanley already had some experience with the older boys. He had played football with them, was good at it, and did in fact want to take over.

From the discussions it emerged that girls were a problem. Mr. Howard had never been able to handle them, and Mr. Stanley did not intend to let them in at all if the club was reopened under his leadership.

It was decided that the visiting chairman, Mr. Wilson, the worker and Mr. Connolly should meet on neutral ground and review the whole situation, in order to advise the Northside estate committee. The following suggestions were made:

(a) That Mr. Howard, the former worker, be asked to open a club on two nights a week for a new group of young people aged 12–14. He should be given complete freedom and responsibility for this new beginning.

(b) That Mr. Stanley be asked to work with the older boys on two different evenings a week.

(c) That for both ventures an attempt should be made to find a woman assistant leader to work with the girls, if Mr. Stanley could be persuaded to admit them.

After a discussion with the association's chairman, it was decided that an emergency general meeting on youth work be called for the whole membership. The neighbouring youth leader, whose club had been damaged, should be invited to come and give a short talk on 'Current Youth Work Problems'. It was agreed that the worker should visit him to fill in the background, and that the visiting chairman and Mr. Connolly for the committee should present the plan just outlined to the emergency meeting.

The meeting was only partly successful, as neither the worker nor the visiting chairman nor Mr. Connolly had foreseen the pressure that both Mr. Stanley and Mr. Howard would be facing in an open meeting with their supporters present. They were compelled to act out the role of being the main protagonists in the struggle, and the general meeting was unable to resolve the conflict. Separate meetings were subsequently held with Mr. Stanley and Mr. Howard and some of their supporters, and as a result the plans became acceptable. It was then obvious that the meetings had been held in the wrong order, and that the conflict might have been resolved at the general meeting if the small, separate meetings had been held first. In the end the plan went into operation except for the woman assistant leader for the girls. Mr. Howard said he did not need one and that he would try to work with some of the younger girls in a mixed group. Mr. Stanley said he did not want one, and that under no conditions would he allow girls into his group.

This illustration is important in showing that help for the group came not only from the worker but, through her, from two sources outside the Northside estate—from the chairman of another estate group and from the neighbouring youth worker. It also shows that the five stages of helping to resolve conflict were clearly identifiable:

Help all parties to see all sides of the situation, not just the one they themselves are concerned with.

Help them to bring the conflict out into the open and to make explicit each point of view.

Help the several parties to recognise that strong feelings are 'in order' and acceptable in such situations.

Suggest and try out alternative courses of action and various solutions.

Encourage remedial action so as to get the parties past the conflict point.

These steps are not a formula, but they can be a guide to help a worker analyse and make suggestions in similar situations.

# 5 The Role of the Worker: Skills and Techniques

From illustrations in the last chapter on field-work practice, an attempt is now made to generalise about the role of the worker, what he does and why, and to suggest some of the skills needed. We also discuss the importance of recording and one way in which it can be done.

## THE ROLE OF THE WORKER

The worker is concerned with five inter-related activities:
Giving information.
Passing on simple social and technical skills.
Acting as a go-between.
Giving direct aid.
Encouragement and support.
All these services may be given to a single group over a period of time.

### Giving Information

The worker is frequently asked for all kinds of information that is not readily available within the group. He must be aware of *who* is asking the question before deciding how to answer it. If a treasurer asks for information about keeping the books, a more detailed answer would be given than to someone not directly concerned. The worker must also bear in mind the use that may be made of information. A very careful answer must be given if it seems that it might be used to provoke or further a conflict.

Sometimes the worker is asked for simple information, and the answer might be a letter such as the following:

'You should write to the Road Safety Officer, Mr. C. E. Jameson,

at the Town Hall, and ask if you could go and see him or if he would visit the estate to discuss the problem with you.'
Or:

'We haven't any information in the office about running a summer fete on the estate, but I know two associations which do this very successfully. I suggest you get in touch with . . . who will give you information about what they do.'

Sometimes there is no simple answer to a question. For example, 'How do I start a children's club on the estate?' It depends on the age range of the children, the number of residents who can help, the physical accommodation, the amount of money that can be spent on equipment, the amount of storage space, the personal abilities of the helpers, and how often they intend the club to meet.

Or, the worker is often asked for information he cannot possibly have and which he cannot find. For example, 'Why can't we get more collectors? At one time we had a collector for every 25 flats.' Here the worker must indicate the various elements in the situation that need to be explored before the question can be answered. He cannot answer the question but can only suggest to the questioners how they might set about working it out for themselves.

The worker must be aware of the setting in which the information is requested.

Many groups telephone for information. It is important to be available, to have time to talk, and to offer to visit if necessary. Ordinary office hours are not the most convenient time for people at work all day. It is a help to be able to identify the caller immediately, and to be up to date with information on the group he represents, without having to look up a file.

When visiting, the worker may be asked a variety of questions. It may be a routine visit, or by invitation of the association for some special purpose, or the worker may have a special purpose of his own. He should be aware of the state of development of the group, the services which have been given previously, and the quality of the relationship between the group and the worker, or other members of the field-work team.

Sometimes groups need to discuss a special problem, perhaps concerning one of their members. There are times when an invitation to the group to come to the office may be better than a visit to the estate. Sometimes a small meeting is arranged in the flat of one of the officers.

### Passing on Skills

Field-work experience suggests that groups need to acquire skill in working with individuals, groups, and social institutions. Secondly, they need to know how to administer an organisation. Thirdly, they need a more conscious awareness of both their own and other people's social attitudes. This involves acquiring a greater capacity to understand another point of view.

There are several ways in which the worker can pass on simple social skills to the groups. He can use formal or informal methods—for example, by his own behaviour in a situation or by his interpretation of another's behaviour. He may introduce a third party who can pass on the relevant social skills, or he may set up a situation where the person or the group needing the skill has the opportunity to try it out. The worker will consider:

*What Has to be Learned?* What does the individual or group need to learn about a particular process in order to set it in motion?

*The Level of Intellectual and Emotional Awareness.* This will condition the receptivity of the learners and the methods used to pass on the skills.

*The Skills to be Passed On* are those needed by the person in the exercise of his role or by the whole group. If these skills replace an already established pattern of action, the transmission will be more difficult than the straightforward learning situation where these are an ingredient in a new series of actions.

*The Resources Available.* The worker may pass on the skills himself or may involve others—from the association, other estates, the Association of London Housing Estates, or the wider community. Outside experts may also be called in.

*Are Changes in Social Attitudes Involved?* It is more difficult to help people become aware of social attitudes than it is to pass on simple technical skills.

### Acting as Go-Between

Part of the worker's role is his availability to the group as a go-between in its contacts on the estate, but particularly in its relations with outside bodies. This is sometimes a difficult situation. He must represent the group's interest, as well as consider the interests of the larger community.

The worker's role is an extremely difficult one to sustain. He may identify so easily and completely with the group as to find it difficult to understand the misgivings of the statutory or voluntary bodies. On the other hand, he may so completely share the values and standards on which their misgivings are based that he cannot understand the difficulties of the groups.

The situations in which he is most often called upon to act as a go-between are:

## Between Individuals and Groups within the Association

Within the committee, between the chairman and the treasurer or secretary; or between the self-appointed leader and the elected leader. Where misunderstanding or conflict has developed between the committee and the association members or estate residents.

## Between the Association and External Bodies

This is a situation in which misunderstandings or conflicts occur between the association and outside bodies, about their respective roles in providing a social welfare or recreation service. Personality conflicts are relatively rare in situations between groups compared to situations within groups. This kind of situation is often difficult for the worker because, unlike the community group which will usually accept his services as a go-between, the statutory or voluntary body does not always feel called upon to do so.

The following techniques have been found helpful to a worker acting as a go-between in a situation between groups.

*Selection of Focus.* The misunderstandings as expressed by the contending parties are nearly always put vaguely. 'They (the voluntary or statutory bodies) won't help us, but they will help other people.' 'It's no good arguing with them, you don't get anywhere.' 'You have to stand up to them.' Therefore, the focus necessary for useful discussion is either not established or is lost in mutual recrimination. The worker's first job is to establish from conversations with each party the real point at issue and to help them state it in terms that make its solution at least feasible. If the two parties can agree what the negotiations are to be about the task can usually begin.

At first the worker must find ways of helping each party separately to come to some agreement on the meaning of the point at issue, on why it has become an issue, and what they feel can and should be done about it. The next step is to arrange for the two sides to meet and state their case. The worker with the community group then faces a long and complicated affair involving not only the facts of the case, but the social attitudes that colour and support the group's interpretation of the facts. In such discussions the worker must never 'let the group down'. They must know that he is on their side, even

H                                                                                                     93 if he has to say that he does not agree with their point of view. In extreme cases he might have to say that he could not support them. If he has a good relationship with the group, this in itself may lead them to reconsider the problem.

The worker should strive towards the clarification of alternative courses of action. Both sides may agree on one alternative and accept the practical implications of acting on that agreement or (and this is more likely) they may continue the exploration until new alternatives have emerged.

The role of the worker therefore as go-between usually passes through the following phases:

Helping each to understand the other's point of view and helping the group to think out and prepare its case, sometimes helping both parties to do so.

Joint discussion—where both parties are encouraged to state their case and consider possible courses of action.

Reconsideration—where each party reviews its position in the light of what the other side has put forward.

Follow-up. The worker often needs to find some way to follow up the work with both parties in order to encourage them to keep the lines of communication open, to persevere, or to implement the arrangements agreed upon.

After a suitable interval, the worker may have to encourage a second round of talks.

So far the worker has been acting as a go-between in differences and conflicts arising from functional relationships of the various elements in the situation. To act as a go-between in purely personal conflicts is very much more difficult and little by way of generalisation, which is all that can be offered here, can be of much help. No worker can avoid situations hampered by personality conflicts and so the following points are offered as general guidance.

The worker should rarely, if ever, offer himself as a go-between in a personality conflict situation without the acceptance of both parties and then only with the backing of the group. Indeed, his attempts are rarely successful unless the group itself, or at least a representative portion of it, has asked him to participate.

Often the most useful work he can perform is to clarify the roles of the conflicting parties, avoiding any attempt at personal social case work.

In acting as a go-between where personality conflict arises, the worker should always attempt to use the group or committee to help to resolve it. Firstly, where it is possible to clarify the work roles of the conflicting parties, the worker should be conscious that a social role depends not only on the acceptance of a particular role by the person concerned, but on the fact that the group accepts the person in that role. This suggests that the worker's task is to clarify the acceptance of the role by its holder and then to work towards the reinforcement of it by group approval. Secondly, the worker should attempt, by his behaviour, to suggest that proper criteria for adequate role performance is not only the personal satisfaction of the person playing the role, but the adequate accomplishment of the task. Therefore the group's approval and support should be related to the satisfactory exercise of the role in the furtherance of the group's work.

## Direct Aid

Community groups often need direct aid in the form of clerical help, the duplication of publicity material, legal aid, the services of an insurance agent or auditor, and on some occasions the loan of equipment. If direct aid is part of the service it causes little or no difficulty and this service can be handled by the most inexperienced of workers.

Direct aid services are important early in the development of the group because the group has not yet found its own resources, and they are important to the worker in giving him something concrete to offer at a point when the group has not yet seen the full implications of his role or the scope of the service.

The worker should always make it known that it is the agency and not he himself that is offering the direct aid. This makes it clear that he is not a completely free agent but part of an established service, and it is also an indirect proof (the worker need not verbalise this) that there are established bodies that can be counted on to help.

The worker must be careful in offering and giving direct aid not to overdo it—that is, not to offer direct services that the group could and should find within its own resources. Sometimes the inexperienced worker is tempted to use direct service over longer periods than are necessary in order to be thought generous or for other personal motives. This sometimes robs the group of some of the material it needs to achieve a proper relationship to its task, and makes the group over-dependent on services it should already have developed by its own efforts.

## Encouragement and Support

The fifth aspect of the worker's role that requires a special consideration of skills and techniques involved is that of offering and giving recognition, encouragement and support. At every stage of his work with the group and in almost every contact with it, the worker is offering recognition to both group and members, including:

Individuals—who need to be supported in their work for the group, and in the roles they must assume. Activity volunteers may easily become discouraged and not realise that all groups run into difficulties. The professional worker expects problems and tries to work through them; the volunteer may think that he has failed and be tempted to give up.

Committees—inexperienced committees may want outside confirmation that they are working on the right lines. They are encouraged when they find that other groups have similar problems or that something that they have succeeded in doing may help another group.

Special events and activities often need the worker's approval so that the group itself may experience the positive effects of its own efforts. This is particularly important in the early phases of development when the group has no adequate criteria for judging its own success.

In its search for identity as a community group, it often has no mirror in which to see its own reflection. The worker's respect and recognition of its independence is an important factor in establishing its identity. It is also important to the worker himself, as it defines for the group one aspect of his function and it offers him a positive base from which to help the group when difficulties arise. The worker can only question what the group does if there is an established relationship of mutual good will and support.

In offering recognition and support the worker may offer it directly, indirectly, or by reflection. In offering it directly he acts as an outside agent whose support and approval are based on his own knowledge and understanding of similar situations in other community groups on other estates. He will make his approval known in such a way that individuals not only experience it as approval of themselves, but use it in their relations with others as an indication of the usefulness or appropriateness of their contribution to the work of the association.

Indirect approval comes from an outside source, perhaps a visit from another estate group to compare methods of work or a visit from students to find out more about the organisation. Approval of the method is assured if others can be invited to regard it as the right way of doing something. A community group committee whose report on a subscription-collection system is presented at a week-end conference knows that it receives approval and support of that procedure.

To offer support and approval by reflection, the worker describes the work of the association to people whose roles or opinions are seen as relevant and important to the group, for example housing officials, councillors, professional social workers, overseas visitors, the local youth officer or university students. The worker's description reflects his support and the agency's recognition.

Some of the problems most often met in offering and giving support and recognition are:

Relating approval to effective and efficient performance. This is often especially difficult in the early days of the group's development when a generalised approval and support are required, that is, approval and support simply for the idea of coming together in order to begin work. The worker must move from this generalised support to more specific support for particular aspects of the work as the group develops. This is one of the ways in which the worker helps the group to be aware of the stages of its own development, and the processes and procedures most appropriate to each stage.

Avoiding sectional difficulties. The worker, in the various stages of his contact with the group, offers his support to specific persons or specific sections of the group, and unintentionally may cause internal difficulties. As his primary role is to help the group to do a better job, he must sometimes be prepared to give a frank opinion on the people and situations that seem to hinder the group in its work. But in doing this he must realise that in praising one section of the group and by inference blaming another, he could make for additional conflict within the group and also damage his relationships with the group, so that his ability to give help would be lessened.

Withdrawal of the worker. In the early days of an association the worker may attend several meetings and then must gradually withdraw. The aim is to maintain a regular contact and to be available if wanted. The worker is never responsible for the group; it is always autonomous, and has to develop the necessary criteria for judging its own success and for giving its own approval and support for work well done. Also, it is in the working out of relationships with outside bodies that the community group comes to terms with the complexities and subtleties of inter-group and institutional relations. The group can then achieve recognition and support on its own initiative as an equal partner in the network of social welfare agencies.

One of the functions of the worker, which is implicit in what has been said in this section, is to help to resolve conflict. This is not to suggest that conflict is the main concern of the worker, but in the many situations where conflict prevents the group from achieving its objectives, it becomes a very important factor in the worker's appraisal of the situation.

If the conflict cannot be resolved, help can be given in understanding the differences in values and standards, interests and needs that gave rise to the conflict in the first place. The worker cannot expect complete resolution of the problems or even long-standing agreement. Conflict has to be seen as normal in the growth and development of the group and in the everyday give and take of

97

community life. Most important, the worker has to pass on to the group some understanding of how conflict comes about, and when it can be resolved, and when it must be accepted, so that on future occasions the group can go into action on its own.

In field-work practice, the actual social pressures at play can never be described, much less controlled, as simply as is suggested here. But however complex or disorderly the actual situation may be, the worker will have to learn to use many of the elements in the social process, in whatever sequence, combination, or timing pattern, in order to try to pass on to the groups the skills which have been discussed here.

## THE FUNDAMENTALS OF THE FIELD-WORK PROCESS

The role of the worker in giving information and direct aid, passing on skills, acting as go-between and giving support, will most often be concerned with facilitating three fundamental field-work processes—communication, interpretation and evaluation.

### Communication

The meaning of communication in this context is the process whereby the flow of information and opinion is maintained throughout the life of the association. Information and opinion have continually to be exchanged between leaders in the various areas of operation; for example, between sections of the committee and the treasurer about expenses, between the chairman and the publicity worker about publicity, between the resident with a complaint or a grievance and the proper committee official. The lines of communication must also be kept open between the various groups and outside bodies. Problems that sometimes grow into conflict situations within the association and between the association and the adjacent community are often basically communication problems, when the conflicting bodies have failed to exchange adequate information as a basis for discussion and compromise. The recognition and acceptance of the various roles in the work of the association, and the opportunity of recognising social attitudes and the part they play, depend on adequate and continuous communication. Three illustrations based on field-work records show some of the basic problems in maintaining communication.

*Illustration 1. Inadequate Communication Within the Committee.* This shows the breakdown of communication caused by confusion of roles in the committee.

98

Date . . . . . Mr. Phillips, the youth work volunteer on the Draw-bridge Estate, phoned the worker asking him to find out why his forms for entry for the sports day hadn't come. He said he had several groups of young people who had been spending their week-ends preparing for the events. He had written to the Association of London Housing Estates twice and phoned once in the last fortnight, and each time he had been informed that the forms had been sent. Would the worker check on this for him, as the young people were already prepared and very much wanted to take part.

Date . . . . . Worker phoned the organiser of the Sports Day and was told that three separate sets of sports forms had been sent to the secretary of the estate association. The worker suggested that in addition to sending the forms to Mr. Phillips he might phone to see what had happened to them before.

Date . . . . . (same day). It became known that the secretary of the Drawbridge association had decided, without consultation, that there was too much paper work involved, that the young people would not be interested since they were to travel some distance, and that the association couldn't afford a coach. He therefore had not passed the forms on to the volunteer youth worker.

At the next meeting of the Drawbridge association there was a heated discussion about whether the secretary could decide on his own about the entry for the sports day, whether it was all the fault of the youth volunteer for not informing him that they wanted to enter, or whether the organisers of the sports day should have sent the forms to the person who had requested them and not to the secretary of the association.

*Illustration 2. Communication with the Association.* These extracts from a single visit record show the effect of bad timing on communication.

A committee was considering having a children's play scheme on the estate for several weeks during the summer instead of the usual outing to the sea. The idea had been suggested at the previous meeting, but there had been no time for full discussion and no decision had been taken. But news of this discussion had leaked out and was talked about among the membership as if a decision had already been made.

Several of the parents among the members organised an informal protest meeting, demanding to know what was going on and why so important a decision had been made in secret. They called for a general meeting to discuss the whole affair of the midsummer outing.

*Illustration 3. Inadequate Communication between the Association and a Statutory Body.* The following paragraphs are extracts from a series

99

of records about difficulty in communication between an association and a statutory body, in this example the local Housing Manager. Misunderstanding often arises when communication is by letter and not face to face.

The worker was told by the local Housing Manager that he was concerned about a certain estate. It seemed that the local tenants' association had been pressing for temporary accommodation, since they were an old estate with very little room for a permanent building.

The Housing Manager admitted that the tenants had in fact something to complain about, as a hut had been promised some months previously. He had received a very aggressive letter from the association saying that unless the hut was up by a certain date they would not be willing to use it. He took exception to the tone of the letter, since he was doing all he could to help them. He asked the worker whether she could make some opportunity to meet their committee.

The worker agreed. The picture she had from his description was of a highly belligerent and angry committee, very difficult to deal with. She arrived on the estate and called at the house of one of the officers, said who she was, and was well received by his wife. Within 15 minutes at least half of the committee had been assembled.

The worker was frank about why she had come: she had happened to be in the Housing Manager's office, and he had told her of his difficulties about the delivery of the hut and that he was upset at the letter they had written. She said it was her job to try to help associations to get club-rooms and to work as co-operatively as she could with both the Housing Departments and the local groups. They were courteous in telling her their story. They said they realised that the Housing Manager had problems. He always wrote to them in a friendly way, but they thought that if they were to get anywhere they would really have to write a strong letter.

As a result of the discussion that followed, the worker was able to convey to the Housing Manager that the committee understood his problem, that in fact they were quite willing to wait for the club-room providing they knew he was doing all he could to get it quickly, and that they had no animosity towards him at all.

The following general considerations should be pointed out by the worker when trying to help groups to understand the importance of good communications:

Keep to the task in hand.

Plan the discussion. This means encouraging the committee to plan an agenda, helping the chairman to establish some control so that members do not all talk at once, and keeping to the rules of committee procedure.

Groups need to understand that unless they keep in touch with their members they will find that interest flags. It can be very profit-

100

able for a group to discuss what are the channels of communication (news sheets, personal contact, popular events, the local press and so on.) This also applies to their relationship with outside bodies.

The worker should try to give information in small 'units': too much information given at one time and relating to different things may well only add to the group's confusion. He should also try to maintain regular contact with a group even when they have no special problems. The nature of the group and its stage of development will determine how frequent this contact should be.

### Interpretation

For the purpose of this discussion 'interpretation' is defined as the attempt to bring about understanding between the various elements in the field-work situation. (This use of the word should not be confused with other technical usage, as for example in psychiatry.) These elements were defined in Chapter One, page 10, as the estate, the tenants' association, the committee, the relevant statutory and voluntary bodies, the worker, and the agency.

Three illustrations are given to clarify this:

*Illustration A.* A community group which had been established for some time had a very active old people's section, which was run very largely by a woman member of their general committee. She was a good organiser, had managed to get around her a small band of volunteers, and the club, which met two afternoons a week, was very popular. The committee decided it would be a good thing to hold an open meeting, when they could invite representatives of the Borough Old People's Welfare committee to come to a social put on by the Old People's Club. There would be a small exhibition of their craft-work, and they could hear the choir which had taken part in a festival specially arranged for members of old people's clubs.

There was a lot of discussion about date and time. The leader of the Old People's Club wanted it to be in the afternoon, since the weather was cold, and this was the time at which the club usually met. Members of the committee however said it was difficult for them to come in the afternoon, as most of them would be at work, and finally it was decided to hold it in the evening. The secretary of the main committee sent out the invitations to local officials and members of the association.

There was consternation when, on the night of the event, the secretary, who had gone to the club-room early, found the door locked and a notice pinned on it saying that the event had been cancelled. The committee and the association members were very upset. One or two of the statutory and voluntary workers from out-

101

side the estate who came regarded this as typical of the unorganised way in which things were often done by tenants' associations.

Usually situations like this are resolved by the natural play of events on the estate and in the local community. In this case the Executive Committee held an enquiry, to which the community development worker was invited. The leader of the Old People's Club was attacked by all the members. At the meeting the worker did what she could to help the leader of the Old People's Club explain why she had cancelled the event at the last minute. (She had to do this without losing the confidence of the rest of the committee.) Eventually it came out that the leader was not feeling well and had been in bed with influenza earlier in the week. She genuinely thought that an evening meeting was not ideal for the old people as the weather had been exceptionally cold, and she had not been able to get all the necessary organisation done in time. She had resented the main committee making all the decisions and sending out the invitations, which she thought should have been her job, and had not stopped to think of the very bad impression her action would make, when she told the old people not to come but did not inform anyone else.

In this situation the worker tried to help the leader of the Old People's club to interpret her action to the committee, and to help them decide how they could best interpret what had happened to the membership and to the representatives of the statutory and voluntary bodies who had been invited. As a result, letters of apology were written to the various people who had been invited, explaining as tactfully as possible what had occurred.

*Illustration B.* The worker had suggested to a new association which had just formed a youth section that they might get in touch with a certain agency concerned with youth work. The tenants' committee accordingly wrote to the agency and asked if one of their officers would visit them.

A few weeks later, when the community development worker was visiting the estate, she enquired how they had got on with the agency representative. They said it had been no good at all. They had been told that they could not get any help unless they had a separate management committee for the youth club not connected with the tenants' association, and a separate membership subscription.

The community development worker apologised and said that she had probably not made clear to the agency the nature of their organisation, and of course it had a right to make its own conditions about which organisations it could help. Most of the clubs with which it would be dealing had management committees and a separate membership subscription, and therefore the representative

102

would not have seen how difficult this would be for their association. The committee obviously felt upset that they had not been regarded as a 'proper' youth club, although they had been trying very hard to establish a programme to meet the needs of their own young people.

The worker then had the problem of explaining to the agency why their conditions were so unacceptable to the group. She explained that the main committee was prepared to spend money on the youth section and did not want it to be quite separate from the tenants' organisation. Their objective was to provide activities for all the members of the family. Secondly, since they had a family subscription collected weekly, they did not think it fair to ask the young people for a separate subscription, since they were already entitled to the benefits of the association under the family subscription. It was true that the young people paid for their own records, and contributed a small amount towards the heating of the hall, but the tenants' association were not prepared to ask for more.

In this illustration the worker had failed to interpret the nature of the group to the agency in the first place. She then had to try to explain why the agency felt these conditions were necessary because of their experience with clubs of a different nature, and to explain to the agency representative why the groups had considered the conditions quite impossible for them to accept.

*Illustration C.* On one estate the committee was interested in providing play space for young children, and had suggested a site which the community development worker and the mothers thought would be suitable. On several occasions committee members spoke informally to the Housing Manager, who asked that the request for the site should be made formally to him in writing. Several months went by and the committee did nothing about the formal request. At the Annual General Meeting a new committee was elected, and at its next meeting the mothers interested in play space took the opportunity to press their case anew. The new committee, anxious to get started and to prove its worth, decided not only to write direct to the chairman of the Housing Committee, but to include in the letter a complaint that the Housing Manager was unco-operative in this matter and had been for the last six months. The Housing Manager was understandably annoyed that they had acted in this way and thought they were going over his head simply to get attention or to make trouble. The chairman of the Housing Committee replied that the Housing Manager would however be willing to discuss the matter with the tenants' committee.

Knowing that the community development worker was interested in the play space, the committee invited her to accompany them when they went to see the Housing Manager. She said that she would be willing to go, but would they have any objection to her telephoning the Housing Manager herself and asking if he would mind if she came as well. This gave an opportunity to explain to the Housing Manager what she knew of the circumstances, and to try to prepare the way a little for the interview. She was also anxious that he should not think she had had any hand in the action they had taken. She explained about the new committee and that it was possible that there had been a genuine misunderstanding. The new committee was probably not aware that the Housing Manager had asked for a letter to be written before he could go to the Housing Committee. She also made an opportunity to speak with the chairman of the tenants' committee, asking whether he thought that some explanation should be given to the Housing Manager about the misunderstanding and some apology made.

From the material outlined in these three illustrations it can be seen that the necessity for interpretation in this work arises from different appraisals of events and situations, and of administrative procedures, and from differences in social attitudes.

## The Content of Interpretation

*Events and Situations.* Interpretation in this work is often concerned with the difference in construction put upon events and situations by the various field-work elements. It is important to create an atmosphere in which there can be open discussion about how a situation arises, why certain things were done, and to what extent they can be undone.

*Processes and Procedures.* It is not surprising that autonomous community groups should, in the process of creating an independent identity, evolve processes and procedures that are sometimes at variance with common practice as defined by the established statutory and voluntary bodies; or that different methods of work should grow up and be championed by different elements within the association (the committee, the membership, the activity volunteers); or that occasionally interpretation should be needed in order to ascertain the relevance of certain of these to the work of the group. The important questions are: What is the process or procedure meant to achieve? How did it grow up in practice? How does it differ from the 'accepted standards'? Should it be modified; if so how, and by whom?

Interpretation here is the attempt to achieve a working agreement between the elements in the field-work situation about particular processes and procedures, and their appropriateness to the group's objectives.

104

*Social Attitudes.* All interpretive work, whether of events and situations or of processes and procedures, involves differences in social attitudes, for example, about money or authority. Helping to interpret an event or a situation, or an administrative procedure can be relatively easy, since the discussion is centred for the most part on rational elements in the situation, the work of the group, its difficulties, its aims and objectives. But the differences in social attitudes between the various field-work elements are often, as was pointed out earlier, a much more difficult affair since emotions come into play which often do not allow of compromise. It is not so much a problem of understanding the other person's point of view, as in more rational areas of discourse, as of learning to accept that other people have a right to their point of view.

Where conflict occurs over strongly held social attitudes, the worker might well use a case work technique, and allow, or even encourage, the expression of deeply felt attitudes before attempting to help the contesting parties towards the acceptance of each other's differences.

## The Levels of Interpretation

The illustrations above suggest that interpretation in this work is necessary on several levels:

*Within the committee.* Interpretation within the committee is often needed in respect of the role of individual members, the relations between the committee and the various sections, and the committee and the association itself.

*Within the association.* Interpretation is sometimes required in respect of the work and behaviour of the different elements in the association, e.g. of the membership and its problems to the committee, or of the leaders of the various sections.

*Between the association and the estate.* Sometimes differences arise between the association (its committee, various sections, and membership) and the estate as a whole, as well as people not living on the estate, over matters of programme or policy, which require interpretation to help the parties concerned to appreciate both sides of the story.

*Between the association and outside statutory and voluntary bodies.* A constant factor in this work appears to be the need to interpret, each to the other, the programme and policies of the community group on the one hand, and of the statutory and voluntary bodies on the other.

### Recurring Factors in Interpretation

There are several factors that always have to be taken into consideration by the worker when trying to bring about a better understanding between the various elements in the field-work situation.

### Differences in Objectives and Frames of Reference

Fundamental to all problems of interpretation in this work are the difficulties that arise from the differences in objectives of the various field-work elements. These differences affect both their ability and willingness to understand one another's point of view, and to consider the situation objectively.

The differences in objectives, interests and concerns of the various field-work elements give rise not only to different ways of working (e.g. formal and informal, short-term and long-term procedures) but to differences of viewing, explaining and rationalising their work to and among themselves, and to and with outsiders. The same situation is therefore seen by each element in a different context and is fitted into a different frame of reference.

When the same situation is seen from different points of view, and judgments are made from within different frames of reference, the participants are likely to fear, distrust or shy away from any attempt at a full interpretation of the situation. They fear that they might have to change their presuppositions or their institutional set-up, and this might involve losing cherished privileges, prerogatives and status. This applies to individuals, groups and agencies.

### Evaluation

Evaluation, as we are using the term here, is the attempt to assess the performance of the various elements in the field-work situation in respect of their effectiveness in helping the community group to achieve its objectives.

The following three illustrations have been selected to show something of the kind of situation requiring evaluation.

*Illustration A.* On an estate the executive committee had been in office for six years, re-elected year by year. During the first three years it had built the association 'almost from nothing', as the chairman put it, into an association well respected on the estate and in the local community, with a wide programme and a good record of support from the membership—payment of subs., attendance at activities, adequate volunteer leadership to do the work. During the fourth year the association began to decline, old activities to be less

106

well attended, volunteers to be less ready to take on the work, and subscriptions becoming difficult to collect. After the annual meeting, at which the committee was once again re-elected almost in its entirety, the chairman said to the worker, 'The life seems to have gone out of the association.' As the result of a series of conversations with various committee members, activity volunteers and key figures in the membership, most of whom shared the chairman's feelings and anxiety, it was agreed that the association should do a self-survey in an attempt to get to the root of the matter. Perhaps the association had done its work so well that its services were no longer needed in the same way as they had been in the past. Perhaps the age of the resident population had brought about a change in their out-look and needs. Perhaps, now that families were settled in on the estate, they felt free to use services further afield.

As it turned out, each of these appeared to be at least one aspect of the problem, but on the whole what emerged was that the member-ship and the residents had become so used to having the service provided and so accustomed to the routine of the association as it now stood, that many had lost active interest. Even some of the statutory and voluntary bodies in the wider community had come to see the once flourishing association as going downhill. As a result of the self survey it was seen that:

New needs had arisen which had not been adequately recognised. The junior club, which had once been a flourishing part of the programme, was now much reduced in size, and a large teenage population had grown up on the estate unprovided for by the association.

The committee, six years in power, had developed the ability to 'settle things before they got troublesome', a useful ability but one that had contributed to the 'lack of colour' and interest for the members.

*Illustration B.* In this example the worker is able to help the com-mittee evaluate their work as a result of a problem arising in one section.

A youth work volunteer had been running a good club for two years, well respected by the young people and the members of the association, when a series of incidents occurred which the committee thought were giving the estate a bad name. They held a special meeting and criticised the committee member who took general responsibility for their youth work. He resigned and said that he would find a shop or room off the estate and take the club there with him. He phoned and made an appointment with the worker. She discovered that although he was a member of the general com-mittee he never felt welcome and never attended unless especially asked to do so, and this was only when something went wrong. His suggestion that there should be a separate budget for the youth section had not been accepted, so that he was always running to the treasurer to find out how much money they could spend. Also, on the first occasion that he had prepared a short report for the committee, the chairman had not made time to discuss it. The youth leader added that the incidents in the youth club had been very much exaggerated.

The worker asked if he had any objection to her telling the chairman that he had been to see her, and whether she might discuss the situation with him. This was readily agreed to.

Discussion with the chairman and later with the committee suggested that the present officers were mainly concerned with money raising events. They had a large bank balance, and apart from generous parties and outings relatively little money was being spent on regular activities such as the youth section, the children's club or the old people. The treasurer in the course of the discussion remarked that if the youth club moved off the estate they would have another night free to play Bingo.

Subsequently the worker, after congratulating the committee on their secure financial position, attempted to open up a discussion on how much money they thought they ought to have in the bank for a 'rainy day', and on how far they thought each age group on the estate was benefiting from their success. Were they interested to compare their annual statement of accounts with any of the other community groups', and what had they in mind when they raised their money?

Once some of these questions had been aired on the basis of the worker asking for information, a small section of the committee gained confidence and one said that he thought they spent too much time and energy just raising money. A process of evaluation then started, which led to temporary conflict in the committee but also to an evaluation of objectives over a period of time. In fact, at the next annual meeting how much money was raised and how it was spent became a live issue.

When the youth club had been closed for a few weeks and the leader had failed to find other premises, the young people and several of the adult members went to him and asked if he would continue to organise the club. When he agreed, they approached the main committee together and the club was eventually reopened and a better relationship worked out.

*Illustration C.* The worker was in touch with an association on a small, very pleasant new estate. She was surprised to find that they had requested the housing authority to remove the sand pit which had been provided for the young children. She asked the chairman of the association what had happened. He went into a long explanation. He said he was sorry about it himself, since his own child had played there, but there had been complaints.

The caretaker said that the sand got into the washing machines in the communal laundry, that a woman in a nearby flat found it too noisy, and that the older children played there instead of in their own playground. Some mothers had said that the sand got into the children's eyes, and others that it might not be clean. He thought the sand was the cause of a lot of trouble on the estate and it would be better taken away.

The worker then tried to suggest to the chairman that it would also be interesting to discuss why there appeared to be so much discontent on the estate, and whether the association could do anything to overcome this. Had the committee considered trying to get people together to discuss this problem? The chairman said he hadn't thought about it in this way. Some people seemed to have found it difficult to settle down. It hadn't occurred to the committee to try and solve the problem of the sand pit among themselves: probably they should have called a meeting of the mothers and had a discussion with the caretaker before taking any action.

In the example the worker tried to get the chairman to make a more thorough evaluation of a situation, and to see that there was a problem of relationships on the estate as well as a problem about a sand pit.

## The Objectives of Evaluation

It can be seen from the above illustrations that in this kind of work the major objectives of evaluation are:

To explore individual roles with a view to helping the person carrying out the role (chairman, activity leader etc.) to do so more effectively and efficiently and in relation, not only to personal satisfaction, but also to the aims of the group and the roles of other individuals pursuing the same aims.

The second major objective of evaluation is to explore the role of the group with a view to helping the group to carry this out more effectively and efficiently. In practice this is primarily an evaluation of the work of the committee.

The third area in which evaluation is often necessary is that of methodology: how useful and efficient are established methods and procedures, ways of working, ways of interpreting the work, what needs to be changed, why, and how?

Lastly, often as an ingredient of the evaluation of role and methodology, there is the evaluation of objectives, both general and specific.

I

Contrary to what might be expected, the evaluation of failure by the group is easier for them to undertake than the evaluation of success, because the group can more readily see the need for holding an inquest about a failure than about a success.

### The Process of Evaluation

The steps found useful as a guide to evaluation in this work are:

Collecting information about what went wrong, what needs to be done, what isn't being done, from the participants.

Getting the information out into the open for discussion between the participants and relevant outsiders.

Helping the group to assess the information in relation to the light it throws on the behaviour and the work of the participants in relation to the objectives of the group.

Pin-pointing the specific trouble spots, bottle-necks, areas of misunderstanding, or areas so ill-defined as to be capable of conflicting interpretation. This last area of the work is more often a cause of difficulty than might at first appear. Sometimes one of the most primitive results of an evaluation is simply to have achieved common agreement about methods, privileges and responsibilities in an area of the work where participants have felt uncertain.

Helping the group to suggest alternatives. Evaluation as discussed here does not simply mean finding out what has gone wrong and leaving it at that. It must move on to suggestions of possible alternatives in the hope of avoiding the difficulty under discussion next time.

Helping the group to decide which alternative to choose. In the same way, the evaluation process should include the agreement of the relevant participants as to which of the suggested alternatives should be given a trial.

### The Role of the Worker

Several different aspects of the role of the worker come into play in evaluation:

To help de-personalise discussion. Very often evaluation is seen by one or another of the participants as a matter of avoiding blame or handing out commendation. Part of the role of the worker is to help keep the process impersonal, i.e. to keep it task-centred, to keep the discussion as far as possible on the difficulty and alternatives as they help or hinder the objectives of the group. On the whole evaluation should not be about persons but about roles, administration, methods and objectives. The worker's job is to help the participants to see this.

To help the group to see that the alternative chosen and agreed upon will most likely involve changes in the ways in which individuals and groups behave and work. A good deal of evaluation in this work goes wrong because once the participants go back to work they find that the alternative they agreed upon requires changes that they had not foreseen and are not willing to accept. As often as not they revert to their original behaviour and the evaluation has accomplished little.

The worker should recognise that the evaluation process is not complete until the new, agreed-upon alternative is in operation and has been built into the situation. This may require a good deal of follow-up. The worker helps the group to see that evaluation is a continuing process. Too often the group will see the need for the evaluation of a specific problem, carry this out, but not see that it involves follow-up to ascertain whether or not the agreed-upon alternative has been successfully grafted into the work situation.

In this discussion of skills and techniques necessary in field work it is assumed that what the worker is doing is helping the groups to evaluate on their own.

## RECORDING

Recording is an important part of the field-work process. It is a necessary ingredient for in-service training and in the supervision of community workers. It is fundamental to the development of field work, its adequate evaluation and interpretation.

The system that follows is offered here only as an example of one way of using records. Different field-work circumstances, agency support and policy and different kinds of clientele would require that those working in this way adopt or devise their own system of recording to meet their own needs.

### Observation, Awareness and Recording

Observation, awareness and recording belong together and form a basic part of the worker's skills and techniques. Everything the worker does at every stage in the group's development is partly determined by his observation and awareness. Ideally, in order to be of optimum help to the group everything should be recorded, either in note form or in more detail. Only by purposive observation and objective awareness can the worker hope to know the situation well enough to offer the right kind of help at the right time.

*Observation.* By observation is meant that the worker consciously takes note of those aspects of the field-work situation about which he needs accurate information. These include the various elements in the field-work situation referred to in Chapter One, page 10. The most important aspects include:

The physical environment and general social conditions in a particular neighbourhood and on the housing estate.

The community group as residents attempting to come to terms with the problems of social life in a particular area.

The committee, the formalised instrument of the group.

The statutory and voluntary bodies, the services available or not available.

The resources of the agency he represents.

Within a larger context, some of the social, economic, political and cultural factors that influence the work.

The worker also needs a considerable degree of self-awareness.

*Awareness.* By awareness is meant an attempt to note objectively the changing patterns of the various aspects listed above, in relation to the need of the group, the performance of the task and the role of the worker and the service. This awareness relates to:

The behaviour of individuals. Awareness of what they do, why, what role each plays; the effect of the roles they play in helping or hindering the situation; the leadership potential of individuals; their social background as it affects their work. How do they function in the group as committee members, association members or activity leaders.

Methods of work. Channels of communication: what are they, where are they open and where closed? What processes are used to reach decisions, resolve conflict, set priorities?

Social attitudes: in-group and out-group feeling; class attitude; social and cultural differences; ideas, ideals, values, as they affect social attitudes about money, authority, conflict and co-operation.

Movement and change: the growth and development of the group towards or away from self-chosen goals. What determined this movement? Integration within the group, disintegration of the group, either as a committee or as an association.

The role of the worker and his purposes; the attitudes of all concerned towards the worker and the services he is able to offer.

Relationships: relationship between members, between committee and association, association and all the residents; relationship of the association to the adjacent community.

The items listed above are not separate or isolated, but part of the helping situation. They are interacting, inter-related aspects of any attempt to help a community group by this method of work. Similarly, observation and awareness are not two sets of behaviour on the part of the worker, but aspects of the same process, the gathering of information and impressions necessary for deciding how best to help if needed. As the worker develops through training and experience he brings a more professional approach to the helping

112

situation. The question of what to observe, what to be aware of, for what reason, and purpose, becomes less self-conscious; he learns almost intuitively to select from the complex field of data what is most appropriate to his needs and function. An inexperienced worker however, could well profit from a list similar to the above, as a guide to observation and awareness, at least in the early days of his field work.

*Recording.* Recording is important and necessary in community development work just as in other methods of social work. The purposes of recording are:

An aid to efficiency. The primary purpose of recording is to help the worker to do an effective and efficient job. Recording contributes to this by holding together, in a proper perspective, all the various elements in a work situation.

A focus for field-work conferences. The field-work sessions with individual community development workers and the regular staff conference require a focus for discussing and analysing the short- and long-term problems involved in the work on a particular estate. Individuals, specific problems and method need to be discussed in the light of detailed, accurate information. This information can only be supplied by keeping adequate records.

A basis of evaluation. As the work develops on a particular estate, questions arise about the approach and method of work and its adequacy in a changing situation. Problems once solved recur, apparently insoluble problems solve themselves. Any useful evaluation of this complex situation must be based on accurate written information.

A basis for planning. Recording provides the basis on which to plan the use of the worker's and the agency's resources most effectively and efficiently. Records are needed of an estate that will be ready to use the services of a worker in a few months' time when their club-room is nearly ready; or, of an estate whose committee has given up once again, and is likely to need several visits during the next few months.

For influencing policy. The professional field worker is in a privileged position with the statutory and voluntary bodies concerned with social welfare and recreation. Information that he can give may be useful in determining policy since it represents a consumer point of view. It is of importance to the supervisor, the agency administrator, the teacher, the social worker, the student learning the job, and some of the statutory and voluntary organisations. Problems of confidentiality can arise as in other fields of social work. Records are the reservoir of information which the worker can consult when required.

113

Public interpretation. Grant-aiding bodies, public bodies, private individuals and residents have to be kept in touch with the work. Records provide the information necessary for public interpretation.

Building a professional body of knowledge. The worker in the process of developing the skills, concepts, principles and procedure necessary to the work must have a body of recorded material from which to generalise. This helps to improve his own practice, and is important in the training of colleagues and of association members.

## The Principles of Recording

Objectivity. The worker must try to maintain the necessary detachment to ensure that personal prejudices, class or cultural bias, or preconceived opinions are kept to the minimum. If they do appear they must be clearly recognised as opinions or value judgments. He learns how to be objective by recording and then eliminating what appear to be unwarranted subjective elements in his appraisal of the situation.

Controlled Comment. The experienced community worker should be able to make on-the-spot judgments in selecting the events to be recorded, and showing the relation of these events to the processes of the growth and development of the group. This should result in a consecutive record of the work. He only learns to do this accurately by writing the record and pruning the irrelevant detail.

Meaningful Questioning. Through studied objectivity and controlled comment the worker should be able to ask himself questions directly related to the problems outlined in the record. These questions, and a knowledge of the resources available, should enable him to state and assess the alternatives open to him or to others for further action.

Imaginative Planning. The portion of the record that covers suggestions for further action requires the worker to imagine what will happen if he performs such and such an action, and to weigh the pros and cons of that action.

Continuity. In order to plan out time, evaluate the work already done and suggest alternative courses of action, there must be continuity. There must be no gaps. If illness or a concentration of visits makes recording at the time impossible, the links must be supplied later. Ideally records should be summarised regularly at six-monthly and annual intervals.

## Different Kinds of Recording

No one kind of recording will take note of all that needs to be documented over a series of visits. Most written records are made up of several types of recording.

114

Narrative. A narrative recording is a simple statement of the sequence of events.

Episodic. Episodic recording is a short narrative of a single incident chosen to make a particular point.

Anecdotal. Anecdotal recording is the writing up of a single remark or set of remarks, abstracted from conversation, to highlight an important point of a social attitude.

Essay. An essay recording is a discursive composition on a particular subject covering facts, figures, notes and concepts, and is used in summarising a number of narrative recordings.

Check Lists.

Factual statements.

*Usefulness to the Worker and the Agency*

Recording is one of the most important tools for the worker in the development of his practice and to the agency in the development of the service. It enables the worker to:

See the elements in the situation separately and so understand its constituent parts.

See the separate elements in relation to each other and to the total situation so that a choice can be made between the alternatives for action.

Make sense of his own role and of his short- and long-term offer of service to the groups.

See his work in relation to other workers in the statutory and voluntary social services and in the larger context of social and cultural change, as it affects the aims and behaviour of the group.

Evaluate his own development as a professional worker.

Recording is the only way of providing the sponsoring agency with material which enables it to:

Evaluate the usefulness and appropriateness of its service;

Decide on policy for future development;

Influence administrative and policy decisions at local and national level as and where appropriate;

Base public and professional interpretation of its work on accurate information.

The description and examples given in the sections on observation, awareness and recording are all drawn from the field-work experience. Different circumstances will probably suggest and require different methods, but much of the material in this chapter could well be a point of departure for further discussion and enquiry for those working in similar fields.

115

## A System of Recording

The recording system described here was not used consistently during the field work on the housing estates, partly because the limited resources meant that the focus of attention had to be elsewhere. It was impossible to do all the work involved. The system however appears to be consistent with the approach and method used in the field work, and might prove useful for training purposes.

It is assumed that the central office will contain a file for every community group, with entries for:

(1) Estate facts and figures.

(2) Community group facts and figures.

(3) Names and addresses of officers and other relevant details about the association and the personnel in the related statutory and voluntary bodies.

(4) A single-visit record in four parts:

    (a) Single-visit narrative recording of the session or interview that the worker participated in.

    (b) Single-visit check sheet, reason for visit, problems resulting, etc.

    (c) Single-visit summary sheet.

    (d) Analysis of the visit and statement of future plans.

(5) Notes from field-work conference with colleagues.

(6) A half-yearly summary of the group's growth and development.

(7) An annual summary of the group's work and development.

(8) List of all the correspondence with or about the group, and list of all material about the group in other files.

(9) Visit, consultation and conference schedule sheet, making a record of the frequency of visits to the group, telephone calls and so on.

From these entries, a complete file on the life and work of the group, its growth and development, and the nature and content of the service, would be available to the worker, the agency and to others with a legitimate interest. The heart of the system is the single-visit record sheet. The other information sheets could be filled in gradually over a period in order to develop the necessary background. The single-visit record has to be written after every visit. An integral part of the recording system is the weekly case conference and the monthly field-work conference, both of which use field-work records. The discussions at such conferences modify or add to their content. The weekly conference would normally be about particular estates; the monthly conference would be concerned with the whole range of field work.

116

*Field-work Illustrations of Recording.* The following is an illustration of a single visit record, one of which should be written up after every visit to a group or every consultation.

### Illustration No. 1. A Single-Visit Record

(a) *Single-Visit Narrative Recording*

As a result of a telephone call from the new secretary of the Riverside Park Estate, the worker sent another form setting out details of the special insurance scheme, and agreed to attend the next committee meeting. Previous secretary has resigned because of change of work.

About 14 people were present. The worker spoke to the new secretary before the meeting started, and noted his name and address. She checked that he had received the insurance form. The chairman welcomed the worker when the meeting started. There was no agenda for the members, though the chairman had a note in front of him. The Minutes of the last meeting were read. They had decided not to affiliate to the Association of London Housing Estates at present, as they had a great many expenses in the early days of the association. At an appropriate moment under 'Matters Arising' the worker said she was sure the Association of London Housing Estates would realise that they had to get on their feet before they could take much interest in outside organisations, and perhaps they would want to affiliate later. The membership of the association was 230 families. They were planning a social and dance.

The secretary read a letter replying to their request to the housing authority for notice boards and the removal of some contractors' material, which they thought dangerous for the children. The letter said that notice boards would be provided at various places on the estate and stated the cost. There was nothing that could be done about the contractors' materials, which they did not consider to be particularly dangerous, and it was impossible to prevent children from climbing over the fence to get to them.

Discussion of the last point followed, with some indignation. The worker asked about facilities for children's play, and said how much children enjoyed building materials. She agreed to look at the site after the meeting and try to find out from the housing authority what the plans were for playgrounds. She suggested that the group also write asking for information.

The treasurer gave a financial statement. The association had £40 in hand, apart from the money for the outing. The accounts appeared to be well kept. The treasurer said that the canteen was losing money. Mrs. T. said in a rather aggressive way that she always paid in all the money. She knew they ought to be making a profit, but if she didn't have a key to the store cupboard she couldn't make sure that other

117

people were not helping themselves, and it was no good blaming her. The chairman then had some difficulty in controlling the meeting, but eventually said that no one was being blamed for anything, and asked the treasurer to continue. A long discussion followed, which from time to time became rather heated. At the end of the discussion it had been agreed that the secretary would undertake to get a lock for the store cupboard and Mrs. T. would be responsible for the key.

A new representative was needed to take over the collection of subscriptions from the flats, for which the former secretary had been responsible. The new secretary said it was impossible for him to do both jobs. Another member offered to do the collection temporarily until a permanent collector could be found. Several others had given up because they found it difficult to collect regularly.

The committee discussed the outing, coach arrangements, provision of tea, and where to stop for drinks when they went on their visit to the coast.

The meeting ended at 10.30 p.m. The worker spoke to Mrs. T., who looked as if she were still feeling hurt, and asked if she received a receipt for the amount she paid in each time she served in the canteen, and when did she pay the money to the treasurer. As there was no formal arrangement about paying in the money, the worker suggested she should ask the treasurer if some such arrangement could be made. The worker also tried to get to know other members of the committee, while waiting for the officers to complete their business.

The worker, with two members of the committee, then looked at the site where the contractors' materials had been left. It was too dark to see much. Address of new secretary: Mr. T. Roberts, 11 Shrewsbury House, S.E. Telephone (Home): TAN 5366; (business, can be used in emergencies) LON 4455.

[Note: In this narrative the worker refers to herself as such, but some others are written in the first person.]

(b) *Single-Visit Check Sheet* (This could be filled in first and the narrative written later).
  1. Reason for Visit: Requested by . . .
     Suggested by the worker during telephone call from the secretary of the group.
  2. If requested, why?
     Information requested on insurance. Worker took opportunity to visit the group again.
  3. What was happening when she arrived?
     Regular committee meeting.
  4. What was the most pressing problem they felt they had?
     Three problems were mentioned: safety of children, need for a playground, an adequate number of collectors for each block.

118

5. What did the worker feel the problem was?
Group is still in early stages and not very stable.
6. What type of help did they ask for?
Factual information. Support for their contention that the housing authority ought to insist on more fencing of contractors' material or removal of same.
7. What help did the worker give?
Factual information (on insurance). Encouragement (by attending the meeting and listening); no direct help on amenity problem as the group saw it; worker focused attention on the positive side of the problem, i.e. providing the children with alternative playgrounds.
8. Have they started any new activity or are they intending to do so?
Planning first outing.
9. Have they stopped any activity or are they intending to do so—why?
Not known.
10. Changes in the committee. Who, why?
Secretary resigned. Reason given: change of job and work in shifts.
11. New contacts with surrounding community.
Not known.
12. Other problems raised.
a. Problem of organisation of the canteen.
b. How to fill gaps left by resigning committee members in relation to collecting subscriptions.
13. Lists, communications, letters, phone calls, etc., received or sent in connection with the visit?
Insurance form sent in advance of visit. Phone call to be made to the housing authority. Discussion to take place with the Organising Secretary of the Association of London Housing Estates.

(c) *Single-Visit Summary Sheet*
Estate: Riverside Park.
Visit Number: 6.
Date: August 19, 19 . . .
Worker's Name: Mrs. A. Brown.

General Comment: The association seems to be going satisfactorily. The chairman gets on well with the committee members. Some tension between canteen organiser and treasurer. Try to visit again soon.
Questions: Ought to be more definite recommendations in a news sheet about the committee structure in relation to volunteers who collect the subscriptions?

To Be Done: Alter records—new secretary. Telephone District Officer re playground sites (casually mention contractors' materials). Mention to Secretary of the Association of London Housing Estates the group's reasons for not affiliating yet; suggest they continue to receive information but are not pressed to join; suggest they might welcome invitation to attend any meeting that might be arranged for new groups; notify him of change of secretary.

Comment: The treasurer may resent the worker suggesting to Mrs. T. that he should have a definite system for collecting the canteen money. It might have been wiser to speak to them together. At the meeting, however, feelings were running rather high and afterwards the treasurer had not been available.

(d) *Analysis of Visit, Comments and Notes on Future Plans*
[The paragraphs correspond to those under section (a) above.]

The number of shift workers on the estates contributes to instability of committees and the high turnover of committee members.

How necessary is it for everybody to have an agenda? It is difficult for associations if the agenda has to be written by hand. This could be brought up in the next appropriate training course. Suggest that the chairman reads the agenda at the beginning of the meeting if necessary.

The worker decided to ask the Secretary of the Association of London Housing Estates if they could arrange another informal meeting for new groups at the office.

Why do some housing officers still send such very formal letters? Rising standards are often reflected in what it is thought fit for the children to do or not to do. A consciousness of amenities and dangers which are not commented on in the old surroundings becomes extremely important in the new.

It is very desirable that playgrounds should be provided at the same time as the estate (though no doubt children will always prefer a building site.) This is a point which must be taken up whenever possible.

Mrs. T. seems very conscientious but easily upset.

The worker felt dissatisfied about the principle by which collectors are always committee members. The committee becomes too large, or committee members have far too much to do. Consideration is needed of what might be recommended as a solution to this problem —compare Barrow Hill estate. The worker felt that some members of the committee were a little sore with the new secretary for saying that he could not collect as well as do his other work.

No comment.

The worker wondered whether it would have been better to mention the question of receipts for canteen money in front of everybody rather than to mention it to Mrs. T. afterwards. She had refrained because the situation seemed rather explosive. It may not improve relations, however, between Mr. T. and the treasurer that she discussed the matter only with Mrs. T.

The site did not look more dangerous than most. One could see where the children had repeatedly climbed over the fence. There is very little that can be done about this; there were no pickaxes lying about! Remembered that no mention had been made about insurance at the meeting, although the new secretary had phoned rather urgently because he had found they were not insured. Decided not to mention this. Realised that they had not had the usual cup of tea at the committee meeting; no doubt this was because Mrs. T. was too upset.

*Plans*

Find a way of interesting the officers and committee in attending next club room course on committee management.

Ask that they get literature regularly from the Association of London Housing Estates, and an invitation to the next meeting of new groups.

*Questions*

The worker did not become involved in the issue of the contractors' material, except to use it to introduce the need for some sort of play space. How can local authorities be persuaded to plan play space at the same time as the estate?

Is there enough written information available to new groups about committee procedure, including simple practical suggestions for the treasurer?

It should be noted that many of the items listed in the description of observation and awareness are present in this illustration, e.g.:

Behaviour of Individuals. The worker noted the attitudes and abilities of the officers and their effect on the committee.

The Committee. The problems it faces because of changes in officers and the difficulty of getting collectors.

Social Attitudes. The incident about the contractors' materials, which the worker feels would have gone unnoticed by the same residents in another environment. She sees this as evidence of a change in social attitude.

The Role of the Worker. Inability to give direct advice and help in sorting out the canteen situation because of the feelings of the

121

treasurer and the canteen helper. Some effort made to do so indirectly afterwards.

The Larger Context. The influence of shift work on the stability of a committee.

*Illustration No. 2. A Continuity Record*

A worker's visits, telephone conversations and office consultations with a group may, for various reasons, be very irregularly spaced. He may visit weekly or only once every three or six months. But the work with the group goes on and the worker keeps sufficient contact so that he can pick up the threads at the next visit.

In the illustration that follows, the community group had recently moved out of its formation stage and was entering the development of the programme stage. This is the time when many groups are glad to have continuing support in the background. The continuity record bridges the spaces between single-visit records and gives the worker a more comprehensive picture of the group's needs when the time comes for more intensive service.

*Estate: Knights Cross Common. Last visit: September 19 . . .*

*October 5.* Sent a letter to the secretary of the Old People's Welfare Committee for the Borough, saying that she would probably be hearing from the Knights Cross Common tenants' association, asking if a member of the staff could meet the committee and explain all the services to which their elderly residents might be entitled. Explained this was a new committee on a new estate, and there might be some useful co-operation if she could visit.

*October 20.* Letter received from secretary of Old People's Welfare Committee saying she had heard from the association, and would go herself. She was glad to have this contact with the estate.

*October 21.* Wrote to the association and asked if two students might also attend the meeting, since it would be interesting for them to hear about the Old People's Welfare services and to meet members of the association.

*October 23.* Telephone call from the secretary: they would be delighted to welcome the students, and would they like to come early for a cup of tea and then her husband would show them round the estate.

*October 23.* Visit from the treasurer of the association, who said he would have to resign because the various sections were not keeping their accounts properly. The worker suggested that perhaps they did not know very much about keeping track of the money and needed help. The treasurer doubted this and seemed to feel it was

122

wilful carelessness. He didn't want the auditor to see books not properly kept. It seemed that 'nothing was really missing'. The worker suggested that he might like to compare his system with that of some of the other treasurers. He said he would, and the worker suggested two people he might get in touch with. (The problem may be that the treasurer expects too much of the sections, and that it might be a case for lowering his expectation rather than raising their standards.)

*November 4.* Worker phoned Stanton House Residential Settlement in response to phoned request from the Warden. She arranged to go to the Settlement for tea to discuss some of the plans the Settlement had for working on the Knights Cross Common estate.

*November 4.* Wrote letter of thanks to the association on behalf of the two students, who had very much enjoyed their visit. Apologised that it was not possible to accept the invitation received through the students to attend the Guy Fawkes day celebrations.

*November 11.* Put note in file about visit to the Residential Settlement. Some difficulty in explaining why the estate wanted an organisation of their own.

*December 3.* Letter received from association asking if an enclosed notice about a social and dance at Christmas could be duplicated quickly.

*December 3.* Phoned secretary and agreed. Tactfully suggested a slight alteration in the wording where it was not clear. This was readily accepted.

*December 5.* Decided to deliver the notices to the secretary by hand, and had a short discussion with him. Things seemed to be going well. They were busy getting ready for Christmas.

*January 7.* Invitation to attend children's party on the following Saturday week. The mayor had been invited. Where could they get more trestle tables. Unable to attend, but gave information about tables.

*January 18.* Telephone call to say a large window had been accidentally broken at the party: were they responsible for replacing it, or the housing authority? Gave information.

*February 1.* Asked if the worker might attend their next committee meeting, as she was likely to be in the district that day.

During routine visit:

See if there have been any developments following the visit from the representative of the Old People's Welfare committee.

Enquire about the Christmas parties. Explain more fully why it had not been possible to attend.

Enquire if there had been any difficulty about replacing the window. Try to find out how the treasurer was getting on.

As this record suggests, the worker is able, by simply noting his continued work with a particular group, to step in again at the next meeting, without having to begin all over again. This is important, since the worker, simply by reading the record before attending the meeting, can:

Know something of what happened since his last visit or discussion.

Account if need be for his actions to the committee or to others concerned.

Have the material ready to hand to interpret to the group, if necessary, the problem they are facing, as he sees it.

### *Illustration No. 3. A Case Conference and Training Record*

The field-work staff holds a weekly meeting to discuss work on one particular estate. Often some recurring element in the field-work situation is discussed in detail, in the hope of establishing principles on which to base further discussion and improvement of practice.

### *Monks Gate*

This record is an abstract from an anecdotal report of a meeting between a community group sub-committee chairman, the warden of a local youth club, and the field worker, together with notes and comments from a weekly field-work conference record.

*Background.* The worker was asked by the Junior Club and Youth Sub-committee of the Monks Gate estate to come with them to a meeting with the warden of the youth club. This club, with premises in the adjacent community, had been sending a youth leader to the estate to help the association during the past three months. But the warden had now decided not to continue this service. The worker phoned and asked the warden if he might attend the meeting. The warden did not seem very enthusiastic. The worker, however, said he thought it might be as well if he understood the whole story, just in case another way could be found of helping with the junior work if his club leader didn't feel he could continue on the estate. The warden seemed to see the point of this and invited the worker to attend. The worker phoned Mrs. Wilks (the chairman of the Junior Club and Youth Sub-committee) and said he would be happy to come along.

*Mr. March* (*Warden*): It's just because we are opening another junior club here; has nothing to do with any ill-feelings, I assure you [*etc.*] But of course [*in jolly mood*] your committee wasn't much help, you know; didn't really understand junior club work at all. You

124

can't just have all those age groups together. We are very strict about that here. With those numbers you need much more money and equipment. Our leader is responsible to us, but I understand from him that some of the parents kept interfering, and that your committee tried to tell him what to do.

*Mrs. Wilks:* No one really explained to us what you wanted. We thought one thing and your leader another. We had a hard job with the main committee to get enough money for equipment, and it's difficult for the mothers to come regularly just at the time they are cooking a meal.

*Mr. March* (to the worker): You can't expect us to work with these volunteers: they don't know what they are doing; they won't listen, and there is no discipline in the place.

The worker accepted this comment and then said:

You see, Mr. March, the main committee itself didn't fully realise the size of this junior club problem, and probably didn't fully understand that more money and help were needed. As Mrs. Wilks points out, the main committee hasn't always been very helpful to the sub-committee.

*Mr. March:* Well, that may be. [Meaning, the worker thought, 'That's no concern of mine'.]

*Worker* [after a slightly embarrassed pause, during which no one spoke]:

Well, Mrs. Wilks, you have come with a suggestion from your committee, haven't you?

*Mrs. Wilks:* Yes, I have. Couldn't you let your leader come to Monks Gate two evenings a week, and then we could split up the numbers so that the young ones came one evening and the older ones the next?

*Mr. March:* I'm afraid that's quite impossible. We won't be able to continue sending our leader to Monks Gate at all, but the children can all come down here to the new club we have formed, and we will continue to provide the leadership.

*Mrs. Wilks* [in somewhat of a huff]: The children won't come this far. There is the main road to cross. Besides, we want to be able to do this in our club-room on the estate.

*Mr. March* [on parting, in an aside to the worker]: It is so difficult to work with these groups. The children would be far better off here.

The worker agreed that it was possible this might be so, and did not argue.

The worker took Mrs. Wilks home in his car. On the way she said she was thinking of giving it all up: the general committee didn't understand how difficult it was for her helpers to look after so many

K                                                                     125 children, and complained when there was some damage; and the outsiders didn't understand either, they always wanted to do things their way.

The worker asked if Mrs. Wilks would like him to be present at the next meeting of the main committee, saying that since he was with Mrs. Wilks when they spoke to the warden, he might be able to help her explain her point of view.

Mrs. Wilks thought this was a good idea, but that it really wouldn't help. The warden of the youth club phoned the worker the following day and said he was pleased that the worker had come to the meeting, and it was a shame that the association didn't take his excellent advice. (The worker thinks that the warden had considered the previous day's meeting and thought that more explanation was necessary. The part about 'excellent advice' was quite gratuitous, since he hadn't given any.)

### Comments from the Field-Work Conference

A. *The Problems of the Sub-Committee.* Sub-committees or sections often have an even more difficult job than the main committee. The main committee either refuses to give the sub-committee real responsibility and insists on going over the ground again at its own meeting, or it tends to leave everything to the sub-committee and not give enough support or take enough interest. The outside bodies, who know little of what the sub-committee is trying to do, and under what circumstances, tend to by-pass it and deal with the main committee instead. The worker has to know when to deal with one and when the other.

Sub-committees also tend to suffer from not having a clear and definite mandate, as well as from pressing problems of leadership. The most capable people tend to find positions on the main committee. Part of the worker's job, then, is to help clarify and interpret the relationship of sub-committees or sections to the general committee, and to consider the terms of reference within which the sub-committee operates; in particular how it budgets and accounts for its money.

B. *The Sub-Committee and the Voluntary Agency.* The type of situation outlined here is not untypical. The professional social work agency offers to help; its offer is accepted; it moves in and begins to set up its own programme, setting the standards it sees as necessary and working with those people it feels fit into its programme.

The result is usually disagreement and, in some cases, the withdrawal of their voluntary service. This may be for the following reasons:

The committee does not ask the voluntary body for a detailed presentation of its plans before the work begins. This is further complicated by the fact that, even if it got such a detailed presentation, it might not be able to see the implications of the proposed service of its work.

The unwillingness of the voluntary body to explain in any detail what conditions they want to make.

The unwillingness of the voluntary body to see that its standards may not be the same as those of the association. (Its greatest contribution would be to work within terms of reference jointly worked out with the main committee in relation to their particular needs.)

The unwillingness of the committee to see that the voluntary body is also responsible to its own national or regional agency, and that work with the voluntary body requires at least a minimum of routine and orderliness, and conformity to a standard.

The unwillingness or inability of the voluntary body to train or work with local leaders.

C. *The Voluntary Body*. The voluntary body may have a set of standards that probably work well for the people it normally serves. It is now presented with a different situation, under different circumstances, not of its own making. It cannot understand why people living on the estate are not prepared to walk as far as some of their other members, or why they do not attend training courses, or why they have to work with a main committee as well as the subcommittee.

This type of organisation is responsible to its own committees, perhaps to a national body, and also to a grant-aiding local authority. The problem is now to develop an approach to such a body that will convey the attitudes, understanding and skills necessary to work in a changing condition.

As a result of discussing this illustration, the workers became more aware of the problems connected with sub-committees and with groups accepting professional help.

The following illustration shows how this knowledge was used.

During a visit to a group intending to form a sub-committee on work with the elderly, in co-operation with the local authority, it was suggested that: (a) The sub-committee be given an agreed and well-defined job, including some financial responsibility; (b) The channel of communication between the sub-committee and the professional worker outside should be laid down and agreed from the start; (c) Both the committee and the sub-committee should find out what was involved in co-operation with the local authority before starting out; agreement should be reached among themselves and with the local authority about the general terms of the service, including the cost and the roles of all concerned.

The purpose here has been to help the community worker, especially the inexperienced worker, to see something of the principles and purpose of recording, and to suggest the types of records appropriate to this kind of work.

# 6 Conditions of Field-work Practice

This chapter will consider some of the conditions of field-work practice. These are, firstly, the recognition of the factors affecting the development of the groups (size, location, age of estate, etc.); secondly, recognition of the different stages of group development and the phases of service appropriate to each stage; and, thirdly, a recognition and understanding of some of the difficulties of the worker and the agency in attempting to work in this way.

## FACTORS AFFECTING THE DEVELOPMENT OF THE GROUPS

The needs and problems of the groups, including the need for autonomy and identity, and for help with committee work, finance and public relations, are themselves affected by a number of other factors which the worker must recognise as part of conditions of field-work practice.

### Location, Size and Age of Estate

The developing community group and the field-work service offered to it are both affected by the location, size and age of the estate. If the estate is situated within or near the old neighbourhood from which most of the residents came, much of the old pattern of social life is likely to continue. The distance to work, school, shops and other amenities will be roughly the same and the pattern of social life will remain comparatively undisturbed. The old neighbourhood appears to support the social life on the estate 'naturally'. Even so, a group may form in order to establish the identity of the newcomers and to meet new needs.

When people are re-housed relatively far away from the old neighbourhood, all the conditions of unfamiliarity described in Part

129

I are present. The new social environment and the need for neighbour-liness encourages the growth of an association; on the other hand, if it is not too far away residents may return to the old neighbour-hood for shopping, to see friends and relatives, and for special occasions, so frequently that they may feel little need to create new social patterns.

Although neighbours can sometimes be re-housed together, this is frequently not possible, even if they wish it.

*Size*. Some estates are too large to be served by a single common enterprise. Where the geographic area covered by an estate, built at high density, is small, the difficulty of organising an association for a potential membership of three or four thousand people may not be realised by those who undertake it.

If the estate is small, e.g. less than one hundred dwellings, it may find it difficult to support an association with a variety of activities. There can be no general rule. One estate with about 120 dwellings sustained a rich variety of activities for about ten years and managed a club room throughout that time, but on a small estate there is a narrower range of potential leadership.

*Age*. The completely new estate presents a whole range of problems and opportunities to residents and groups. Where a new section is added to an old estate, the old estate may already have an associa-tion. The new residents may feel that it does not represent their interests, or, in an enthusiastic attempt to come to terms with their new environment, they may throw all their energies into the existing group and give the impression of making a take-over bid.

If the old estate has no community group and feels no need for one, the new residents may take the initiative and the problem arises of including the established residents. Part of the work of the associa-tion may then consist in establishing good relationships between the two areas.

### Amenities

The absence of amenities thought to be necessary by new residents can provide a stimulus to development. Such an absence immediately provides something specific to complain about and, therefore, an objective to work for and an incentive to set in motion a programme of community action. This in turn produces some of the social interaction necessary for the development of community feeling and community cohesion. (But it can hardly be suggested that estates should be built without essential amenities in order to provide the residents with this stimulus.)

130

## Club-room or Meeting Place

If a club-room has been built with the estate, the first tenants will probably ask questions about its use. 'Who will run it?' 'What activities will be offered?' If they are told by the Housing Manager that it is for their own use and can be run by them if they are interested, it obviously provides a reason for individuals to come together to explore the possibilities.

Although the absence of a meeting place can be a hindrance to the development of a group in the early stages, it can also spur the group to common action. Amenities built with the estate are important, but the development and work of a community group does not depend entirely on the existence of such an amenity from the start.

## Social Origins and Social Attitudes

On housing estates, the sharing of similar traditions, customs, values, standards and ways of behaviour may make common action possible. If the shared traditions and customs do not include ideas about self-help or the value of common action, group development may possibly be hindered.

If the residents come from mixed social and economic backgrounds, the development of groups depends very much on the proportions of the mixture. If the balance is not equal, the larger proportion may frighten off, or tend to exclude, the smaller. Where the proportions are evenly matched, a struggle for power may develop.

Whatever the background of the group, it will affect the kind of indigenous leadership available, the kind of training that is needed and acceptable, the rate of development of the group, the possible programme and the relationship of the agency to the group.

A new group is affected by the varying attitudes of groups and organisations in the wider community. Where organisations welcome the newcomers, accept them and offer opportunities for co-operation, the community group will develop, although there may be a period when the welcome is rejected while the new group establishes its identity. If the organisations ignore or reject the newcomers, then the community group on the estate may remain isolated and make little use of the existing facilities.

The attitudes of the statutory and voluntary bodies in the established community are important. However welcoming and co-operative they wish to be, there is always the possibility that a struggling new group may feel itself rejected or resented, and then its growth is slowed down. The housing authorities may either encourage a group as an aid to the development of community life on

131

the estate, or see a vigorous group as a challenge or a threat to their authority. In the long run, the success of a group depends very much on the attitude of the housing authority.

## Leadership

*Experienced Indigenous Leaders.* Leaders of this kind have usually been 'trained' by their previous experience. They may have been members of a trade union, a political party, a residential settlement, church or other body, and have been in a position of some responsibility, perhaps as a group or committee officer within a larger organisation. This kind of leader can often bring knowledge of how things are done, of committee procedure and an understanding of organisational matters, as well as an extremely valuable intuitive ability to get people to do things together.

In the early stages, the group may be so dependent on the experienced leader that he tends to dominate. Because of their dependence, the group may feel resentment at their need of his skills. If the leader has gained his experience in a more highly organised group, like a trade union, with set standards and objectives, he may push the more informal housing estate group too hard, attempting to reach standards inappropriate in their circumstances. He may be intolerant of relatively trivial mistakes or over-estimate the resources available and the capabilities of group members. If he becomes discouraged, he may leave just at the point when his skills are essential if the group is to continue at all. An experienced leader may arrive at the stage when a group is stable and cohesive, and he is likely to be able to use his skills without endangering the group or disappointing his own expectations. Should an experienced leader come at a later stage, he may be extremely valuable in helping the group to achieve its aims. On the other hand, if he needs to prove his leadership, he may try to persuade the group to begin all over again, and this could lead to its break up. The experienced leader is often either unwilling or unable to pass on his skill to others. The way he emphasises his leadership may even drive out others whose service the group needs; the circle into which other leaders could come is not enlarged, and when he leaves the organisation collapses.

*Inexperienced Indigenous Leaders.* Most of the local leaders encountered during the field work were inexperienced when they began to take part in the work of a group, and this affected their leadership in one of two ways. First, such a leader might feel hesitant and inadequate, fearful of making a wrong decision, slow to see what was needed, unable or unwilling to take sufficient responsibility for making things happen, in order to match the expectations of the
132

membership with the activities of the committee. This kind of inexperienced leader either gradually developed the necessary skills and confidence, or grew anxious about his inadequacy and withdrew.

The second effect of inexperience was to lead to an over-estimate of the need for positive, visible leadership and for the 'boss' to make all the decisions, and to be in on everything. This conception of leadership was sometimes due to insecurity in the new role, fear of failure or a genuine misunderstanding of the work of a leader in a self-programming group. This kind of leader can stunt the growth of a group and deter other potential leaders by his own fear of displacement or of losing control.

This fear can also hamper the group's relationship with the worker, who is seen as a threat by the insecure leader, and this may prevent the worker from offering effective help. There is less danger of an established group being, or feeling, threatened or overwhelmed by this type of leader, whose skills and energy can then be used to advantage.

*The Sociopathic Leader.* All leaders bring their own personalities into the work of the group and sometimes the personality is more valuable than any knowledge or expertise. Even a richly gifted personality, a charismatic leader, needs to bring something other than his personality to the group—some knowledge, skills, insights into human behaviour; also a recognition of the existence of a group as a group, and of the individuals within it and its responsibility to the membership, the residents and the community.

By contrast, the sociopathic leader usually comes to the group determined to remake it in his own image. He uses his endowments —sometimes neurotic, occasionally psychotic—as the sole instrument of leadership. This can involve an almost total disregard of the personalities of other members, of the validity of existing aims, objectives and procedures, and of the already existing pattern of social action. The sociopathic leader is not necessarily psychologically disturbed, but may be imprisoned within a particular situation, whether at home, at work, or in the social environment, that offers no scope for his potential abilities. He may suffer from inadequate educational opportunity and resent having to live below his potential. On the other hand, he may hold an exaggerated idea of his social role, far in advance of his ability to perform. He may try to act out a phantasy of leadership, without the necessary personal resources and with inadequate understanding and appreciation of the situation in which he is actually set.

A newly formed community group often suffers seriously from the presence of such a leader. At first it feels the need of his determination and drive, only to discover later that his energy is disruptive

133

of co-operative effort and that the group cannot extricate itself from his attachment. There were examples during the field work where the leadership behaviour of sociopathic leaders who had attached themselves to community groups led, or almost led, to the destruction of the group. The sociopathic leader often feels the need to deprive the group of the worker's services, as the worker is seen as a rival. The sociopathic leader can define leadership only in the singular. No other leader at any level must provide any service to the group but himself. All other leadership is unacceptable and, if it appears, is seen as competition or rebellion.

*The Indirect Leader.* The indirect leader is important to the work of the community group and is frequently present in the membership or in the wider community. He does not seek office as a committee member or as an activity leader but works quietly behind the scenes. He is often someone with previous experience of leadership in organisations unconnected with the estate. He encourages association among members and residents or, if he is from the adjacent community, he may help in the formulation of opinions about what is needed and what should be done. He may even be asked to speak at membership meetings and may often be useful as a mediator, helping informally to interpret the conflicting views. An indirect leader may sometimes be a disrupting influence on the work of the group if, for some reason, he has been wrongly excluded from the affairs of the group, is by nature a lone wolf, or is even an incipient sociopathic leader. It is important for the worker to find ways of helping the group to use the indirect leader to the best advantage in order to extend the opportunities for leadership as widely as possible.

## The Wider Context

Neither community groups nor new housing estates are cut off from the influence of wider social conditions. For example, the changing level of aspiration and pattern of social life visible in the country as a whole will have some impact and effect on even the smallest group. It is probably fair to expect that the tempo of social change since the last war will be maintained, if not increased, and that aspirations of all kinds—educational, economic, social and vocational—will continue to rise. For example, the familiar changes in the traditional role of husband and wife are already reflected in community group life, where more women are taking administrative responsibility, being recognised as leaders in positions previously considered as exclusive to men. It is probable too that traditionally middle-class activities for married women—homecraft, cookery, dressmaking—provided by various voluntary organisations, will develop in housing estate communities, although, formerly, such activities were extremely difficult to start and maintain.

Again, most community groups working with youth have already moved away from boys' work towards mixed work, which has as part of its content 'boy/girl relationships'. Such groups may be concerned about the gulf between the generations, the differences in values and standards and the differing levels of aspiration in attitudes towards work, sex and education.

These general changes in the pattern of social life may also affect the recreational activities of the groups and there may be a movement towards formerly 'middle-class' recreational patterns—music and drama, political discussion groups, and informal adult education.

## THE STAGES OF GROUP DEVELOPMENT

From the discussion of field work so far, and especially of Paisley Common and the typical cases of helping the group, it will be seen that housing estate community groups usually pass through stages of development, each characterised by a different pattern of social interaction between its members, its sub-groups and other groups in its social environment. The worker must recognise this and use this recognition in working with the group.

For the purpose of field-work discussion, six stages of group development were agreed upon:

1. Starting point
2. Exploration
3. Formation
4. The development of programmes
5. The established association
6. Integration with the wider community

These six stages are not seen as exactly parallel to the social reality of group life, but are guide lines to help consider the changes that take place in the life of the group as it attempts to carry on its task. None of the six stages can be seen as a separate, isolated phase, and not all groups pass through all the stages—for example, some never progress from exploration to formation. As it is important for the worker to be aware of the various situations, it is helpful to discuss each stage separately and in some detail.

### (1) The Starting Point

In fact, there is often no visible starting point. Spontaneous social interaction, the raw material from which groups develop, happens from the moment the new residents move on to an estate, and the worker's role is simply that of an observer.

## (2) *Exploration*

At this stage, individuals meet informally, at first without definite purpose, in the ordinary occasions of social life. This loose network of personal relationships, from which the community group gradually emerges, is characterised by:

Several small, nebulous, informal friendship groups, each with some idea about what should be done.

No firm agreement within or among the groups on any one proposal or on any set scheme for co-operation to achieve any of their aims.

The presence of indigenous leaders—individuals with a definite idea, often without a formal following, or with a very small, loosely knit one.

*Role of the Worker.* At this stage the worker is occupied in making personal contacts, taking and creating opportunities for establishing his own role and probably only offering specific information.

The worker must be able to draw on his experience of what other groups in similar circumstances were able to do, and to offer the necessary information should the group decide to take on a new task. Even before the group has reached any depth of cohesion and is still more or less a collection of individuals, the worker must make it clear that his service is offered to the group. Often a strong indigenous leader will attempt to 'use' the worker in the exercise of his leadership, especially if his authority is not already established.

The worker must make it clear that he is advising the *residents* and that the group, or groups, he is working with are to him representative of the entire resident population.

## (3) *Formation*

By now the loosely knit informal group has become more organised and is concerned to do something for the estate. They may even have regular meetings with a temporary chairman and have a fairly well worked out proposal for some kind of activity. The gradual emergence of group feeling enables a definite programme to take shape. Some characteristics of this stage are:

The group has begun to attract new members and it is possible for sub-groups to form, usually on the basis of common interests. age or place of residence on the estate. The group may choose a name for itself and may elect a chairman.

Difficulties in getting co-operation. Occasionally after the initial enthusiasm has waned the sub-groups may compete with the larger group for status and power. Sometimes this takes the form of a
136

conflict about what is to be done, or the nature of the authority vested in the officers.

Deciding on aims and objectives. Many difficulties are partly resolved when the organisational forms are agreed upon and a general committee elected. Some difficulties may then be centred upon the roles of the various officers and the relations between the committee and the membership.

*Role of the Worker.* The worker should be able to show why formalisation is helpful, and to suggest forms of organisation which have been tried and found useful.

The worker should recognise that, at this stage, some conflict is possible. The worker can point out that conflict experienced by the group is part of its development and not a sign that it will never work or that it is becoming less neighbourly. He should also be able to suggest how the conflict can be used, when it is recognised and accepted, to clarify the aims of the group and its preliminary tasks.

The worker should explain to the group the time and care necessary to establish the organisation. Often elements within the group want to begin work before the resources, manpower, money and organisation are available. The worker can suggest that the best thing is to concentrate on building an organisation capable of offering services. The social interaction arising from the attempt to build an organisation is just as valuable as that which occurs later when the service is offered.

### (4) Development of Programme

With some kind of organisation agreed upon, and something of its structure achieved, the attention of the group usually turns to the provision of service to its members. This period is characterised by increased cohesion and a sense of purpose. Early in this phase there is often pressure to make a vigorous start and to begin all the activities at once before the necessary money or manpower is available.

When the membership is fully informed and all the volunteers are available, then the committee is faced with the need to prove its usefulness. Excessive demands for service come in from the membership; the residents have exaggerated expectations, and dissenting groups within the membership add to the committee's problems. In such a situation the committee often overstretches its resources in order to offer bigger and better service, to exercise its authority and to prove itself. The committee, the membership and the association are attempting to establish an identity in their own eyes and in those of the statutory and voluntary bodies. It can be that so much is

137

being done, so much attempted, that there is a general breakdown in communications.

*Role of the Worker.* The worker should suggest caution by pointing out the difficulties that may come from attempting to do too much.

Anxiety can be allayed by assuring those directly concerned that the difficulties encountered are only to be expected; that going more slowly will increase the stability of the group and not endanger its 'identity'; that one activity well done can achieve more than several that 'don't quite come off'.

The worker can show the group methods of keeping the lines of communication open so that the various sections of the association and the community can be well informed and stress the importance of this.

Help may be needed for the group to develop appropriate criteria for evaluating its work. Good evaluation is an aid to better service, a way of helping the group to see the value of the work and to achieve their own experience of 'success'. Often the criteria used are not relevant to the activity evaluated; for example, an outing does not depend for its success only on the numbers in the bus or the cost per person.

### (5) *The Established Association*

This phase of the group's development produces strong group feeling stemming from established procedures. There are also relatively well-defined rules for individual and sub-group behaviour, and a sense of identity resulting from the successful attainment of some goals. Some characteristics of this stage are:

Established Procedure. The group has settled down to a routine of group life; the role of the committee members, the work of each activity volunteer, and the channels of communication have been established. A tradition of how to do things in the association has grown up, a balance of responsibility and privilege has been achieved, and the provision of service to the membership and the estate has become almost a routine affair.

Contact with Outsiders. The security of the established community group makes for easy contact and co-operation with the neighbouring statutory and voluntary bodies, with other housing estate community groups and with the Association of London Housing Estates.

Changes in Leadership. At this stage in the development of the group, it is possible that some of the early leaders have retired and have been succeeded by a new set of indigenous leaders. This may happen without undue difficulty, simply by the election of new officers. On the other hand, the group may experience a short period

138

of adjustment while the new leaders are settling in, but usually leadership is replaced gradually.

*Role of the Worker.* In the early stages the worker had to help the group to come to terms with the intricacies of relationships between the elements that made up the association. Now he has to help the association to develop a pattern of response to the neighbouring community, and to help those in the established community and in the statutory and voluntary bodies to understand the nature and problems of the group.

In the early stages the worker helped the group to establish ways of dealing with recurring difficulties and to agree on principles of procedure. He may now have to encourage them not to become too set in their ways and so unable to respond to new circumstances or new needs. The worker should also encourage the group to offer service to less developed groups so that the association concerned has the opportunity to widen its sphere of activity by helping others.

### (6) *Integration with the Wider Community*

In the final stage a community group can undertake wider responsibility on the estate in providing service to the members and residents and in its relationships with official bodies. It has a wide variety of activities with an equally wide variety of indigenous leaders and can often take comparatively heavy responsibility in the Association of London Housing Estates and in local affairs. The group is now one among many community groups and is, in fact, an established voluntary body which can associate and negotiate on an equal footing with other statutory and voluntary bodies in the community.

*Role of the Worker.* At this stage the role of the worker is to recognise and support the group as 'an established body' and to change the character of the service offered to the group from a *community development* service to that of *community organisation.*

### *Phases of Service*

As the group develops so the service offered by the field workers changes to meet new needs. The development of a group has been described in six stages and something has been said about the role of the worker at each stage of development. Under the heading of six phases of service, the role of the worker is now discussed in greater detail.

*Phase One: Observation.* If a worker has occasion or opportunity to

139

be present on an estate before Phase Two his role is simply that of an observer, trying to recognise as many aspects as possible of the milieu in which the group will later form and develop.

*Phase Two: Preliminary Contact.* This usually takes place in the preformation stage of the group's development, when interested individuals on the estate ask for help. The one or two interested residents may seek advice directly, having come to hear of the service available, or perhaps indirectly, for example through the Housing Manager.

The help or advice may be seen as an official service to which they are entitled, since the field worker is often regarded as a representative of the local housing authority. The service may even be seen as the attempt of a voluntary body to 'get in on the work' on the estate to further the aims of a preconceived programme. Sometimes the service is seen exclusively in terms of the first kind of help given. For instance, if the first help was with play space for children, the service for a while is seen as only concerned with the needs of children.

The preliminary contact may appear to be a direct request for help about getting a particular amenity, but underlying this request may be a basic need for residents to come together and to do things together; the co-operation necessary to achieve some improvement helps to satisfy this basic need.

The preliminary contact should be guided by the following considerations:

Begin where the residents are, with the problem they present, accepting their statement of it, and offering service to meet what they say are their needs.

Try to allay fears of outside influence, to reduce outsize expectations, to establish identity, and to be clear and precise about the help that can be offered. This kind of communication is only possible if the worker can make opportunities for getting these ideas across.

Avoid over-involvement in the everyday affairs of the group. The worker is an objective participant with a definite purpose for being there, and a definite service to offer.

Keep the contacts open. Often in the preparatory phases, misunderstanding arises between members, between the small informal groups, between the worker and one of the indigenous leaders or one of the smaller groups. If this cannot be resolved, the worker should withdraw temporarily, in such a way as to keep the contact open. The primary concern in the preliminary phase is to build the kind of relations with the group that will make possible further use of the service as the group develops.

140

## *Phase Three: Initial Advice*

This phase of the service corresponds roughly to the formation stage of the group's development, and is often characterised by the need of the group to use the services of a person from outside. The worker comes as a friendly, knowledgeable outsider who 'can be trusted to advise without attempting to impose', and who does not have 'an iron in the fire'. He can be adviser, consultant, or informant, but without being part of the group conflict which is an inevitable and a natural part of this stage of the group's development. For example, the worker knows what kind of person might make a good first chairman for the group, but he has no vested interested in any particular person being selected. He knows from experience in working with other groups what activities might be best to start off with, but his suggestions are not conditioned by his involvement in the life of the newly formed association or the social life of the estate.

During this phase the worker is usually able to suggest a variety of uses the group can make of the service of the agency, offering help with account books or duplicating, with the first activities for the member and in making contact with the statutory and voluntary bodies.

The worker has to offer support to both individuals and the newly formed committee, which will be faced with unfamiliar duties and may be in need of support and encouragement as well as information, advice and guidance. The worker should then begin the process of helping those concerned to seek support from, and give support to, each other in their common efforts to lay secure foundations.

## *Phase Four: Intensive Service*

This phase of the service is roughly parallel to stage three in the group's development, the building up of the programme.

More work and responsibility fall upon the committee as the programme develops, and the roles of the committee members can no longer be safely played out in the domestic issues of drawing up a constitution, holding meetings and discussing association policy. As the programme expands, money has to be raised and spent, activity leaders have to be supported in their work, the membership has to be actively involved, and in all this the roles of the committee members become more complicated and sometimes confused. Particularly competent activity leaders might appear to be, and might in fact be, a threat to the officers. Questions of responsibility and privilege accorded to committee members, activity leaders and membership need clarifying as the circumstances change. Individual committee members can be helped to understand their new roles by

L                                                                              141

encouraging them to attend training sessions and weekend conferences, such as those organised by the Association of London
Housing Estates.

It is important that the services offered should help to establish
committee procedure, to maintain the balance of relationship
between committee, membership, activity volunteers and the estate
as a whole, keep open the channels of communication and also
allocate responsibilities and privileges within a commonly agreed
frame of reference.

At this stage, the worker and the service have to be constantly
available, especially during the early days. It is important that the
group should feel there is constant support in the background; the
mere knowledge of this is a valuable kind of help.

During this phase of intensive service, the worker should attempt
to broaden the field of educational opportunities open to the group.
This should include not only week-end conferences but visits to
estates facing similar problems, contact with relevant statutory and
voluntary bodies (the old people's welfare worker, the youth officer).
He should also help the group to use other sources of information,
encouragement and support.

*Phase Five: Specialised Service*

By this time the group has successfully established a programme of
service for its members, has more or less agreed upon committee
roles and procedures, and has to some extent learnt to seek advice,
guidance and support from sources other than the worker. The
worker can now offer a specialised service, concentrating on one
particular activity or difficulty, for example, youth work on the
estate or the annual general meeting, and give detailed consideration
to its planning, programme and evaluation. In doing this he will try
to pass on some skills to the group. In discussing the evaluation of,
say, old people's work, he will help to bring out the criteria for such
an evaluation and at the same time see that something is learned
about how to develop criteria for other activities.

*Phase Six: Gradual Withdrawal*

The worker has made it clear that there are other sources of support
and help, and has assisted the group to ask for information, guidance
and support from other estate groups and from the relevant statutory
and voluntary bodies; and also to look for information and help
within its own association.

It is part of the worker's job to strengthen the ties with statutory
and voluntary bodies. He can then gradually withdraw, making it
142

clear that he is available if wanted. During this phase the worker should begin to work with the community group as an established voluntary body similar to others in the community and to his own agency. This is often a problem phase if the worker is reluctant to cut down his visits.

## The Worker

*Doing Too Much.* The worker is continuously tempted to do too much for a group. Their many requests for help and advice may be phrased in such a way as to convince the worker that the situation is an emergency. The temptation to 'do it for them' is very strong. There is the odd occasion when only the worker can fill in and do something of importance in a group's life, but this is an exception. In the early days, for example, a worker may find himself chairing the first Annual General Meeting, or taking the minutes. He may do many other practical things, but always with a view to showing the group how and helping them to do it for themselves.

If the worker does too much himself the group is deprived of opportunities of learning by doing. If he is too deeply involved with decisions made in the group and a project fails he will be blamed, and the group will miss the opportunity of assessing the failure in broader terms. When a project succeeds, the group may miss the full force of the experience of 'having done it ourselves'. This does not mean that the worker is not available to give information and advice, but that he has to develop a shrewd sense of how much or how little is actually needed compared with what the group actually requests. A worker is often driven by anxiety to do too much; anxiety about getting things started, getting something done, about his own failure with this or that group. This is rarely a disaster but it usually means that the stock of material available to help a group come to terms with its own problems is diminished.

*Acceptance.* It may seem strange to suggest that a group's acceptance of a worker may be a problem for him. Experience in the field has shown this to be so, especially if the worker has been successful the first few times in helping the group to get something done, to work out a problem or to overcome a difficulty.

The worker is invited and then expected to attend every meeting, take an interest in every affair, help in every situation and finally to take responsibility as a member of the committee and association. This is often a difficult situation because it may be the group's way of thanking the worker, and because it offers the worker an access he

143

needs, a freedom and depth of contact that is beneficial to both parties. It may indicate that the group feels free to ask for, and take, advice and the worker can more effectively offer it. Yet it has its dangers on two counts, which the worker must learn to cope with. The first is that if he becomes too involved in the affairs of the committee of the association he may lose objectivity, and even if he does not, he may be thought to have done so. To be too directly associated with choices and decisions, which can in most situations not be unanimously arrived at, or equally accepted, by all sections of the membership means that he will inevitably become so involved in the situation as to be unable to 'offer help from the outside'. The second is that an unskilful rejection of the group's offer to join fully in the work of the association might be seen by the group as a rejection of themselves as persons and of their work. This can be especially disappointing for the group and the worker in cases where early acceptance of the group by the worker played so large a part in the group's development.

If the worker is aware that this stage is a passing phase, he may be able gradually to give less attention to the group without giving offence. This is the time for the worker to show the group a wider context of the work by discussing, confidentially and with care, his relations with other groups, his 'office work' commitments and other aspects of the work. This will also emphasise the necessity for strict allocation of time in his work schedule, and serve as an illustration of the worker's role as 'consultant' rather than full member of a group.

*Rejection.* Rejection is sometimes easier to handle than acceptance. Of course the inexperienced worker is often disappointed by rejection, but so often it is a sign that the group has worked out a satisfactory way of doing things and is ready to reject the worker in order to show that they have 'arrived'. (Rejection may be too strong a word to use.) It might be simply a temporary measure designed to get the worker out of the way while a 'private' affair was settled.

The worker's response to rejection will vary according to the situation. Where it seems to indicate independence, there is agreement. If the rejection appears to be temporary, the worker will find ways of leaving the door open so that the group will not 'lose face' should they want to return for help. Whatever the situation, the worker will try to leave the impression that help is always available, if not from him, from someone else. On no account must the onus of rejection be put on the group. The worker must rely on his knowledge of the group to make the break look natural. If this is quite impossible, the fault must be attributed to the service offered and not to the group. Rejection may come from only one group or section of the association, from a single individual, or a clique. It may stem from a struggle between the committee and the association, or the association and the estate. Usually it is temporary, and the appropriate response may turn it into a phase of development.

The workers met a number of groups who felt that they had been rejected by official bodies. In their words, they had been 'told off', 'accused' or even abused for 'not doing what was suggested' by agencies whose advice had proved unacceptable. Here the worker had to try not to increase the feeling of rejection but to use the situation to emphasise the group's right to accept or reject him and the service offered. In this way, approval and recognition of the group's identity and independence could begin to build up confidence again.

## The Agency

If a worker undertaking this kind of work has special problems and opportunities, the same is equally true of the sponsoring agency. New methods of work make new demands on the agency as much as on the worker, an important point when considering the relevance of this approach and method in other parts of the community.

Before any departure can be made from a traditional method of working, the agency must be willing and able to work in a different way. It must be willing to change, to alter patterns of service, to develop and adapt new ways of thinking and working. New criteria have to be worked out to define the areas in which the new service can be offered, and to assess the effectiveness and efficiency of the work. The agency may need to make only slight modifications to some of its established ways of working, but there may be real conflict with some of its traditional standards and procedures.

A willingness to alter and adapt must be present at every level of the agency operation. It must be shared by the management or executive committee, by the executive and administrative staff, and by those directly concerned with the day-to-day problems of the service and its operation in the field. But willingness alone is not enough. Willingness alone will not always provide the necessary support. The agency must also have the ability to offer the field workers adequate supporting services, supervision, in-service training, clerical help, and acceptance and support for the work in the field. The agency must also have the resources necessary to allow the worker to offer direct services in the field (duplicating, help with book-keeping, etc.).

Even when the agency sponsoring the service has the necessary willingness and ability to do the work, there are still other conditions that must be fulfilled. For example, the 'image' of the agency must be one that enables the individuals or groups concerned to accept the service. The sponsoring agency, and therefore its workers, might be seen as a charitable organisation giving help to the poor. This might, in fact, make the establishment of contact and the development of a relationship between the worker and the group either more difficult than it need be, or outright impossible.

It is possible that an agency which appeared to fulfil all the conditions for providing a service might still be inappropriate. For example, if the groups needing help were youth groups, a youth-serving agency might seem to be the obvious choice. But there would be a danger that their familiarity with youth work might prevent their seeing the groups' needs in the terms presented by the groups themselves, who might in turn resent what they saw to be a pre-conceived programme being 'pushed' on to them. Also, the selection of one youth-serving agency to do this particular work might cause friction with other youth work agencies.

There is no hard and fast rule about this, and a youth serving agency might be just the body to do this work. It is therefore extremely important to consider the role of the agency with the same care as the role of the worker, before the setting up of the service and during its operation.

*Administration.* Social work agencies never expect to operate within a strict 9 a.m. to 5 p.m. five-day week schedule, but the other extreme of 'constant availability' brings its own problems of staff and office routine. At the beginning of this service and especially in the early stages of field work, it was very important for staff to be available at all hours, evenings and week-ends, 'simply to be there so that we can talk to someone when we need to' as one committee member described it. To the onlooker, this seemed like spoon-feeding. 'Why can't it wait till Monday?' 'It's only a petty quarrel, it will sort itself out.' What seemed trivial to the onlooker might have been a momentous issue for the struggling group. Even the obviously trivial requests could not be dismissed, as they often represented a kind of testing out, 'Can we count on them if something were to go wrong?' 'Will they be there in an emergency?' To convince the groups that the offer of 'constant availability' was trustworthy was as important a part of the service as the more practical assistance with duplicating, publicity and accounting. The price of success was a certain amount of havoc in the office.

A typical day and evening in the central office of the London Council of Social Service may find field workers, office staff and consultant occupied in checking transport arrangements for an old people's outing, drafting letters of invitation to a residents' social, discussing with a delegation from an association the legal implications of a lottery they proposed to run. Treasurers from two different groups may be wanting to discuss the audit before the annual general meeting; someone may want advice on buying sports equipment, and someone else may want help in drafting a request to the local Council on behalf of the committee. One group may have taken a decision to circularise the whole estate about a special activity due to take place in four days time; as it is the first event for the whole estate to be attempted by the committee, it is important that it should be a success.

The necessity to take things as they came strained even the most flexible office routine. But even the overcrowding and confusion had some positive effects in introducing residents to a quite different set of problems from their own and also, incidentally, to residents from other estates. Residents came to the office when they could fit the journey in with their day's work, night shift, or home commitments. They came when there were crises in committee or association, or a quick turnover in leadership. All this required an office and an administrative set-up as responsive to the needs of visitors as the field workers tried to be to the needs of the groups on the estates. In this situation the efficiency of the sponsoring agency had to be put at the disposal of those who came for help rather than be maintained for its own sake.

*Interpretation.* Every social work agency is in partnership with others engaged in social welfare work in the area and in the whole country. As a partner, an agency is responsible for explaining and interpreting its work to its colleagues and to the local and wider community, especially to those who provide the grant aid. In a Council of Social Service the necessity for interpreting the work is brought nearer home by the fact that many social welfare bodies are members of the Council. An example of providing a playground is given to show the difficulties of interpretation even within a Council of Social Service.

A social agency concerned with recreational needs, after long and difficult interpretation to the local authority, had arranged for a playground to be provided in a neighbourhood that was shortly to have a new housing estate. The playground was to be in the old neighbourhood, adjacent to the estate. It was thought that it would be as convenient for the residents on the new estate as for those in the older neighbourhood. This scheme met with approval since it would encourage the two neighbourhoods to mix and come together. The estate was built, the new residents arrived, a community group was started with help from the field workers from the Council of Social Service, and one of the group's first requests was for a playground on the new estate. Mothers found the existing playground too far away for the children; they themselves felt more at home on the estate and did not want to mix with 'outsiders'. The community group organised a delegation to the local authority to ask for a playground on the estate. A meeting took place of the community group, the Housing Manager, and the social agency responsible for the original playground. Immediately afterwards the agency was closely questioned about the work that it was sponsoring on the new estate. Three sharp questions were, 'Why do you encourage the community group to upset our carefully laid plans?', 'Why don't you explain to the group what has already happened and how difficult it was to get a playground at all?', 'Don't you think, if you help them with a playground on the estate you will only emphasise their isolation from the rest of the community?'

These were valid questions, which had not occurred to anybody before the new residents arrived. Afterwards the social agency which had planned the playground found itself in conflict with the wishes and needs of the community group at that particular stage of its development. The residents had already gone through the first phase of the settling-in process, had come to know some of the other residents, and were prepared to work together to improve the amenities on the estate. The community group needed to establish itself, to create its identity in relation to the adjacent community, and to provide a service for its membership. (In fact, the existing playground was not as convenient as had been thought.) The growth of community feeling enabled the group, in however limited a way, to serve the need of the whole estate even though the decision to try to provide a playground was prompted initially by only a section of the mothers. The mothers seemed to feel that having just got to know one another, they would like to have their own playground, and in any case were worried about the younger children going off the estate. The field workers helped the mothers to express their point of view, and to make a case for some separate provision on their own estate.

This type of situation recurs constantly, as for example the organisation of a youth section on the estate, 'in opposition to youth clubs in the surrounding community' or, 'in spite of excellent facilities a stone's throw from the estate'. There was also criticism of special activities being arranged for old people, young people and children on the estate when recreational facilities were available in the local settlement. The sponsoring agency, through its community development field workers, had to try to interpret in detail what might be called the *sociological* reasons for the behaviour of groups at different stages of development and with different needs, interests and problems. It was also essential to repeat over and over again that the priority for the field workers should be, not the provision of ameni-

148

ties, but the strengthening of the community group, and the encouragement of anything that was seen as productive of neighbourliness on the estate.

*Responsibility without Control.* An agency inevitably attracts problems when it accepts public money for work with community groups when it cannot control the work of the groups. The agency has to justify its work to itself, to its donors and partners, and to onlookers; it has to carry out its work, offer the service, work with groups in the field, and evaluate its work, but with no formal control. The agency cannot 'command loyalty', 'exercise authority' or 'enforce discipline'. (The only possible control would be the withdrawal of the service, a very rare occurrence.) Its constitution might prevent it from raising money by any form of lottery, but this would not prevent the field workers from offering advice to an autonomous group on the legal requirements of running Bingo.

A sponsoring agency which is responsible but not in control must learn to live in an advisory capacity rather than as a superior authority.

## Values and Standards

The problems of the agency and the worker were aggravated by differences and conflicts in the values and standards of all those involved. These were the groups themselves, the neighbouring community, the voluntary and statutory bodies, the agency and the worker.

The values and standards of the groups, especially in their early days of development, might differ considerably from those all around them (professional workers, officials and even the neighbouring community)· The differences might cover a wide range, from attitudes about money, how to raise it and account for it; how to settle arguments; how to distinguish between a 'public' and a 'private' controversy, and between the use and abuse of power. There were differing interpretations of the meaning of 'independence', some meaning complete isolation, others very moderate cooperation. Group behaviour was conditioned by many other social attitudes which gave rise to differences in values and standards, which in turn affected the work in hand and the relation of the group to its co-workers.

Groups are also affected by the values and standards of the neighbouring community. If the longer established community is hostile to the newcomers because they consider their standards to be lower, mutual suspicion arises. This is difficult to overcome. On the other hand, if the settled community feels rebuffed by the new-

149

comers because of their need to establish their own identity and programme, suspicion may arise that will be equally difficult to overcome.

The values and standards of the statutory and voluntary bodies also differ from those of the groups and often give rise to unrealistic expectations about their behaviour and work. It is said, 'They keep changing their officers', 'They don't answer letters', 'They altered the day of the week on which they meet and forgot to let me know', 'Their meetings never start on time and never finish before 11 o'clock'.

The values and standards of the agency and its workers may also conflict with those of the group. For example, a group may decide to raise money by a method of gambling which is only just on the right side of the law; or it may decide to spend money lavishly on something which professional workers may think unnecessary. A more complex situation arises when the field worker supports a group in a course of action from which his agency must dissociate itself.

When a worker is involved in a conflict because of differences in values and standards, he is first of all non-judgmental. He does not reject the values and standards of the group, even when they are obviously 'wrong' either in themselves or in the way that the group applies them. He is non-judgmental, not because he has no values and standards of his own, but because he believes that his acceptance of the group 'as it is', is the only basis on which he can work with it. He is non-judgmental because he is aware that often the values and standards of neighbours, officials and even on occasions of the sponsoring agency, are inappropriate and inapplicable to the group at that particular stage of its development. This may result in a paradoxical situation where the worker is non-judgmental about the values and standards of the group, but considers those of the outside bodies as inappropriate and inapplicable. In fact the field worker must regard this as not so much a question of 'rights and wrongs' as of different pre-suppositions and ways of thinking. (This of course only applies to situations which do not infringe the law.) To say that a worker accepts the values and standards of a community group does not imply acceptance in any absolute sense of their standards and values. Only from an attitude of acceptance can the worker begin to help each side interpret its views to the other. To ascribe non-judgmental behaviour is not to suggest that no judgments at all are made. The worker is constantly trying to assess the adequacy of group behaviour and to be specific in his judgments of the committee's methods and relationships. It is the non-judgmental attitude which makes the judgments acceptable and useful in the group's development.

150

# 7 Further Considerations and Conclusions

This chapter includes suggestions for further study arising out of the field work. There is a discussion on the need for training for community work as part of social work education and of community development as a method of social work.

### Services to Problem Families

On some estates there were small groups of families, sometimes unfortunately described as problem families because of their complex inter-personal, social and economic problems. In some cases they were helped by the tenants' association directly, even if they were not members, for instance by a special money grant in an emergency, or indirectly by the activity of the association and the support and encouragement of the neighbourly atmosphere the association had in part created. But on the whole the work of the association for problem families was far from adequate considering the size and kind of problem presented by these families to themselves and to their neighbours. Two possible opportunities for the extension of this approach might be:

That a special worker should be made available to the community groups who were willing to work with problem families on the estate. The association would be expected to do this in collaboration with, for example, the local Family Service Unit or the local Family Welfare Association and other relevant statutory and voluntary bodies. The worker would attempt to use the 'good will', neighbourliness, etc., of the membership and the residents in whatever 'supportive' programme was developed with the relevant casework agencies.

The same worker would be made available to those estates

151

which wanted to offer intensive personal service to families in need, but in this case the worker would not be in direct contact with the families but with the association's volunteer, to enable her to help the families. The worker would also be a bridge between the volunteer assistant, the case-work agencies and the other channels of help provided by the association on the estate.

In either case, difficulties would almost certainly arise.

Both the privacy of the family in need, and the confidential nature of the helping process, are more difficult to protect the greater the number of people involved. This is especially so when attempting to involve untrained estate volunteers as case-work aides.

The worker might find it difficult to hand over to the group or to the estate volunteer, and might do too much of the work herself for too long. Her presence and activity might also be construed as interfering with the work of the statutory and voluntary bodies.

Great care would have to be taken to maintain good relations with the established statutory and voluntary services in the community already working with, or available for work with, the families. The service suggested here would have to be considered as an added resource to them, as part of the helping programme they had designed and not as an overlapping or competing service. If the originator of the supporting programme was an outside voluntary body, the association would have to be helped to see that it could co-operate without feeling that its autonomy was threatened.

Where could a worker be found with both case-work skills and a community development orientation, who would be able to work with the association, with the outside statutory and voluntary bodies and with the volunteer worker, to whom she must pass on the necessary skills?

### Services to Autonomous Groups in the Wider Community

This whole presentation has been centred on the autonomous group on the housing estate. (No mention has been made of the presence of autonomous groups in the wider community of which the estate is a part—sports, arts, garden clubs, women's groups, immigrant groups etc.) If helped in the way discussed here they might be expected substantially to enrich the social environment of the estate and to provide points of contact that would at once be welcoming, useful and non-threatening. They would be non-threatening because as autonomous groups themselves they could be expected to understand something of the importance of independence to the newly formed housing estate community group.

If an offer of this kind of help to autonomous groups in the adjacent community were successful it might improve the quality of the social life in the whole neighbourhood. It might lead to a more varied programme of activities for both the housing estate community group and the autonomous group in the wider community, and perhaps make possible the exchange of information and encouragement which would be useful to both kinds of group. The difficulties here might well be:

Getting permission from the relevant parties in the adjacent community to offer the service to autonomous groups in 'their community', or even their agreement to try to find the potential for the creation of such groups. Often the housing estate is seen to be in need of such help in contrast to already established communities with no such need.

The possible hostility of a housing estate community group especially in its early stages, to the settled community which might make them suspicious of a service that offered the same encouragement to community groups off the estate as was being offered to them. This would complicate the role of the worker and the service. Part of this difficulty might be met by using a different worker based in a different agency to help the other groups.

In the later stages of their development the near certainty that the 'on Estate' and 'off Estate' groups would find common problems and interests drawing them together to exchange experiences and perhaps plan joint activities. In itself, this would be good but it might be seen as a threat by an Association of London Housing Estates: the emerging pattern of local co-operation between community groups leading first to accommodation and perhaps later to assimilation, could be seen as an indication that its own existence was no longer necessary.

### Possibility of Working with More than One Organisation on the Same Estate

In all the work described there was an attempt to work with only one community group on each estate. On large estates a number of different interest groups sometimes developed. These were related in different ways to the community group. Sometimes informal groups were encouraged to merge into the larger, more effective community group. Sometimes when a second group appeared on an estate the established group tried to include the second group in the association. Sometimes it had to accept it as a rival.

More thought needs to be given to the possibility of several groups offering different kinds of opportunities for inter-personal relations and service (not necessarily of a specific social welfare nature) on the same estate. On a large estate this might then lead to an organisation with the same structure as a community association.

153

The question then becomes at what point in the development of a tenants' association on a large estate can other groups of other kinds, with other aims and objectives, be encouraged and helped to come together and develop? How can their existence and work be related to the structure, function and programme of the association? What kinds of help would these groups need, and could the service be provided?

### *Need to Extend and Enrich the Programme Offered by the Groups to Their Members*

Little has yet been done to offer programme resources of a more imaginative nature to the committees and the activity volunteers. It is true that the associations provide their members and the estate residents with services which would not otherwise have been offered. But on the whole the programmes of most of the groups included few cultural activities, which suggests that considerable thought might be given to the possibility of: (a) Explicitly adult educational activities on the estate, e.g. discussion groups on human relations; marriage and the family; early childhood education; current events; and especially opportunities for participation in the arts, holiday planning, and vocational advancement. Some of these activities take place on or near the estate through classes organised by the Education Authority. (b) Consideration should be given to the possibility of a counselling service for young people which would include giving information about recreation, further education and vocational guidance.

Any attempt to enrich a service from outside, to stimulate interest in the association for the new services, to get the service itself on to the estate, is liable to create conflicts within the committee and the association because the new ideas and activities are seen as an imposition from outside. This might be avoided if the Association of London Housing Estates itself were developed as a resource body for new programmes and new activities.

### *Provision of Trained Indigenous Leaders for Work Outside their Own Immediate Locality*

On the whole it is difficult to encourage the trained and experienced indigenous leaders to give up active work in the association and take on similar work in the wider community. Family problems, the development of new interests, retirement from active participation, and change of job, all play a part in the decision of the indigenous leader to withdraw. Yet a number of indigenous leaders could well have been encouraged to offer their experience and skills elsewhere,

154

and so to enrich the pool of indigenous leadership available in the local community. In this situation, questions such as these are posed:

How to prepare the 'retired' indigenous leader for service elsewhere?

How to help him in his new field of service?

How to encourage the adjacent community to ask for his help and to accept what he has to offer?

If work has already begun with autonomous groups in the adjacent community, would they accept the skills and experience of an indigenous leader from what to them would be 'outside', or would they be more likely to see him as a threat to their own independence?

Could a 'retired' indigenous leader be prepared for more intensive service with an already established statutory and voluntary body? Could he help on another estate? How could this be done?

### Possibility of Sharing In-service Training with Staff Members of Statutory and Voluntary Bodies

The main emphasis in the field work was on enabling the groups to acquire sufficient skill and confidence to handle their own affairs. This included the ability to converse and negotiate with statutory and voluntary bodies. Examples have been given of difficulties and breakdown in communication in this area and have suggested that the worker's skill as a go-between and interpreter is of importance.

Communication between the worker and the agencies could have been improved, given more time, and one idea which was tried successfully for a short period was to include some staff members of the agencies in field work training sessions. There were many practical difficulties, but the mutual understanding of methods of work and the possibility of discussing problems in informal surroundings were extremely valuable.

### Relations with the Wider Community

On the whole it was difficult to help the association, even in their more developed stages, not to be estate-centred only, and to be separate, but not isolated, from the social life in the adjacent community. This needs further thought and enquiry from the point of view of the hindrance and help to such a balance coming from within an association and, equally important, from the opportunities that can be brought into being in the wider community itself for enlarging the area in which groups would feel able and willing to participate.

155

Something at least is known about the possibilities of work on housing estates, but little is known about the relevance of this particular method in other settings. The second area of study which needs consideration would entail a series of field-work enquiries specially designed, organised and evaluated. The field work would provide some of the answers to basic questions about the problems encountered, the methods used, the results obtained, and the modifications necessary. Suggestions for working in one particular area of need are outlined as follows:

### Community Care for Mental Health

A community development worker in this setting might find that the work could best be done by a team including a social group worker, a family case worker or psychiatric social worker. The sponsoring agency for this work could be the local Health Department.

Possible objectives of a field-work enquiry in this area of need are:

To contact those receiving out-patient treatment or in need of after-care in a given community with a view to forming groups that would offer both support and a programme of activities. The groups should not be formed without considering how far to involve parents, relatives, friends, neighbours, landladies, etc. In the process of helping to develop and support such groups, social and other skills should be passed on so that eventually the group might become self-supporting.

To act as a bridge between the groups and the other statutory and voluntary bodies who are offering services to the mentally ill.

To act as a bridge between the groups and other services necessary for rehabilitation and adjustment, e.g. employment, probation, marriage guidance, etc.

To act as a bridge between the groups and other groups in the community, both autonomous and formal, involved in other aspects of community life (sports, gardening, the arts, and other activities).

The primary emphasis in this field-work enquiry would be the help given by the field workers to the groups to enable them to provide their own members with appropriate services. The field-work service would be based on the recognition that those in need of after-care require more than individual help, and benefit from interaction with other members of a group.

The purpose of a field-work enquiry might also be to provide adequate documentation to show the kind of individual needs best

156

met in this way, the particular problems of this kind of group, and the role of the worker and the agencies in helping groups to start and providing them with a field-work service.

This example suggests a basic pattern for broadly based community work which, with some modification, could be equally applicable in other areas of need. It is not difficult to see the relevance of this pattern to youth work, work with the aged, or with ex-prisoners for example, and it is suggested that field-work enquiries of this type could also lead to changes in such areas of common concern as road safety or economic productivity. Although the community development worker is seen as the initiator in these areas of need, this may not in fact be so, and in any situation community development work is only one of many partners engaged in initiating social change and in implementing a social welfare programme.

## COMPARATIVE STUDIES

If this approach and method of work are to be more widely used with community groups other than housing estate groups, a number of comparative studies need to be made. 'Comparative studies' here means the documentation of a number of different attempts to use this method in a variety of situations, which could include aspects of the continuing work on housing estates and the areas suggested for field-work enquiry.

Before a comparative study can be made it is necessary to have more information about community groups other than those on housing estates. The questions that will be asked are similar if not identical to those already discussed.

### Community Groups not on Housing Estates

Information of the following kinds is needed about autonomous groups not on housing estates:

In what social environment do groups of this kind arise?

What are the needs, problems and potentialities peculiar to this kind of group in its several stages of development?

How can these groups best be helped to do a more efficient and effective job and to interpret and evaluate their work?

What is the break-up rate of this kind of group; at what stages, and for what reasons does the break-up occur? Apart from the natural reasons such as a group breaking up because it has done its job, how can groups which have not finished their work be supported in such a way as to avoid a break-up? At what point is help most necessary? What kind of help would be most acceptable?

What kind of social welfare provision can groups of this kind be reasonably expected to undertake successfully?

In situations where such groups are needed but do not spring up naturally, how can they be helped to come into being, and by whom?

*Indigenous Leaders.* It has become clear that community groups on housing estates cannot spring up and develop without leadership drawn from their own social environment. For other groups therefore it is important to know more about how to find, encourage and support such indigenous leaders.

What circumstances give rise to indigenous leaders? How are they 'called forth' by the situation and the groups? What are some of the more general personal and social reasons for their willingness to take responsibility?

What are some of the personal characteristics of indigenous leaders that differentiate them from other members of the group?

What social skills does the indigenous leader already possess and what training does he or she need?

What are the most widespread and pressing needs of the indigenous leader who works with autonomous groups? How best can these needs be met, and by whom?

What can be done by the group itself or by the worker to lessen the difficulties caused by the ill-equipped or destructive indigenous leader?

*Training for Community Participation.* We have described something of the training necessary to help housing estate community groups see their work in relation to the whole estate and to the wider community. To make a comparison with non-housing estate groups, the following questions arise:

How much of the housing estate training methods is appropriate and adequate for non-housing estate community groups?

What further techniques have to be evolved to help the group with management problems, interpretation, etc.?

What special training is needed to help indigenous leaders and activity volunteers?

To what extent will the role of the worker differ in offering training to these groups? To what extent can she use the interview as a teaching technique and the conference and study group as training situations, to meet the needs of non-housing estate community groups?

What should be the role of the sponsoring agency in offering the service?

To what extent are the problems and needs of non-housing estate community groups similar to those of estate groups to make a basis for general approach to training for community participation?

### *Social Work on Adult Education: the most Appropriate Sponsoring Body*

Considering the problems of the agency offering the service and those of the groups receiving it, what kind of agency would be best suited to offer the service?

Some of the problems already mentioned of the sponsoring agency doing this kind of work are:

Under or over-estimation of the capabilities of the groups.

The role of the worker differs from that traditionally understood by the parent agency.

The interpretation to other agencies of the work of groups for which the sponsoring agency has responsibility but not control.

The personal and administrative problems caused by the need for constant availability and direct services.

The problems involved in being held responsible for failure and in taking no credit for success.

Would a sponsoring agency face these same difficulties in work with non-housing estate community groups?

Should the service be offered by an agency directly related to the need or situation? For example, should the Housing Department offer service to housing estate community groups, the Youth Committee to youth groups, the Health Department to community care groups for the mentally ill, or should the service be offered by an agency not already at work in that field?

Is it possible for a local statutory and voluntary body to offer service to all kinds of autonomous community groups, for example the Further Education Committee of the local council, or the Adult Education Department of a university; or should a special agency be founded, a centre for Community Development?

If it is agreed that the most appropriate agency is one not directly concerned with the groups to be served, should the local Council of Social Service or the Further Education Committee have social development officers who use the approach described here, so that the service is available to all community groups in any one geographical area?

The work on the estates was started within the framework of a social work agency. But much of the work was in fact 'detached' adult education. Should a frame of reference be used with a more definite Adult Education content?

Should the work be regarded as belonging to both social work and education, or should some kinds of service be seen as social work and others as adult education?

These are important questions because the answers given will influence the decision on the points at which to enlarge the frame of

159

reference for the work. This decision will also affect the kind of training to be offered and the kind of agency expected to undertake it.

## Experience in New Towns and Overseas

A good deal of information and experience about work similar to that on housing estates is already in existence in New Towns, especially about the work of social development officers.

On the basis of this information, what kind of comparison can be made with the work on housing estates and with the suggestions for further enquiry? How would it fit into the larger frame of reference with an emphasis either on social work or on adult education? Is there any possibility of including aspects of town planning and urban renewal within this framework?

There is even more information available about community development work overseas. Some of it is directly applicable to work in cities and towns in the United Kingdom and it has certainly influenced our thinking and approach to this work. Comparable work in Holland, Canada and the U.S.A. requires more careful study than it has yet received. A detailed study of work being done with autonomous community groups in urban areas in those countries, comparing the behaviour of groups and indigenous leaders, their needs and problems, the role of the worker and the agency, the methods and techniques used, and their successes and failures—such a comparison would do much to broaden the base of the theory and practice of community development in this country.

This kind of study might also help to answer the question facing agencies doing community development work in this country. The question is how best to formulate the findings in the field-work experience so that they can make an effective contribution to social policy.

The suggestions in this chapter for continued work on the housing estates, for field-work enquiries and for comparative studies, could help to produce a body of information and experience which could well result in community development being seen as a useful and necessary partner in the renewal of urban life.

The following questions are fundamental to field-work practice because the aims and character of the work depend on what the agency, the worker and the participants see to be the potential of each group within a particular community.

### THEORETICAL STUDY

Is 'community' the proper designation for the loose network of informal groupings that make up a community group as defined and described in this Report?

160

Should we speak of a 'social welfare community' since social welfare is the main focus of the community development process described here?

What is the optimum size for such a social unit? Which of the structural and functional characteristics listed in Appendix II must a social unit possess before it can properly be called a community?

Returning to the example of the housing estate community group, can we legitimately refer to the housing estate itself as a community?

Should a social unit have power to make decisions in a much larger area than that of social welfare before it can legitimately be called a community?

If practice is to be affected by the answers to these questions, then the answers must be sought from material derived from the continued work on housing estates, from field-work inquiries and from comparative studies like those outlined in this section.

## PROFESSIONAL TRAINING

One of the conclusions drawn from the field-work experience is that specialised training is needed for community work of this kind. We have come to see that community work in the context described here can be regarded either as adult education or as social work, depending on the nature of the sponsoring agency. Because the work was sponsored by a social work agency, the discussion of the need for specialised training is set within the framework of social work.

### New Perspectives

At this point it is perhaps necessary to say something about the nature of current social work training.

A discussion of community work might well begin with a recognition of the case-work bias of contemporary social work training and practice. Among the reasons for this are:

The cultural context within which social work originated, the Protestant ethic in middle-class society, which tended to see the individual client as the point at which change needed to take place. Consequently the role of the worker and the case-work situation were seen in the same terms.

The growth of depth psychology (Freud, Jung, Adler and Rank) gave added support to the importance of ego-functioning and the adjustment of the individual to his environment.

It was, and to some extent still is, easier to offer help in modifying or changing individual behaviour than it is to attempt to change the structure and function of social institutions that in part condition that behaviour.

161

The point here is not that the Protestant ethic, the contributions of the various depth psychologies or the difficulties of influencing community behaviour are inappropriate aspects of the case-work orientation, but that these elements do not provide all the background necessary for other areas of social work concern and practice such as social group work, community organisation and community development.

This suggestion of a case-work bias in social work theory and practice is in several ways an over-statement. In point of fact, the early settlements, the Councils of Social Service, the Community Centres and the Youth Service have all recognised and used more than the purely individual approach to providing social work services.

It is obvious from the discussion now going on in the field of social work that social group work and community organisation are now recognised as complementary aspects of the whole field; yet a number of residual attitudes remain that need to be kept in mind in any discussion of appropriate training for community work:

That often community work and social group work are seen merely as an extension of the case-work approach and method.

That group and community factors are usually seen as secondary in any treatment programme rather than as complementary aspects of the same service.

That it is widely believed that the above can be substantiated by reference to basic human needs, etc., which put the 'individual' almost as an isolated social unit in the centre of the frame of reference. This allows the problem situation, and therefore the treatment programme, regardless of the group or community factors present, to be defined as 'basically a social case-work situation'.

As a result the belief is widespread that training for social work should be 'predominantly case-work orientated'.

These factors often tend to conceal the complex nature of social problems and the various helping processes. They also obscure the complementary nature of the various social work approaches and methods.

Alongside these attitudes, a new perspective is emerging in both social work theory and practice that recognises the inter-relatedness of the social problems, and also the complementary nature of the various fields of social work practice. Examples of this are the findings of the Bristol Social Project about the importance of working with groups and the community in any attempt to help the problem family; the beginnings of group consultation for problem families and for those on probation; the interest in community organisation in the work of Councils of Social Service, which are now seen as more than an administrative framework for the provision of case-work services, and as capable of offering a social service in their own right in respect of community-wide planning for social welfare provision; the willingness of the London Council of Social Service to sponsor this work and this report.

It is within the context of these new perspectives that we offer some suggestions about community work training.

These suggestions also spring from the experience of working with students.

### Students

During the course of the field-work, students from five different universities, who were reading Social Administration or allied subjects, studied our work with the estate community groups. Sometimes they visited the groups at work or in committee session. Sometimes they attended case conferences and shared the in-service training of the staff. Sometimes they attended workshops or week-end conferences. It was only possible to take a limited number. Since it was so difficult to get staff who could use this approach and method, it was decided to try to stimulate interest among social work students and to use this contact to try to clarify what kind of training, if any, was necessary for those wanting to do this kind of work.

A beginning was made by agreeing to take a limited number of students, in the main from three universities which wanted to place students for a limited period for field-work or visits of observation, usually for two weeks or a month. The groups of students were balanced between those from overseas reading Community Development who would eventually go back, and students reading Social Administration who might decide to work in this country. A programme of observation and discussion was worked out including the analysis of case material.

It was found that sometimes the students felt they were part of a vicious circle as regards this work: 'Even if I wanted to do this kind of work, there is no adequate training for it. And if there were, I couldn't afford to take it, because there would be no job waiting at the end'. This situation is changing rapidly.

From experience with the students three points arose about training:

Training in urban community development would eventually have to be offered in a systematic way as part of general social work training.

Training would have to be separate from, but related to social case-work and social group work as well as social administration and community organisation. There would have to be opportunity for field-work placements and supervision.

163

Because relatively little is known about this approach to community work at the present time, and because of the literature from overseas, publication of material about work in progress here should be encouraged.

## A Suggested Training Course in Community Work

For the purpose of this discussion it is assumed that this suggestion for a community work training course is seen as one part of a professional social work training course. It would be preceded by courses on the physical, social, and cultural environment, on human growth and behaviour, on man in society, and on human relations in industry and the professions. It would be followed by a course on the field of social work and concluded by one on social policy and research, and would of course include field-work placement and supervision.

The course would cater for students intending to work:

'Within' institutions doing community work and local authority departments whose work relates to environmental conditions (settlements, residential centres, hospitals, hostels, community centres, housing departments, public health, child care, etc.)

In the field 'between' institutions and the community (Councils of Social Service, rural community councils, regional councils, etc.).

With community groups, either as self-programming groups needing help or in relation to an overall community care programme.

This community work training course would draw from both the community organisation and the community development approach, and would offer opportunities of practice in both methods.

## Suggested Structure and Content of Course

Section 1. *Community Behaviour.* This course provides discussion of specific community problems and the conceptual tools necessary for the student preparing to work with communities and community groups. It might include study and discussion of:

The satisfaction of basic human needs in a community setting.

Levels of community behaviour (within and between groups.)

The social processes (co-operation, competition, conflict, accommodation and assimilation in community behaviour).

Relations within and between groups and social institutions in respect of social welfare needs in a community setting (the intergroup work process).

Social problems in the community setting, and social work as an intervention in the community process for social welfare provisions.

164

Community behaviour would be the core of the community work curriculum in the same sense that individual growth and behaviour is the core of the case-work, and group dynamics is the core of the group work curriculum. For a more detailed consideration of what the content of this study might be see Appendix II.

Section 2. *Problem Situations in Community Work.* A selection of problem situations in community work should be studies from records illustrating field-work difficulties:

Within an institution or agency.

Between institutions or agencies.

Within and between community groups.

These problems should be studied from the point of view of the possibilities of treatment by either community organisation or community development methods. Records should illustrate the following needs:

To bring about co-operation between existing statutory and voluntary bodies or community groups.

To help community agencies or community groups to identify their needs.

To help community agencies or community groups to mobilise the necessary resources of leadership, money, public understanding and support.

To help community agencies and community groups to train leadership, lay and professional, for work with the statutory and voluntary bodies and with community groups.

To interpret the needs of community agencies or community groups to each other.

To gather, correlate and use information about social welfare needs in order to influence social policy.

To define and explore the role of the community worker in doing these things.

Section 3. *Tools and Techniques in Community Work.* Working with committees—the committee as a task-centred group.

Helping committees and community groups to identify social welfare needs, design and carry out various kinds of self-survey.

Record keeping and report writing as part of the job—the techniques of recording.

Techniques of evaluation for the community, the committee, the worker, the agency.

Professional interpretation to, or on behalf of, community agencies or community groups in respect of their needs, work or problems.

Public interpretation to, or on behalf of, community agencies or community groups in respect of their work or problems.

165

Section 4. *Educational Methods.* The social worker in either community organisation or community development work will need some understanding of informal adult education. Section 4 is an introduction to the methods of Adult Education, so that social workers may become acquainted with the skills and techniques relevant to work with adult community groups. A closer acquaintance may reveal opportunities in the field work for co-operation with an adult education specialist. In community organisation, the worker will be required to help statutory and voluntary bodies singly or together to clarify objectives, collect, analyse and interpret information, develop plans, planning procedures and criteria. Agency staff will need to learn new ways of thinking and working, so that the worker must help to create a 'learning situation'.

In community development, the worker will do similar work but in relation not to the needs of established agencies, but to those of autonomous groups. In both cases the worker will be in part an adult educationist.

Courses in Section 4 might include: Learning—visual and other adult education aids; psychological and social aspects of learning. What inhibits learning, what induces it? How is this study relevant to the worker in an established voluntary body or to the indigenous leader who is a member of a community group?

Methodology—what are the most appropriate tools and techniques in informal adult education? What kind of teaching situations are most appropriate in this kind of work? How can they be organised? (Workshops, week-end conferences, seminars, study groups and reading parties, etc.)

Section 5. *Community Organisation.* Community organisation as a method of social work is concerned with relations between established statutory and voluntary bodies. There would be a study of the particular role of the worker; the nature and content of the work; the particular application of the method to the problems listed in Section 2 and the tools and techniques in Section 3; the responsibilities and limitations of the role.

Section 6. *Community Development.* Community development as a method of social work concerned with the relations in and between autonomous groups and community groups and established agencies.

Section 7. *The Social Work Continuum.* This section would cover the continued exploration of the helping process in relation to the complementary nature of community organisation and community development as methods of social work. It would emphasise the inter-dependence of social problems and the inter-dependence of social work methods, including the possibilities of jointly planned and executed programmes undertaken in collaboration with social case-work and social group work services.

The Sections in the Community Work Training Course need not follow any set order, but could be seen as concurrent learning opportunities. The course would include lectures for theoretical and conceptual material and for factual information; placement in several kinds of community work situations to give experience of different kinds of community problems requiring different kinds of treatment; and supervision during field-work practice, as well as seminars during and after field-work placement.

The Course might be organised in such a way as to explore the experience arising from the various field-work placements, relate that experience to the conceptual and theoretical material being offered, and work on the development of skills and techniques necessary to do the job (including committee participation, record keeping, etc.)

Within a generic social work curriculum, this community work training course would be optional.

*Supervision, Placement and Training.* The following items included in the suggested Training Course need further consideration:

Supervision in community work.

Placement opportunities for community work students in training.

In-service training in the field.

In so new an area of social work as community development, students frequently find discrepancies between what is taught in the training course and what is practised in the field. It is, therefore, very important that students in placements should be offered supervision that would bridge the gap between their training and their field-work experience.

*Supervision.* Supervision in community work is only different from supervision in case-work and social group work in its frame of reference. Both supervisor and student or worker operate from their understanding of the community process and the possibilities of intervention in it. Apart from this, supervision has the same purpose of helping the worker to be more objective, to see his work in a proper context, to develop and improve skills and techniques and to come to terms with field-work problems. Supervision also helps the agency to use its staff resources as effectively as possible, and both agency and staff should regard the offer and acceptance of supervision as a mutual responsibility.

Supervision in community work is an integral part of the method, as part of the resources made available by the agency to the student

167

in each of his placements and recognised as such. This raises the question of where the supervisors are to be found and how they are to be trained.

*Placement Opportunities.* A satisfactory placement requires:

That the agency's approach to the work should coincide as far as possible with that of the training course.

That proper supervision should be available to the student.

That there should be good liaison between student, tutor, agency and supervisor.

That community work tutors should be available who can supervise as well as teach.

That information from the practical work and from supervision should be fed back into the teaching process.

*In-Service Training.* It seems that what is necessary to deal with the problem of finding placements with adequate supervision lies in providing in-service training, or professional staff in agencies which are doing community work and who when trained would offer supervision to students in training.

An in-service training programme could be carried on using the day-to-day work of the agency as a basis for discussion. Such a programme might well include some of the material from the community work training course.

These suggestions for a training course in community work and for further consideration are inevitably tentative and general, and may offer guide-lines for further consideration about the structure and content of this kind of training.

COMMUNITY DEVELOPMENT AS A METHOD OF SOCIAL WORK

As was pointed out in the introduction to this report, the workers only gradually discovered the best method of approach to the groups. Eventually they came to see the relevance of community development as a method of social work.

The literature on community development came from developing countries, the United Nations, and a small amount from this country, Canada and the United States. To anyone acquainted with this literature the phrase 'community development' is known to be used in several different ways, as illustrated in the following:

'Community development is the most appropriate method of implementing the decisions of the centre in local districts'. Community development here denotes a method of local administration.

'Community development rightly conceived, is about bridges, roads and other physical facilities, and physical artifacts of the

168

community, regardless of how these things have been achieved'. This usage concentrates solely on the material achievement.

'Community development is that aspect of the social process that results from the modification of social structure of any given community'. In this usage, community development is seen as one aspect of the natural process of social change on a local level.

'Community development is the conscious use of the community process by the participants themselves (who may need expert or technical help) in order, through common action, to achieve self-chosen goals'.

This last usage refers to community development as a method of social work. It emphasises both the natural process of community development and its conscious use in order to achieve self-chosen objectives. Variations on this last usage are as numerous as the circumstances in which this method is used. Some usages emphasise rural and village life; some, one or other of the particulars of rural life, agriculture or the position of women in the village. Others emphasise the neighbourhood, the block or the street as social units in an urban setting.[1] This is not the place for any detailed examination of the differing interpretation of the fifth usage, except to note that the objectives for which the method is used will naturally determine the precise contents of the process. The common elements in all variations on the social work usage are:

That the basic unit of development is the community.

That the approach is to the social group rather than to the individual or the social institution.

That the basic objective is self-help by the participants to achieve self-chosen goals.

Community development in the sense described above is sometimes seen as 'the widest possible approach to community problem-solving, reaching out into the whole community at every level concerned, with the wide variety of felt needs'. Secondly, it may be seen as one approach to a particular problem, or set of related problems within the community, one aspect of a much larger or wider effort to help with or solve a social problem. The second approach is under consideration here, and the term 'community development' can be assumed to cover the following elements:

The conscious use of the community process by the participant and others called in for advice or guidance.

The approach to the social group and not to the individual.

Self-help, seen both as an objective and as a method.

The social setting throughout is urban.

Currently in British society community development is not a

[1] See *Community Development in Urban Areas* New York: United Nations—Department of Economic Affairs, 1961).

generic process attempting intervention at every level of the community process as might happen in rapidly developing areas overseas. It is an attempt to work at the level of a local project. These projects are usually related to social welfare or recreation.

The consideration of community development as a method of social work is divided into three sections, first an examination of the helping process, second, a discussion of the role of the worker in the use of this approach, and third, a working definition of community development, which attempts to draw together the other two sections.

### *The Helping Process*

The helping process is described by outlining the most important contents of each of its five phases:
1. Observation and enquiry.
2. Formulation of the problem.
3. Suggestions for modification.
4. Evaluation.
5. Re-planning.

In the description of the helping process, it is assumed that the worker has been called in for consultation by the group because they have a problem, on the understanding that he is an outside adviser with no authority over the group, with no preconceived programme to implement, and that he agrees that the objective of the group and its method of work will be self-chosen. The process here is outlined from the point of view of the worker.

*Phase One—Observation and Enquiry:* Preliminary observation and exploration:

How does the group state the problem? How do they account for the problem, whom do they blame, what do they think can be done, how, and by whom? What is the history of the problem in the community, in the group, who is involved in it, why are they involved in it, in what way?

What is the community context of the problem? What parts have individuals, groups, social institutions played in causing, recognising and solving it? What suggestions do they make for solving it? How do their varying definitions of the problem and its solution differ from those of the group asking for advice?

How can the group itself be involved in collecting the relevant information, discussing its implications? At what stage can the group be helped to compare the various definitions of the problem, and the various proposed solutions?

Phase One has several objectives. The worker has to collect the

170

relevant information, to involve the group in its collection, to help the group to involve other interested parties in the discussion of the problem situation. At the same time the worker is getting to know the group and its individual members, and the members are getting to know one another and others involved.

*Phase Two—Formulation of the Problem:* Statement of the problem.

The worker attempts to help the group to formulate the problem from the information, attitudes, opinions, already collected. This formulation should enable the worker and the group to move on to further discussion and enquiry, which in turn should be understood and accepted by all those involved.

As well as the main problem, the formulation should include some recognition of new problems that are likely to arise during any attempts to solve the main problem. What persons, groups or social institutions are likely to be adversely affected by an attempt to solve the problem? What new sub-groups will be created by a solution of the problem?

What changes may result from a solution of the problem? Where will they take place, and for what purpose?

What resources will be necessary in persons, money, expertise? Which of these are available, and in what amount?

What further enquiry is necessary? Why? Who should do it, how should it be done, in what form should it be presented?

During Phase Two the worker is attempting to help the group to formulate the problem in terms of its own needs, understanding and resources, and to interpret it to individuals and to interested parties whose help or approval is one factor in the solution. During this phase, the worker will have, to some extent, proved his usefulness to the group by the help he has offered them and by the way in which he has worked with them. The group members will have learned something of how to get on together in performing a task, and have come to understand some of the needs and opinions of others in the community.

*Phase Three—Suggestions for Modifying the Situation:* The formulation of the problem will suggest various solutions, plans of action, different approaches and methods which will need to be examined, discussed and agreed.

*Structural Setting.* What form will the operation take? Who will take responsibility, and on what authority, for each part of the operation, and how will the parts relate to the whole?

*Procedure.* How will the work be carried out in the most effective and efficient manner; how can communication be established and maintained between the relevant roles, groups and bodies?

What are the specific goals to be attained by the whole group; by individuals (officers); by sub-groups (working committees); by other local leaders? How are these goals best stated, what criteria are most appropriate for the evaluation of their successful operation?

When the group has been working together for some time, and has accomplished some things and failed in others, a re-formulation of the problem may be necessary. The formulation of the other ancillary problems that arise as the work progresses will probably need to be undertaken by the group.

During Phase Three, the worker will have attempted to help the group to understand the various suggestions for the modification of the situation and to select and to try out various procedures in order to make progress. In this process the worker will have helped the interaction between the group and the community. This may result in the group achieving an identity, recognising its primary task and to some extent agreeing upon the method of fulfilling it.

*Phase Four—Evaluation:* Where have the desired changes been achieved, those desired by the whole group, those desired by individual members, those suggested by interested parties?

What was learned that will be useful to the group's growth and development and to its performance of future tasks?

Has the group settled down in its work in the most effective and efficient way? Has it settled too deeply into the work, tending to become too settled in its ways?

Has it made the best use of resources, human, financial and social?

Were as many as possible of the individuals and sub-groups concerned with the problem included in the solution?

Did the work offer opportunity for the recognition and growth and use of the indigenous leaders, and the widest possible opportunity for taking responsibility and making decisions?

Did the solution cause more conflict, more ill-will in the community, than the original problem? Why did this happen? How could it be avoided in the future?

*Phase Five—Re-planning:* Phase Five leads straight into Phase One, a new beginning on new problems that are created by the working out of solutions to old ones.

In actual practice, of course, the helping process does not begin at Phase One and move steadily on to Phase Five. Social reality is never as neat, and certainly never as predictable, as this outline would suggest; in reality the phases and steps often overlap. The concept of five phases is useful for suggesting the possibilities inherent in the relationship between the worker, the group and the task to be accomplished in the particular circumstances.

The process that has been described has been operating on several levels at the same time:

Inside the worker's head, as part of his planning and thinking about the work with a particular group.

Within the group itself, as it learns to work out for itself the problems presented by the task in hand.

In the behaviour of the indigenous leaders as they attempt to offer their leadership to the group and to share in the fulfilment of agreed aims.

In the working out of each separate problem, and also in the thinking and work of the worker and the agency with the community group.

## The Role of the Worker

The role of the worker is that of helping the group to use the natural social processes in the group and in the community, in order to achieve self-chosen aims and objectives.

*How the Role is Established.* The role of the worker is established in general as a method of social work, and in particular in any given situation by the interaction between the policy of the agency, the needs of the group, the available resources, and the worker's own knowledge and skills.

The policy of the agency is determined by its understanding of the need for this kind of work, the approach and method necessary for such work, and by the resources available with which to do it. These include traditions, an established method of work, and a recognised position in the community within the network of statutory and voluntary social welfare bodies.

The needs of the group have to be assessed by taking into account the point of view of the group itself, of other interested parties and of the agency and the worker. These needs have to be seen in the context of the adjacent and larger communities of which the group is a part.

The resources available include individuals and indigenous leaders within the group; the presence or absence of shared interests, needs, values and standards, and the degree to which these are recognised by the group; the skill, knowledge and understanding of other groups and social institutions in the community, and the extent to which they are willing and able to help the group concerned; the knowledge, skills and understanding of the worker from his training and past experience.

N

### Characteristic of the Role of the Worker

*Promoting Participation.* The worker first has to ease himself into the situation, and then to promote participation between individuals and groups, between individuals and sub-groups within the group, between groups and between the group and other social institutions in the community. This is done by passing on to the group the skill it needs in order to participate, by helping to resolve or by-pass problems that inhibit or limit participation, by helping to find and train indigenous leadership, by offering acceptance, approval and support, and by helping the group to feel that participation is worth-while. The worker tries to help the group make possible a wider participation for concerned persons and other groups.

*Promoting Agreement.* The second objective of the worker's role is to promote agreement within the basic unit, the committee, so that decisions about aims and possible choices can be adequately made. He does this by helping to work out the roles of committee officers and the relationships between the roles. He also attempts to promote agreement between the various sub-groups that make up the complex group on whose behalf the committee operates. He does this by helping to open and formalise channels of communication, and by helping them to assign sub-group responsibilities and privileges.

*Strengthening Autonomy.* The third objective of the worker is to strengthen the autonomy of the group to enable it to continue as a self-programming community group. He does this by helping it to achieve an independent identity in its own eyes and in the eyes of others in the community, by establishing and formalising its role in the community vis-à-vis the other groups and social institutions. He helps the group to strengthen its own decision-making powers and procedures, its ability to mobilise and use the available resources, and its ability to do a job to its own satisfaction.

### The Mode of Participation

The worker can be seen in various modes of participation in the group and community process. For example:

As an objective observer. The role of a community development worker is that of an objective observer of the community process. Objective observation is not meant to imply any 'scientific' way of making infallible judgments about what is happening, but simply implies that his role includes attempting to 'see both sides of the story' and to help the groups to do the same. This may seem too obvious to mention, but only those who have attempted to do social

174

work for an established agency, offering established service to people who obviously need it, but will not take it, or who have worked with an autonomous group, will know how delicate a requirement this is.

Controlled participation. Perhaps the single most important characteristic of the worker attempting to help the group to use the natural social process is by controlled participation. This means the worker's conscious control of his own behaviour within the helping situation, in order to offer the group the most effective and efficient service. In this he is not a natural participant, a member of the group; his participation is controlled in such a way that the group understands his function and is able to use the service he is offering.

As an agent of social change. The worker should realise that he is an agent of social change and accept responsibility for this. His service to the group will, it is hoped, strengthen it, increase its capacity to get the job done and so change its position in the wider community. This process will not always be welcomed by other groups in the community, not even by some of the relevant social institutions. The worker's presence and behaviour will sometimes represent the cause of change within the group itself as seen by the different participants and sub-groups.

As a resource person. The worker participates in the group's work in so far as his knowledge, insight and understanding are adequate to his needs and useful to the group. He participates as a resource person on the understanding that the resources necessary to do the job are in fact available, but as yet unrecognised or unused, and that his usefulness to the group will terminate once the resources necessary to do the work are organised and available for that purpose.

*Responsibilities.* The role of the community development worker has in common with other social and professional workers the values and standards on which social work in general is based. The most relevant to this discussion are:

Confidentiality. The worker has the same responsibility to the group and its individual members and the community he works with as a case or group worker in respect of the confidential nature of the work. It has a right not to have its personal affairs discussed without prior agreement. The 'good name' of a group or community is as important to them as it is to an individual and demands the same respect and thoughtful consideration.

Non-judgmental behaviour. The worker should be aware of his personal and social attitudes. In work with the community, he must aim at non-judgmental behaviour in respect of differing values, attitudes and standards.

Exploitation. The worker has a great responsibility to avoid the exploitation of individuals, groups or community for his own social

175

and emotional satisfaction, or for the advantage of the agency for whom he works. The group and the community have an integrity of their own which should not be manipulated to further the advantage of either the worker, the agency or any of the relevant parties.

The role of the worker includes a responsibility to the agency who employs him, and to social work as a profession. This centres on passing on information in appropriate form, so that social policy may be influenced at various points.

The role, like others in social work, involves the responsibility to be a witness to the democratic process that social change is possible and compatible with orderly change in social institutions and society, and that 'ends do not justify the means'.

*Skills and Techniques.* Community development, as a method of social work, has a set of skills and techniques chosen and developed to aid the helping process and to support the worker using the method.

These skills and techniques can be divided into four categories:

1. Observation and Awareness. The worker observes the external physical and social factors in the field-work situation, and tries to be aware of the needs of the groups, their limitations and potentials, the stages of group development and the most appropriate forms of service at each stage. His awareness takes in his own role and that of the agency providing the service.

2. Information giving, passing on simple social skills and acting as a go-between in order to help the groups define their problems, and to find and use the available resources and serve the community.

3. Communication, interpretation and evaluation. These are the techniques for helping the groups, their officers and members to learn to work together to evolve the most appropriate machinery with which to get the task done.

4. Recording. The worker keeps records in order to make sense of the field-work process, and so to improve his practice and his service to the groups. With a recording system, the material about the helping process can be ready to hand to interpret the field work to the groups themselves, to his colleagues, and to the relevant statutory and voluntary bodies.

Each of the skills and techniques listed in the four categories is essential to the work, and together they form the basis of adequate practice.

### A Working Description

It should now be possible to offer a working description of community development and to discuss its relations to other methods of social work. This description is built up from previous points about the helping process, and about the role of the worker. 'Community development is a method of social work through which community groups are helped by a worker to use the social process, in order to achieve more effective and efficient relationships. The method finds and uses appropriate resources for reaching self-chosen goals, and makes a contribution to group and community life'. It is worth setting out the implications of each section of this definition.

'Community development is a method of social work . . .' Community development is part of the social work enterprise and related to other areas of social work practice, case-work, group work, community organisation, as well as to social work research and administration. It is a method in the sense that particular kinds of knowledge, understanding and skills are relevant to its practice.

'Through which community groups . . .' This refers to autonomous groups with common welfare needs capable of being met by the common action of its members The community of which the group is a part must be seen both as the cause of the needs as well as the supplier of the resources, and the setting in which the common action takes place.

' . . are helped by the worker to use the community process . . .' The community and group processes are described in Appendix II. The salient parts of the community process are its shared values and traditions, shared needs and interests, common resources, common organisation and structural forms.

'. . . in order to achieve more effective and efficient relationships and to find and use appropriate resources for reaching self-chosen goals . . .'

Relationships are made more effective between individuals within the group, between the groups and sub-groups and social institutions in the community.

'Finding and using appropriate resources' including the shared values and traditions, shared interests and needs. These form a common ingredient of the knowledge, skills, and understanding of members, indigenous leaders, participants and of the worker.

'Self-chosen goals.' The goals and the means of achieving them are chosen and agreed by the group, recognised and accepted by the worker, and made known in the neighbourhood as goals of the group's own choice.

'. . . as a contribution to group and community life'.

The contribution is made by the members of the group, by its indigenous leaders, activity volunteers, and by its work and the service it offers to the community. The worker and the agency add their contribution by the help they offer the group.

The contribution to individuals comes through the provision of

177

opportunity for taking part in the responsibility for activities, also through the direct services the group offers to its members.

The contribution to the group is in the offer of help in the more effective and efficient performance of its task; in giving recognition, approval and support, and in the willingness of the agency and the worker to offer this service.

The contribution to the community comes from enabling more members to take part in community affairs, from the opportunity which the group provides for training leadership, and again from the direct service which the group provides.

This working description is clearly based on values common to all social work as it operates within the social process seeking to make explicit and effective social welfare values.

## *Community Development and Other Methods of Social Work*

This comparison of community development and other methods of social work, especially community organisation, is made from the point of view of the setting in which they operate, the community itself. Comparisons could be made between origins or objectives of various methods of social work, but the starting point here is the community, with an outline of the different ways of working within the community process. This process is everything that happens among people, within each individual; between individuals; within and between groups; and within and between social institutions.

The following description outlines each aspect of the community process, shows various points at which social work appears to be needed, and the way in which it intervenes in the community process in order to make social welfare values explicit and effective.

*Intra-personal.* This is the level of community behaviour at which individuals internalise values, develop an identity, 'become persons', in interaction with parents, play-, school- or work-mates. At this level the individual takes on part of his cultural equipment, values, standards, ways of speech and behaviour, including the acceptance of 'self' with all its strengths and weaknesses.

When problems become apparent at this level, social work usually intervenes by way of offering case-work help, for instance, probation, medical and psychiatric case-work, family case-work, child guidance, or psychological counselling.

*Inter-personal* behaviour takes place between two persons in the home, the school, at play, at work, and in the community. At this level of behaviour people interact together, give, take and exchange the skills, knowledge, understanding and other personal and cultural

178

characteristics that are integrated in the development of personality and the growth of the individual into a social being.

When problems occur at this level of interaction, the social work method of intervention is again through case-work in an attempt to use the social process of interaction between two persons. This method offers assistance previously unavailable or unexplored within the environment of the persons involved.

*Within Groups.* When a problem occurs on this level, within the family as a primary group, the school, play or work group, the social work method is usually to offer a social group work service, group therapy for a family, social group work for a youth group or a group of old people.

*Between groups and social institutions.* When the groups are simple secondary groups (youth, aged, or special interest groups like sports or the arts) difficulties occurring between them are usually worked with by use of the social group work method. But when the difficulties arising from relations between complex groups or social institutions must be dealt with, the most appropriate social work methods are either community organisation or community development. Community organisation is concerned with the relations between established social institutions, the statutory and voluntary social welfare bodies. Community development, as described above, offers its service to complex community or other types of autonomous group to help with internal relations, and with the relations of the group to the wider community.

These four categories describing the community process show problems arising at particular levels and through particular forms of social interaction. This is in no way to suggest that the problem is located only in that area of the individual's or group's life, or that only one method of social work assistance can, or should, be offered. In fact, the reverse is usually the case, as the following examples may help to emphasise.

### Example One

Mr. Jones suffered a serious industrial accident about two years ago, and found it difficult to get back to normal life. He felt he had nothing to live for, and several times put off re-training, saying that he was not up to it. The doctor suggested psychological treatment. During this treatment it appeared that Mrs. Jones was nervous about her husband's injury, worried about the future of the family, and was beginning to resent his being around the house all the time. As the situation at home worsened, he saw less and less of his old friends and nothing of his old work-mates; he became more and more withdrawn and unwilling to attempt to co-operate.

The treatment programme that was worked out for Mr. Jones was substantially as follows:

Several appointments were made for Mr. Jones with the rehabilitation units, and a psychiatric social worker helped Mr. Jones's wife.

As a result, Mrs. Jones agreed to join a discussion group of other wives facing similar problems.

A holiday away from home for Mr. Jones, after which it was agreed that he would join a discussion group with others affected by industrial injuries who were about to join in a re-training programme.

Re-training away from home, with every other week-end at home.

A job with his old firm doing a different kind of work but in association with some of his old work-mates.

A discussion group after his re-training and return to work, to help him develop outside interests not requiring physical skills (he was formerly interested in sports).

In this example the process began on the intra-personal level—the injured man's problem with himself—but the attempt to help him soon led the worker to use other kinds of social work situations—the inter-personal relation of husband and wife, and group discussion of various kinds that involved other levels of the community process.

*Example Two*

The Elm Street boys were a group of 15–17 year-olds who began visiting the Johnson Boys' Club, but refused to enter into any activities, provoking incidents and then attempting to smash the place up. They would not join, as they said the club was 'kids' stuff', nor would they discuss what they wanted from the club. Mr. Brown, the boys' worker, discussed the matter with his committee and they decided to employ a detached worker to work with the boys on the streets. After six months of work with the Elm Street boys the programme included:

Recreational activities in the neighbourhood and in the central city area specially designed for this age and group.

Work with the local Youth Employment Service to arrange for special sessions in an informal atmosphere, and later more intensive help with the work problems and job placement for those willing to accept it.

Counselling with two of the seventeen-year-old boys about

180

boy/girl relationships, which eventually enabled them to move away from the group and to begin 'going steady'.

Work with one of the sub-groups in the larger group which eventually enabled three of the boys to join the senior section of a local youth club.

Special help—psychological guidance for Tommy, the eldest boy in the group, who showed signs of being emotionally disturbed.

In this example the problem arose on the group level of the community process. But adequate help had to be offered on all levels, to include intra-personal (as in the case of Tommy), inter-personal (boy/girl relationships counselling), within the group (the work with the sub-groups of younger boys), between the social institutions (the club which sponsored the 'treatment' programme, and the local Youth Employment Office).

*Example Three*

A group of immigrants were having a party that the landlady claimed was getting too noisy. Controversy followed between the tenants and the landlady and her husband, which soon involved immigrants and English neighbours. Some younger boys returning from their youth club joined in the disturbance, as did several older men from the club across the street. The police were called, the crowd was broken up, but the tension aroused by the incident could be felt in the neighbourhood for the next fortnight.

The local vicar got in touch with the youth club leader, the head-mistress of the secondary school and the chairman of the local tenants' association, and suggested they form a temporary good-neighbour council and invite representatives of the immigrants in the neighbourhood, and other neighbourhood groups, to discuss problems of 'neighbourliness' in the community. The plan in this case included:

Bringing together key figures in the locality for discussions and fact finding.

Bringing together the groups involved for group discussion of tensions and grievances.

Organising an informal meeting of the opposing sides, with representatives of the local institutions.

Forming a local neighbourhood council to be a forum for public discussion of inter-cultural difficulties and of neighbourliness; making more formal provision for resolving difficulties and airing grievances—all this in the hope of modifying social attitudes.

In these examples it is apparent that as the levels of community behaviour interact in the community process so the fields and methods of social work interact in any given treatment programme. It is now possible to make two statements, one about social problems and one about the different methods of social work, which will help to distinguish between community organisation and community development.

First, social problems in any community are rarely, if ever, separate or isolated social events. They are inter-related, inter-connected aspects of the community process in the same way that *non*-problem situations are. If at first social problems appear to be isolated, further exploration will usually reveal their complex nature, and their close relation to other events and situations in the community process. As a result 'solutions' to social problems usually need to come from many sources rather than a single one.

Second, social work methods. Social work, like any social institution that grows up in response to a particular complex or sequence of needs, has attempted to respond to the social welfare needs of individuals, groups and communities. Its main point of intervention in the community process has been through intra- and inter-personal relations within the community. The method of work, therefore, has been mainly social case-work.

With the growing awareness of the inter-relatedness of individual, group and community problems, social work has recently taken a broader view, and has begun to develop methods and approaches that enable it to effect a wider area of community behaviour. Social group work as a method has been joined by community organisation and community development.

### Comparison of Community Organisation and Community Development

*The Nature of the Concern.* Both community organisation and community development share the basic social work concern, that of meeting social welfare and recreation needs. Both define social welfare needs, individual and community, in the same way, using the same terms as other fields of social work.

Community organisation is mainly concerned with relations with established social welfare bodies. For example, a Council of Social Service is concerned with programmes of service to special groups, the aged, youth, the disabled, represented by special agencies, or with community-wide welfare planning. Community development, on the other hand, is concerned with the less organised, informal, autonomous groups in community life, which provide a service for themselves and for others in the community.

*Objectives.* The objectives of the two methods are similar. Both aim

182

at helping people in the community to recognise social welfare needs, to find and use resources and to provide services.

But the primary objective of the community organisation approach is to strengthen and rationalise the existing network of statutory and voluntary bodies, and to initiate new services within the network. By contrast, the primary objective of the community development approach is to enable the community group itself, at its own pace and in its own way, to accept responsibility and achieve status.

*Approach and Method.* The approach and methods of community organisation and community development are similar. They share basic social work assumptions about individual, group and community behaviour, and they share basic social work tools and techniques, interviewing, the use of the group and community procedures, finding and using community resources. They also share the common ethical standards of non-judgmental behaviour towards the client, and of confidentiality.

They differ in that community organisation uses its method to achieve greater effectiveness and efficiency within and between established welfare bodies on an administrative level, but community development, using a similar method, adapts it to achieve the same ends in work with community groups. Community organisation, therefore, involves work with the statutory and voluntary bodies as established agencies and with trained and experienced social workers, or knowledgeable laymen already involved in the provision of social welfare service. Community development, on the other hand, works with small informal groups and indigenous leaders who need to find out for themselves how to use the same techniques in their work with their own and with other community groups.

*The Role of the Worker.* The role of the community organisation and the community development worker is similar, in that the worker is an objective participant attempting to offer a service to those who need it, and to encourage a more efficient and effective use of natural social processes to achieve agreed aims and objectives.

The role differs in that the worker using the community organisation approach is seen as a social administrator, or a social planning or policy expert, in relation to the needs of the statutory and voluntary bodies, whereas the community development worker is usually a detached, informal 'adult educationalist' whose relations to the community group are much more informal, unscheduled and unstructured. This worker uses his skills and techniques with a view to their being adopted by amateurs and not by professionals.

183

## The Importance of Autonomous Groups

The strength of the approach and method we have been discussing here lies, we believe, in its recognition of the importance of autonomous groups. This recognition emphasises the opportunities for personal satisfaction through service by participation in community affairs, and the additional opportunities offered for doing and being things together, and so making for neighbourliness in situations where this is sometimes a pressing need. It offers support in self-help to community groups providing a social welfare and recreational service, and possibilities for partnership with statutory and voluntary bodies providing these services. This method provides an opportunity for participation in the democratic process, not only in self-government but in opening channels of communication between informal groups and established bodies, and channels through which information from the groups can be fed into social planning and policy.

In short, the autonomous community group should, we believe, be seen as a natural, useful, and necessary buffer or intermediary between the individual and the larger, more formal groups and institutions of society. It provides an opportunity to use often untapped human resources and is a partner in social welfare provision. The autonomous community group has the power to enrich social life and is therefore seen as a much needed resource in present day urban conditions.

## The Continuing Need for This Kind of Work

We have for the most part been discussing community development as a method of social work within a particular context, i.e., that of social work in an urban environment. From a broader point of view it is, we believe, possible to describe the method as a form of social education. Social education in this sense has as its objective the passing on to those individuals, groups and social institutions who need and want them, the social skills and conceptual material necessary to a more effective and efficient use of personal and social resources and of their social environment. Its approach and method is informal, tailored to the needs of the recipients, and offered in terms they can understand and accept.

The role of the worker, and the agency, is that of an outside resource person who helps to create a situation in which learning can take place, and who can pass on skills and help them to take effect in the life and work of those who are learning to use them. This kind of social education can take place in any circumstances, at any

184

time. If for example a firm is about to move from London to a new locality, social education could offer employees and their families an opportunity to explore together what the move will mean to them. It might offer to residents in a village which is becoming a commuter town the opportunities to explore the pros and cons of the change, or to women residents in a hostel an opportunity to discuss together the difficulties and opportunities of the younger unmarried women newly arrived in a large city. In the field work described, the method aims to help community groups on estates in a more effective and efficient pursuit of self-chosen goals.

In all examples the common factor is the attempt to help individuals, groups and social institutions to understand, accept or reject, use and affect, their social environment. If, as on the housing estates, the work is primarily about social welfare and recreation problems, a social work enterprise is the most likely to have the necessary know-how about these kinds of problems. In other situations, it might be the extension of a town planning process, or of industrial relations, or, as we have seen, of adult education.

## Why is it Necessary?

'Is all this detail really necessary simply in order to help a local group to manage its affairs sensibly?'

If, for example, one were to examine an autonomous group in a different environment, say a literary society in a middle class area of a moderately large town, we should probably find that although it had the same difficulties in each of its stages of development, it was in fact able to surmount or by-pass them more or less with ease as compared to the groups we have described here. If, in addition, one were to do a simple survey of the number and variety of similar groups in the same community as that of the literary society, we should probably find that they range from gardening, sports, local history and drama groups to small investor, property owner and community protection or improvement groups. The question then becomes, how is it that on the whole middle class communities give rise to autonomous groups within a wide range of interests, and that they are generally capable of functioning without outside help?

The difference seems to be that middle and upper class communities have 'built-in' resources of indigenous leadership—the lawyer, the business executive, the scholar or teacher—who have the necessary cultural and social accomplishments. Since they share a wider variety of interests, e.g. the arts, current affairs, property, and because in addition they share some of the traditions of voluntary action as a natural ingredient in their cultural heritage, the middle class autonomous group has within the group itself, and within the

185

community of which it is a part, the necessary resources with which to carry on the work.

We are not implying that there is any appreciable difference in the number of spontaneous and autonomous groups in the different social classes. Indeed there is every reason to assume (unless further enquiry should prove it otherwise) that autonomous groups fulfil similar social needs in the several classes. What is clear is the vast difference in the cultural and social resources available from within the groups themselves. This disparity accounts for the need for a service offered by an outside agency, always with the aim that the service should become unnecessary.

But this is not the whole picture. Although it shows grounds for doing the work described, it conveys no impression that the situation is likely to be radically altered by the impact of technological change. One effect of the increasing pace of social change may be that individuals, groups and social institutions in a complete cross-section of society will need 'outside' help in order to come to terms with new conditions of life and work. The kind of service described here will then have a much wider validity.

# Appendix 1a

## RULES OR CONSTITUTION

1. NAME. The name of the Club/Association shall be:

   ............................................................................

2. OBJECTS. The objects of the Association shall be:
   - (a) To provide facilities for recreation or other leisure-time occupation for members of the public at large, in order to improve the conditions of life for the persons making use of those facilities.
   - (b) For the furtherance of the above object, to associate the local authorities, voluntary organisations and the residents of . . . Estate in a common effort to advance education and to provide facilities for training and recreation, and social, moral and intellectual development, and to further health; and to foster a community spirit for the achievement of these and other charitable objects.

3. MEMBERSHIP. Membership of the Association shall be open, irrespective of political party, nationality, religious opinion, race or colour to:—
   - (a) All persons living on the Estate who shall be called full members.
   - (b) Well-wishers anywhere who shall be called associate members. Associate members shall not have the right to vote at members' meetings.

4. SUBSCRIPTIONS. All members shall pay such subscriptions as the Annual General Meeting shall determine.

5. MANAGEMENT.
   - (a) The Club shall be managed by a General Committee to be elected at the Annual General Meeting.
   - (b) The General Committee shall consist of a Chairman, Secretary, Treasurer and . . . other members (or one representative from each block).
   - (c) Any affiliated group or section sponsored by the Com-

mittee shall have the right to be represented on the General Committee.

    (d) If vacancies occur among the officers or in the Committee, the General Committee shall have the power to fill them from among their members.

6. ANNUAL GENERAL MEETING. The Committee shall arrange an Annual General Meeting for the purpose of receiving the Annual Report of the Committee and the Audited Statement of Accounts; of accepting the resignations of the Committee, of electing a new Committee, of making recommendations to the Committee and of voting, whenever necessary, on proposals to amend the Constitution.

7. SPECIAL GENERAL MEETING. The Chairman or Secretary of the Club may, at any time, call a Special Meeting of the Club, either for the purpose of altering the Constitution or of considering any matter which the Committee may decide should be referred to the members in general. They shall call such a meeting at the written request of not less than . . . members who give reasons for the request.

8. RULES OF PROCEDURE. Meetings of the Committee shall be conducted in accordance with the rules drawn up by the Committee and revised by them when necessary. The Secretary shall keep a Minute Book with Minutes of all Committee Meetings.

9. FINANCE.
    (*a*) All monies raised by or on behalf of the Club shall be applied to further the objects of the Club and for no other purpose.
    (*b*) The Treasurer shall keep proper account of the finances of the Club and shall open a Bank Account in the name of the Club.
    (*c*) The Accounts shall be audited at least once a year by a qualified auditor.

10. ALTERATIONS TO THE CONSTITUTION. Any alteration to this Constitution shall require the approval of a two-thirds majority of those present and voting at the General Meeting at which it is discussed. Any resolution for the alteration of the Constitution must be received by the Secretary at least twenty-eight days before the meeting at which the resolution is to be brought forward. At least seven days' notice shall be given to the members that the meeting is taking place.

11. DISSOLUTION. If the Committee by a single majority decide at any time that on the grounds of expense or otherwise, it is necessary or advisable to dissolve the Club, it shall call a meeting of all the members giving them at least twenty-one days' notice and stating the terms of the resolution to be proposed at the meeting. If such a decision shall be confirmed by a simple majority of those present and voting at the meeting, the Com-

mittee shall have the power to dispose of any assets held by or in the name of the Club. Any assets remaining after the satisfaction of any proper debts and liabilities shall be applied towards charitable purposes for the benefit of the inhabitants of the Estate as the Committee may decide and as may be approved by the Minister of Education.

This Constitution was adopted as the Constitution of the.................................................................at a Public Meeting held at..........................................on .........................19.......
Signed................................Chairman.
Signed................................Secretary.

# CONSTITUTION OF THE ASSOCIATION OF LONDON HOUSING ESTATES

1. NAME. The name shall be The Association of London Housing Estates, hereinafter called 'The Association'. The Association shall be non-party in politics and non-sectarian in religion.

2. OBJECTS.
   (a) To promote the objects of the member organisations.
   (b) To consider matters of interest to the member organisations and to exchange and publish information for the further-ance of the above object.
   (c) To promote the training of voluntary and other workers, to hold conferences and to promote inter-estate activities for the furtherance of the first above-named object.
   (d) To enjoy mutual co-operation with the London Council of Social Service in the sphere of their common purposes for the furtherance of the first above-named object.
   (e) For the furtherance of the first above-named object, to associate the local authorities, voluntary organisations and the residents of housing estates in a common effort to advance education and to provide facilities for training and recreation, and social, moral and intellectual development, and to further health, and to foster a spirit for the achieve-ment of those and other charitable objects.

3. MEMBERSHIP OF THE ASSOCIATION. Membership of the Association shall be open to all housing estate community groups within the County of London whose objects are the provision of facilities for recreation or other leisure-time occupation for members of the public at large, in order to improve the conditions of life for all persons making use of those facilities; whose membership is open to all residents on the estate; which are non-party in politics and non-sectarian in religion, and which have a committee elected at an Annual General Meeting.

O 189

Membership shall be open to all such groups in any stage of development. Applications for membership shall be considered, and if approved, accepted by the Executive Committee. All applications for membership whether accepted or rejected, shall be reported to the next meeting of the Association and the decision of the Executive Committee shall there be confirmed or altered as the case may be. Each group accepted as a member of the Association is entitled to vote.

4. MEETING OF THE ASSOCIATION. The Association shall meet at least once a year.

Each member of the Association shall be entitled to send not more than three representatives, who shall themselves be members of groups which are members of the Association.

The Association shall elect annually an Executive Committee of 20, and such other committees and groups as it may, from time to time, think advisable. Nominations for the Executive Committee, limited to one per member group, must be received at least 28 days, and shall be circulated to members at least 14 days, prior to the Annual Meeting of the Association. The Executive Committee shall have the power to fill any vacancies that arise in its membership between the meetings of the Association, from the person with the next highest number of votes among the original nominees for the existing Executive Committee, where the number of nominations exceeds the number of those elected.

Any Executive Member who misses more than three consecutive meetings without apology or without being represented by a deputy properly elected by his own committee shall be deemed to have resigned.

5. OFFICERS. The Association shall appoint from its elected members a Chairman, a Vice-Chairman, an Honorary Secretary, an Honorary Treasurer and such other officers as it shall deem necessary.

6. FINANCE. There shall be an affiliation fee to be decided annually by the Association, the minimum to be £3 3s.

All monies raised by or on behalf of the Association shall be applied to further the objects of the Association, and for no other purpose.

The Honorary Treasurer shall keep proper accounts of the finances of the Association and shall present a statement of accounts to the Executive Committee Meetings.

The accounts shall be audited at least once a year by a properly qualified auditor or auditors, who shall be appointed at the Annual General Meeting.

7. QUORUM. The Quorum at the meeting of the Executive Committee shall be one third of the membership of the Com-

mittee at the date of the meeting, or the nearest whole number above one third.

8. TRUSTEES. The Conference shall appoint not more than three trustees, at least one of whom shall not be a member of the Association. Trustees shall be *ex-officio* members of the Committee. One trustee shall resign every third year and be eligible for re-appointment if he so wishes. The Executive Committee shall have the power to fill occasional vacancies among the trustees. All and any real property acquired by the Association shall be vested in the Trustees, who shall be appointed at the Annual General Meeting.

9. DISSOLUTION. In the event of the dissolution of the Association, any remaining assets after the settlement of all proper debts and liabilities, shall be given to such charitable organisations or organisations with objects similar to those of the Association, as the Association may decide, subject to such consent as may be required by law.

10. ALTERATION TO THE CONSTITUTION. The Constitution was adopted at the first Annual Meeting of the Association. Amendments to the Constitution shall be made provided that:
   (a) Notice shall be given 28 days prior to the meeting at which such amendments will be moved;
   (b) The amendments are agreed by at least two thirds of those groups represented and present and entitled to vote.
   (As amended at the Eighth Annual General Meeting on 29th May, 1965.)


Information
Sheet No. 1

### NOTES ON COMMITTEE PROCEDURE

*Announcements of Meetings:*
It is advisable to send out announcements of committee meetings a week before the date of the meeting. Although many committees have a regular day of the week or month for meetings, so that members can plan in advance to attend, a written notice nearer the date is a useful reminder.
Example: A meeting of the X.Y.Z. committee will be held at 8 p.m. on Wednesday 12th October in the Club-room. Kindly notify the secretary if you cannot attend.

J. Black, Secretary,
40 White House.
Phone: ABC 6789

*Apology for Absence:*
Committee members who are unable to attend the meeting should send an apology to the Secretary.

*Quorum:*
A committee meeting cannot proceed unless there is a Quorum. A Quorum is the minimum number of committee members who must be present before business can be conducted. The number is stated in the Constitution and is usually one-third of the total number on the committee.

*Agenda:*
The Agenda is the name given to the list of subjects to be discussed at the meeting. It should be short and set out clearly. Every committee member should have a copy of the agenda at least 24 hours before the meeting. This may not seem necessary but the purpose of the agenda paper is to give the members time to think over the various items and come to the meeting prepared to discuss them.

EXAMPLE

X.Y.Z. Committee Meeting
12th October, 1959
Agenda

1. Apologies for absence.
2. Minutes of the last meeting.
3. Business arising from the Minutes.
4. Treasurer's report.
5. Children's party.
6. Request from Youth Section for an extra evening.
7. Arrangements for Jumble Sale 26th November.
8. Any other business.
9. Date and time of next meeting.

*Special notes on the Agenda:*
*Correspondence:*
All correspondence should go to the Secretary. There is often a place on the Agenda for correspondence. This item is intended for reading letters which do not refer to other items on the Agenda. It is not necessary to read all the correspondence that has arisen since the last meeting. This item is usually the fourth on the agenda, following 'business arising from the minutes'.

*Any other business*
The Chairman has to be careful about this item. It is intended for bringing up minor matters of business which are not on the agenda elsewhere. Since it is always towards the end of the meeting, the Chairman must take care to see that an important matter is not rushed through without sufficient discussion. The Chairman must be observant about this and if, after reasonable discussion he feels it

is going to need even more time, the item should be put on the agenda for the next meeting.

*Procedure at Meetings:*

1. There *must* be a Chairman. If the elected Chairman cannot, for some reason, be present, his place must be taken by the Vice-Chairman. If it should happen that the Vice-Chairman also is absent, someone must be elected to conduct that particular meeting for the one occasion only. The meeting cannot proceed unless there is someone in the Chair.

2. All remarks must be addressed to the Chair.

3. Discussion must keep to the subject and not wander from the point.

4. Personal remarks and offensive language are out of order.

5. In committee meetings, as well as general meetings, only one person may speak at a time. The rule continues to apply when a speaker stands to address the Chair. This means, therefore, that even the Chairman takes his seat as not more than one person may be on his feet at the same time.

Information Sheet
No. 2

### DUTIES OF THE CHAIRMAN

1. To consult beforehand with the Secretary on all the business to be discussed.

2. To conduct the business according to the order of the agenda paper unless it is altered with the consent of the meeting.

3. To confine discussion to the item actually before the meeting and to see that it is dealt with and finally settled before passing on to the next.

4. The Chairman is there to guide the meeting. He should not force his own point of view on the committee.

5. He should give all those wishing to speak an opportunity to do so; to see that their remarks are addressed to the Chairman and to allow no private discussion or personal matter to be introduced.

6. If two people should speak at the same time, the Chairman should say who is to speak. His decision on such points is final.

7. The Chairman should make every effort to let any meeting over which he presides understand the reasons for and the purpose of his rulings. For example, if he stops a discussion he should explain that it is because the committee is getting away from the point, or that the discussion is becoming too personal.

Information
Sheet No. 3

### DUTIES OF THE SECRETARY

*Before the Meeting:*

1. Make sure a place is available for the meeting.
2. Make sure that the Minutes of the previous meeting are written up in the Minute book.
3. Settle the items of the agenda with the Chairman.
4. Send out notices and agenda to all members.
5. Keep all the papers that may be needed at the meeting, in a folder, if possible. They should be arranged in the order in which they will be needed at the meeting, that is, in the order of the agenda.
6. Have any reports or information ready which may have been asked for at the previous meeting.
7. Have writing materials ready at the meeting.

*At the Meeting:*

1. He should be at the meeting ahead of time with the books, correspondence and other necessary papers.
2. Make a note of those present or have the signatures written in the attendance book.
3. See that a quorum is present before any committee business is done.
4. Read the Minutes of the previous meeting and obtain the Chairman's signature.
5. Take notes of the business of the meeting for the Minutes.
(*Note:* it is not important to write down all that is said at a meeting —but the important thing for the Minute book is that all decisions, as well as important conclusions must go into the Minutes.)
6. Assist the Chairman with information he requires.

*After the Meeting:*

1. Draft the Minutes as soon as possible and submit them to the Chairman.
2. Write any letters, secure any information or take any action on matters decided by the committee.
3. Write up the Minutes in the book after the Chairman has seen the draft and made any comments.

Information
Sheet No. 4

## DUTIES OF THE TREASURER

1. The treasurer is responsible for the proper handling of the finances of the organisation, but not for the actual raising of money.
2. For collection of subscriptions and for paying these and all other money into the bank.
3. For issuing receipts.
4. For paying all bills.
5. For keeping a watch on the expenditure.
6. For keeping the committee regularly informed of the financial position.
7. For keeping proper books, or seeing that they are kept.
8. For preparing a statement for audit at least once a year and for presenting the audited accounts to the Annual General Meeting.
9. It is usual to have three officers of the committee authorised to sign cheques. Two of these signatures are required when cheques are signed.

*Notes for the Treasurer*

1. He should see that, however small the amount of money taken, a receipt in some form is issued in one of the following ways:
   (a) Giving a proper receipt from his receipt book.
   (b) Signing a book or card held by some other member of the Association – for example the book held by the collector of subscriptions for one block of flats, or the book showing canteen takings for an evening.
   (c) By issuing tickets. These may be specially printed or may be specially numbered cloakroom tickets. The number on the tickets is checked with the money later – all tickets should have a duplicate number on the stub. Whatever the kind of ticket used a stub should be kept by the steward or the person in charge of selling the tickets. When the money is checked the stubs and the money should balance.
2. It is a golden rule that all money collected should be *paid in* to the bank and all money paid out should be *drawn* from the bank. Money taken in cash for one thing and immediately paid out in cash for another is not always recorded in the books and this causes confusion.
3. The treasurer should agree with the members of the committee that small sums of money collected by them should be paid in at certain stated times, and once agreed, he should see that the rule is observed.
4. On no account should any large sum of money be kept in the house by anybody.

195

Information
Sheet No. 5

### ANNUAL GENERAL MEETING

Notes which may be useful when preparing for an Annual General Meeting.

*Before the Meeting*

1. Proper notice of the meeting should be given. Members should know the date about a month before the meeting takes place. There should never be less than one week's notice. The meeting should be held at about the same time each year.

2. The Agenda should be prepared by the Secretary in consultation with the Chairman and then agreed by the committee. Any resolution to alter the constitution should be on the Agenda paper.

3. Practical arrangements should be made about the room; it is sometimes useful to have a blackboard and chalk for writing the names of those nominated for the committee, etc.; paper and pencils should be provided if voting is on paper.

4. The Treasurer should see that the accounts are audited and an audited statement should be duplicated, so that each member may have a copy at the meeting.

5. The Secretary should prepare a written report. This would normally include a reference to some of the following:
   *Membership:* including any changes in officers or committee members during the year.
   *Reports of regular activities:* (Sometimes these reports are given separately by representatives of individual sections.)
   *New activities started* and activities which may have failed.
   *Special Activities:* outings, summer fetes, sports days, etc.
   *Social Services:* for example—visiting of old people, gifts to people in hospital, etc.
   *Residents' Problems:* Co-operation with the Housing Authority and other authorities over matters of general concern to the tenants.
   *Attendance at Conferences or Meetings outside the Estate.*
   *Relationships* with other organisations: Help received from local Evening Institutes, Housing Officers, etc.

6. The Chairman should prepare a list so that he can thank those who have worked for the Association in the past year. Great care should be taken about this in case someone is left out. It may be wise to thank people in general terms, and not by name.

7. If the organisation has a President it is usual to ask him to take the chair at the Annual General Meeting.

8. As the Chairman should not take the chair while voting takes place for the office which he holds, it should be arranged for someone else temporarily to act as Chairman.

# Appendix 1b

## ASSOCIATION OF LONDON HOUSING ESTATES

## ANNUAL REPORT 1966/67

It gives me great pleasure to present this report of our tenth anniversary year. Looking back over these first ten years of our association's existence, and surveying the scope of our activities and the needs we have attempted to meet, gives me reason to be proud of our achievements.

But satisfaction in what has been achieved, if it is not matched by a desire to re-assess our aims for the future, will lead to stagnation and less effective efforts to meet the constantly changing needs of a dynamic society.

I am pleased to report that your executive committee, with the active support of our organising secretary, Mr. Graham Riches, has approached all our work in this spirit of introspection and reassessment of our aims and achievement. Mr. Riches, or Graham as he is known to most of us, has, during the twenty months he has worked for the association, entered wholeheartedly into the spirit of our work, emulating the efforts of our previous able organising secretaries and making his own contribution as well. One of the main functions of the organising secretary is to establish good relationships with official bodies and outside organisations and this he has done efficiently.

You will be sorry to learn that Miss Bobbie Montford, who has worked as a member of our Youth advisory staff, will be leaving our services at the end of June this year. Bobbie, who has worked with us from November 1962, will be missed by the large circle of friends she has made at group level in her work for individual associations. We thank her for her services and wish her luck and an easing of her domestic problems. Many thanks also to our secretaries—Miss Jenny Gabb, and Miss Elaine Lamb, who has replaced Miss Julia Stiles.

Other reports will indicate to you the extent and variety of our activities and the new avenues of work and training which are opening up before us. Plans have to be made to meet this new challenge, and these are explained in detail in the report of the

Finance and Policy sub-committee; a report which merits careful reading, and indeed, study.

We have continued to enjoy the active support of the London Council of Social Service through Mrs. Muriel Smith of their Community Development department. We have recently co-opted to our executive committee Mr. J. Beale, M.B.E., who is the honorary Treasurer of the L.C.S.S. His extensive experience of voluntary welfare work in the London area and the closer co-operation he will be able to make between the L.C.S.S. and ourselves promise to make his presence a valuable asset to our committee.

In conclusion I would like to say how much I have enjoyed my term as chairman of an active and co-operative executive committee. Their attendance has been regular in spite of commitments and competing interests. I wish to thank them for their services to the groups. Without our staff and their unstinted efforts, much of our work would not have been possible. We are conscious of having worked them too hard; but when I am reminded to congratulate Graham and his wife on recently having started a family, I am happy to see that our staff are yet able to lead normal domestic lives!

(Signed)

## YOUTH SUB-COMMITTEE REPORT

We have had a full and interesting year and I am going to select the most important parts of our work. In June we held a meeting of youth leaders to meet Sam Field of Adventure Unlimited, who gave a résumé of his work. Also we asked for suggestions for future activities. Many were forthcoming and many of them were very practical. After a great deal of thought and discussion of the ideas put forward, we decided to hold a conference in the autumn, and invite leaders as well as the youth. This was held in October at the Islington Green school and proved to be a great success. We put our suggestions to a joint meeting and then divided into two groups, the Youth in one room and the Leaders in another to discuss the various proposals and then met together again to discuss the findings. The following were the suggestions put forward, and the decisions arrived at:

1. Combined Membership of Youth Clubs within the Association. This would mean that a member of one club could visit other clubs if in a different area to their own club. This was agreed on and the material has been sent to the clubs who were represented at the Conference and we hope to get replies very soon.

2. Adventure week-end for boys between the ages of fourteen and sixteen years, at Woodrow House under the leadership of Joe Lowney. This was specifically for boys who had never done this sort of thing before, and we had room for twelve of them. I do not want to go into detail as to what took place at that weekend, only to say that it was a great success, so much so that some of the boys have asked their leader when the next one will be taking place.

3. Week-end Conference this year. It was agreed that this be held out of London, combining an adventure week-end with a conference, and the subject for discussion decided by the youth was 'Sex and Morality'. After discussion with Sam Field we decided to go to the P.G.L. Adventure Centre, Llangorse, Breconshire for the week-end 8th–10th September, 1967. Full details will be sent out as soon as possible, when we hope to get your full support to make this a success.

From this Conference a youth advisory committee was set up under the chairmanship of Peter Eldridge to advise us on what youth wanted, and it has already come up with two good suggestions. One was that we join Oxfam in their next march and we invited Mr. Eaton of Oxfam to meet us and discuss this. It was agreed that a certain percentage of the money raised would be used by the clubs taking part. By the time you read this the walk will have taken place and we hope it will have been a great success. The other proposal was an inter-estate dance at either Caxton Hall or Brighton. We decided on Brighton and are now trying to find a suitable club for this purpose, and at the A.G.M. we may have something definite to give. I have tried to give you a good picture of what we have done, but cannot show the invaluable work done by all members of the committee and staff during my short period of chairmanship. I thank you all.

(SIGNED)

### INTER-ESTATE ACTIVITIES

This year has been a very busy one for the Activities sub-committee, and all members and co-opted members have worked extremely hard on your behalf. Activities organised have been: Social and Dance, Sports, Swimming Gala, Darts and Indoor games, Cricket and Football. So you see we have had a full programme.

The Social and Dance was well attended and all had a good time. The next dance will be held on November 11th this year, again at Dulwich Baths.

Sports: There will be two sports meetings this year as we have decided to arrange a meeting for the under-elevens. This will be on Sunday 3rd September, at Battersea Park. The senior Sports meeting will be held at Hurlingham on Saturday 24th June. Over-all winners last year were Aboyne Estate.

The Swimming Gala has been arranged for Saturday, 21st October 1967, this time at Kentish Town. Last year's Gala was well attended, and placings were Faylands, Churchill Gardens, and Hallfield.

The Football League was a new venture for us and we are very gratified at the response and enjoyment of all who took part. The games were played in a sporting manner, and we look forward to a larger number of entries next season. League winners were Churchill Gardens, W.G.D. and Tulse Hill. The cups for the League were given by Kingswood Estate, Stockwell Gardens and Flower House estates.

The Knock-out Cup Final held at Honor Oak was well attended, and after a good game Churchill Gardens took possession of the cup, which was personally donated to us by Mr. J. P. Macey, Director of Housing, G.L.C.

The Five-a-Side Football Tournament, held at Camberwell Baths on Saturday, 1st April, was quite an event, and a good afternoon's entertainment was enjoyed by all. Winners in each division were W.G.D., Stockwell Gardens and Churchill Gardens. The cups were donated by Churchill Gardens Estate.

To those associations who gave cups, and to Mr. Macey we offer our sincere thanks.

The Darts Tournaments have not been completed yet, but I should be able to name the winners at our A.G.M.

We are very pleased to welcome new member estates who have joined in activities this year and trust that they have enjoyed participating. All these activities have meant a great deal of work for the staff at the office, and I extend my thanks for all the work done. Also I would like to tender my sincere thanks to all sports secretaries and co-opted members, without whose help and advice these many activities would not function.

My congratulations to all winners and runners-up, and to the less fortunate – better luck in the future! May next year be as enjoyable as this and also may there be more associations joining the activities. It has been great fun.

(SIGNED)

WORK WITH THE ELDERLY

This committee has again been instrumental in helping and advising members who have come to us with problems, and we have advised newly affiliated and newly formed clubs of the do's and don'ts concerning the running of clubs for the elderly.

With the Bulletin we have tried to be constructive and informative with the items contained therein, but we do still need lots more copy from individual estates. It is rather a problem knowing exactly what to include each quarter to provide interesting and informative reading to club leaders and members, for one cannot repeat the same topics too often.

The Annual Conference held on 2nd July at Oxford House was, as always, well attended by club leaders and members. Mrs. C. M. King from the London Council of Social Service was our guest speaker and her topic was Hobbies and Pastimes for the Retired. Mrs. King covered all aspects of hobbies both indoors and out, and the attention of the audience was proof of their interest. We also had a guest panel to answer questions put to them by delegates, and here we proved most definitely that although the body may age, the mind certainly does not. The highlight of the day's events was the concert in the evening, provided by the September Club from Flower House, and what a truly marvellous show it was, thoroughly enjoyed by everyone.

The Olde Tyme Dance held at Dulwich Baths in February was a most glittering affair, dancers being dressed in their finest of evening clothes. Their Worships the Mayor and Mayoress of Southwark honoured us by being present for part of the evening, and although they were unable to stay long, they appeared most interested in our social activities and efforts to help each other. We would like once again to offer our most sincere thanks not only to estates who donated prizes for raffles but to the Borough of Southwark for their extreme generosity to our cause by allowing us to use the hall and its facilities free of charge. The Central Pool Transport Fund is steadily mounting but as so few estates seem to require help from this fund, we shall have to reconsider to what best advantage this money can be used to help the elderly.

Woodberry Down Rose Bowl: This was donated as a memorial trophy to be awarded annually to the winning estate for inter-estate activities for the elderly. We have tried to organise these games, but response has been very poor. Club members seem to prefer the confines of their own halls for games like darts and whist, so with the consent and approval of the donors, this trophy will now be awarded to the winning estate in the Junior Inter-Estate Sports.

Finally, may I add sincere thanks to my fellow committee members for the support during the past year. Particular thanks must go to Miss R. Bush, our secretary, who has most admirably assisted the Chairman through her term of office. The office staff have, as always, been extremely co-operative and have dealt most efficiently with the paper work added to an already mountainous pile.

Thank you all very much indeed.

(SIGNED)


CONFERENCES AND TRAINING

*Annual Conference: Conquering the Concrete Jungle*
This year, due to the increased cost of the Wansfell Conference Centre, our annual conference was based in a London Hotel and was non-residential. It was something in the nature of an experiment to make this Annual Week-end a non-residential event as the tradition of Wansfell has been long established. However, the week-end was attended by over thirty delegates from fifteen affiliated groups and interested organisations and was felt to be successful. Added attractions were the Saturday evening theatre and cinema outings.

The discussions at the conference were as varied and interesting as usual, ranging from the problems of moving onto a new estate to the practical advantages—and disadvantages—of carrying out 'self-surveys'. Some excellent films were shown highlighting differing activities staged by various estates, and these stimulated discussions on the planning of various activities. Our guest speakers were Peter

201

Willmott, Joint Director of the Institute of Community Studies, and Miss B. Wollaston of the Woolwich Ecumenical Project. The conference concluded its discussions by compiling a short list of recommendations to the executive committee. Some of these have been acted upon, others still have to be implemented.

*Study Groups on Community Care:*
At the time of writing last year's report we were in the middle of the Club room courses on Committee procedure. At the time of writing this year, we are holding a course in Community Care, which has been structured with the valuable help and advice of Miss Bell, Lecturer in Applied Social Studies, at the London School of Economics.

Topics discussed at this course have covered a wide field and include such items as the problems of mentally and physically handicapped people, both as individuals and as members of the community; the amenities provided by local and national welfare agencies; and the special difficulties encountered by the deprived child.

The course has not attracted as large an attendance as previous courses on other subjects have done, but this, perhaps is due to its rather specialised nature. However, the measure of its success must, I feel, be judged by the interest and enthusiasm of those members who are attending, and of this there is much evidence. The usefulness of the information received during the discussions cannot be denied —in fact, much of what has been learned has already, at the half-way stage of the course—been put into practice on the estates.

*Courses attended:* Mrs. J. Smith of the Peabody Avenue Association has attended the basic course in voluntary social work run by the London Council of Social Service at Morley College; as a representative of the A.L.H.E. Mr. G. Riches went on a short course at the Overseas Visual Aids Centre and is at present attending a course on Community Development at the Institute of Education, London University.

*Future Plans:* As this is the tenth year of the A.L.H.E., plans are in hand to make the Annual Conference a special event. The conference will be held at Knuston Hall, Northants, from 30th June to 2nd July, and it is hoped will include both interesting discussions and an enjoyable social programme.

Later, during the autumn months, another Club-room course on Committee work will be held. This will be centred in either North or Central London, and will, no doubt, attract groups who are situated in those areas.

(SIGNED)

## THE FINANCE AND POLICY SUB-COMMITTEE

The main business of the Finance and Policy sub-committee for this year has been to evaluate our current aims and objects in order to reassess them in view of our future development plans necessary to meet new needs.

The scope of our work during the ten years we have been in existence has developed into a definite pattern of community work suitable for 'family member' community groups on housing estates. We have helped individual groups with their problems by drawing upon the 'pool of advice' built up by the organisation through its contacts with a large number of groups, of which seventy have affiliated over this period of ten years. Our services are used by groups at all stages of development from embryonic groups who seek our advice and help, e.g. in drawing up their constitution, to more well-established groups who ask us to organise training programmes and help them cope with such complex problems as community care for the mentally subnormal. Alongside our community development work has grown up the supporting programme of community sporting activities, details of which appear in the Inter-Estates Activities Report. This, in broad outline, is the scope of our work at present, but we feel that changing needs challenge us to plan for further expansion.

Our constitution confines our membership to groups within the Inner London Area and under certain circumstances to groups on the periphery of this area. With the creation of the County of Greater London we have been approached by groups and housing authorities in this area to extend geographically our field of activities to allow them to benefit from our experience and services. It is, therefore, recommended that this annual conference considers and, if thought fit, approves the necessary amendment to our constitution to permit our expansion into Greater London. It is proposed that the expansion should take place in stages over a period of time and will be planned so that our resources and finance will not be subjected to undue strain.

We now have to consider the all important question of finance. When our organisation started we were almost entirely dependent upon the London Council of Social Service for our funds. The London Council of Social Service has now generously agreed to help us along the path towards financial independence by making a grant application this year which included our requirements as a separate item. The next stage will be to discuss with the grant-aiding authorities the proposal that we should make separate grant applications in the future.

The Executive Committee proposes to seek approval at this Annual General Meeting for your authority to commence negotiations with the London Council of Social Service, with a view to establishing the financial independence of the Association of London Housing Estates as from 1st April, 1968. A special meeting will be called later in the year to consider and, if thought fit, to approve the necessary resolutions to put this into effect.

(SIGNED)

## THE ORGANISING SECRETARY'S REPORT

It is not only a pleasing but also a healthy sign to know that newly formed associations still wish to become affiliated. This year eight such associations have affiliated and we can now boast seventy-one member groups. However, perhaps we should not let these figures obscure the fact that there are some aspects of associations' problems which we have as yet hardly touched: there are those groups which have been running for a number of years and have developed special problems; those older estates which appear to need associations and yet these are not forthcoming; and there are some areas of London in which we have little or no contacts.

These are not problems which can be solved overnight—we require more knowledge of people's needs, a larger staff, more time for the workers to explore possible lines of work and more contact with other organisations. Since last year we have definitely made steps in these directions—our successful application for increased grant aid will allow us to have three full-time C.D. workers and we have additional office accommodation in which to house them. The purchase of a car will give increased mobility to the Organising Secretary, and our meeting with some members of the London Boroughs Associations has served to strengthen our contacts with the Boroughs. These developments will, it is hoped, be furthered in the coming year.

The A.L.H.E. as an organisation has no authority in terms of the actions of member associations. This being the case it is of particular importance that the A.L.H.E. brings new as well as regular ideas and activities to the attention of member groups.

New events this year have included the Football League, the success of which depended to a great extent on individual team managers and the Management sub-committee. In the League Cup and five-a-side competitions over 120 matches were played and 126 medals and seven trophies were awarded. This is to say nothing of the constructive use to which all the boys concerned were putting their leisure time. The Adventure Week-end for boys organised by the Youth sub-committee was another new idea. Joe Lowney, the Churchill Youth leader, who ran the course said it was one of the best he had ever been on and all the boys were eager for more. Perhaps we can further develop this type of activity.

In trying to tackle the subject of community care in a study group held at the office we may have taken on too much, but though attendance has been small, the discussions have all continued until late in the evening and have served to high-light particular problems facing the mentally ill, physically handicapped and deprived children in the neighbourhood.

The Annual Conference for members of Old People's Clubs is a regular feature in our calendar and one which is always a great success. The Work with the Elderly sub-committee also has strong contacts with other Old People's Associations and no doubt benefits from these contacts.

Finally, a personal note of thanks to Bobbie. If it had not been for Bobbie's kind and sympathetic understandings of the problems facing a new organising secretary, I feel sure my task would have been more difficult. In no small degree the development of the A.L.H.E. has been due to her skill as a community development worker especially in times of great difficulty when we have been without our full complement of staff. It will be a hard gap to fill, but fill it we must if the work is to continue to develop.

(SIGNED)

## SERVICES AVAILABLE TO YOUR ASSOCIATION OR CLUB

1. *Advice*

| | |
|---|---|
| *Free advice* | For committee members and organisers on any problems they might be experiencing. |
| *Free advice* | On starting and running your own youth club. The Association of London Housing Estates employs two full-time youth advisers to help clubs on estates. |
| *Free Legal Advice* | The services are available of a legal adviser for your club if you need the help of a solicitor. |

2. *Direct Services*

| | |
|---|---|
| *Insurance* | At special rates for associations, clubs, club rooms and equipment. |
| *Duplicating* | Duplicating of newsletters, bulletins circulars, announcements to members at *cost price* with no service charge. |
| *Auditor* | The Association can put you in touch with a voluntary auditor who, if given sufficient advance notice, will audit your accounts. |
| *Entertainment* | Bookings can be arranged and information given for the hire of puppet shows for Christmas parties, and other shows for appropriate age groups. |

3. *A Chance to Meet People from Other Estates*

| | |
|---|---|
| *Athletic Sports, Swimming Gala and Table Tennis Leagues* | These are organised annually by the Association for young people. |

| | |
|---|---|
| *Darts and Indoor Games, Cricket League and Football League* | These competitions give you an opportunity to visit other clubs. |
| *Social and Dance* | An annual event attended by estate clubs from all parts of London. |
| *Conferences* | A week-end conference is held where groups on estates exchange helpful information and ideas. Conferences on youth work are held to help those people running clubs. |
| *Clubroom Courses* | These examine the problems of running associations. |

4. *Publications*

| | |
|---|---|
| *Information Sheets* | These are *free* and give information on the duties of secretary, chairman, treasurer, committee procedure, holding an annual meeting, etc. |
| *Conference Reports* | All conferences held by the Association are fully recorded and sent to member groups in booklets. |
| *Broadsheet* | A monthly newsheet containing information about individual associations and the A.L.H.E. |
| *Newsletter* | A quarterly free newsletter *Contact*. |
| *Annual Report* | Detailed information about the year's work of the association. |
| *Membership Fee* | Three guineas per annum. |

WEEKEND CONFERENCES

| Date | Venue | Theme of Conference | Programme: Content | Name and Details of Speaker or Group Leaders |
|---|---|---|---|---|
| 2nd–4th Sept. 1955 | Wansfell Adult College | Committee Procedure and Problems | 1. Welcome to Delegates<br>2. Committee Procedure<br>3. Committee Problems<br>4. Club room Activities<br>5. Publicity<br>6. Looking for Leaders<br>7. Finance<br>8. Fund Raising | R. Clements<br>J. Tilliett<br>General Discussion<br>Mrs. M. A. Smith<br>Miss I. Booker<br>F. S. Milligan<br>B. H. Honeyball<br>B. H. Honeyball |
| 7th–9th Sept. 1956 | Wansfell Adult College | '. . . to bring together representatives from Committees of Housing Estate Groups | 1. Welcome to Delegates<br><br>2. Talking of Teenagers<br>3. Exchange of Information on:<br>(a) Children's Parties<br>(b) A.G.M's.<br>(c) Films<br>4. 'Mock Committee' Meeting: Enacted<br>5. Everyday Life in Holland<br><br>6. 'Old People'<br><br>7. 'Success or Failure—How Do We Judge Our Work?'<br><br>8. Summary and Evaluation | R. Clements, O.B.E., Deputy Secretary, National Council of Social Service.<br>P. Kuenstler and Miss I. Kerner.<br>Discussion.<br><br><br><br>Discussion on 'Mock Committee'.<br>H. J. Barentsz, 'Ons Huis' Community Centre, Amsterdam.<br>Miss D. Halsall, Secretary, Stepney O.P.W. Committee.<br>F. S. Milligan, Secretary, National Federation of Community Associations. |

| Date | Venue | Theme of Conference | Programme: Content | Name and Details of Speaker or Group Leaders |
|---|---|---|---|---|
| 30th–31st March 1957 | Beatrice Webb House | Problems of Organisation | 1. Organisation of an Association | Mrs. M. Smith |
| | | | 2. Youth Work | Mr. Bernard Newman |
| | | | 3. Drama | Mr. F. Sainsbury |
| | | | 4. Old People's Welfare | Mr. R. W. Groundsell |
| | | | 5. Garden Fete | Mr. F. W. Smith |
| | | | 6. Community Organisation in New York | Mr. George Goetschius |
| | | | 7. Service to Groups | Miss I. Booker |
| | | | 8. Summary of Conference | Mr. John Hayes |
| 6th–8th Sept. 1957 | Wansfell Adult College | Breaking Down Apathy | 1. Welcome to Delegates | Mr. J. Hayes |
| | | | 2. The Housing Group and Management Partnership | Mrs. E. Denington, Vice-Chairman, L.C.C. Housing Committee. |
| | | | 3. Making Our Committees Work | F. S. Milligan |
| | | | 4. Keeping in Touch with the Member | J. L. Hayes |
| | | | 5. Relations with Outside Organisations | G. H. Smith |
| | | | 6. Publicity | P. Kuenstler |
| | | | 7. Playgrounds in Stockholm | Miss I. Booker |
| | | | 8. Harlow New Town | P. Kuenstler |

| Date | Venue | Theme of Conference | Programme: Content | Name and Details of Speaker or Group Leaders |
|------|-------|---------------------|--------------------|---------------------------------------------|
| 5th–7th Sept. 1958 | Wansfell Adult College | New Angles on Our Work | 1. Welcome to Delegates<br>2. The Changing Community Life of London<br><br>3. The Medical Officer of Health<br><br><br>4. The Lawyer – His Place in the Community<br>5. The Job of the Architect<br>6. The Police and the Citizen – Their Co-operation | W. Johannes<br>Rev. St. J. B. Groser, Warden, Royal Foundation of St. Katharine, Stepney.<br>Dr. John Kershaw, M.D, B.S., D.P.H., M.O.H. Borough of Colchester.<br>A. L. Diamond, Legal Adviser to the Standing Conference.<br>Oliver Cox, Architect, L.C.C.<br>An Inspector of the Metropolitan Police. |
| 18th–20th Sept. 1959 | Wansfell Adult College | Accent on Youth | 1. The Problems of Youth<br>2. What Makes the Adolescent Tick?<br>3. What is Being Done?<br>4. Discussion 'Brains Trust'<br><br>5. The needs of young people: Adult attitudes – Leadership – Recommendations to Committees on Estates – Recommendations to the Standing Conference | P. Duke<br>R. C. Wright<br><br>P. Winterforde-Young, Duke, Irey, Fyrel, Winterforde-Young, Mrs. Steel<br>Summary and Discussion |

| Date | Venue | Theme of Conference | Programme: Content | Name and Details of Speaker or Group Leaders |
|---|---|---|---|---|
| 2nd–4th Sept. 1960 | Wansfell Adult College | Widening the Programme | 1. Introduction to Conference<br>2. Seeing Is Believing<br>3. Central Council of Physical Recreation<br>4. 'I Want to Go to School': the N.U.T. Film on Children at School<br>5. The Berrymoor Puppets<br>6. What the Local Authority Has to Offer | Mr. J. L. Hayes<br>Mrs. Abercrombie<br>Film Slides.<br><br><br><br>Mr. Aidalberry<br>Mr. Honeyball |
| 9th–10th Sept. 1961 | Wansfell Adult College | Taking It From Here | 1. Keeping in Touch with the Member<br>2. Committee Procedure<br>3. Finance<br>4. Publicity | J. Hayes<br><br>P. Kuenstler<br>D. Fifer<br>S. Clements |

| Date | Venue | Theme of Conference | Programme: Content | Name and Details of Speaker or Group Leaders |
|---|---|---|---|---|
| 7th–9th Sept. 1962 | Wansfell Adult College | The Estate as a Community | 1. Welcome to Delegates | Mr. E. W. Dawes, Faylands Estate<br>Miss I Booker |
| | | | 2. The Estate as a Community<br>3. Housing Management | Mr. R. Randall, L.C.C. Eastern District Officer |
| | | | 4. The Job of the Association on the Estate | Mr. W. W. G. Townsend, Argyle Estate. |
| | | | 5. The Point of View of Youth | Mr. J. Robbins and Mr. K. Carter, Avery Hill; Miss C. Murphy and Mr. A. Reed, Brooklands Park. |
| | | | 6. The Older Person's Point of View | Mrs. Perkins, Flower House; Mr. and Mrs. Jones, Woodberry Down; Mrs. Torp Newman, Hallfield. |
| | | | 7. The Estate as Part of the Neighbourhood | Mr. W. R. Johannes, Clapham Park. |
| | | | 8. General Discussion and Summing Up. | Mr. J. L. Hayes, Churchill Gardens. |
| 6th–8th Sept. 1963 | Wansfell Adult College | Good Neighbours | 1. Neighbourhood and Community Problems | Miss M. J. Wood, Citizen's Advice Officer, London Council of Social Service. |
| | | | 2. The Importance of Neighbourhood Foster Care for Children | Miss B. Drake, Children's Officer, L.C.C. (Area V) |
| | | | 3. Special Services for the Elderly | Mrs. J. Smith, Peabody Estate Tenants' Association. |
| | | | 4. General Welfare Services on the Estate | R. Prewer, Esq., Secretary, Churchill Gardens Tenants' Association. |

| Date | Venue | Theme of Conference | Programme: Content | Name and Details of Speaker or Group Leaders |
|---|---|---|---|---|
| 4th–6th Sept. 1964 | Wansfell Adult College | 'Planning for Living on a Housing Estate' | 1. Two films on The City and Problems of Urban Life, by Lewis Mumford, Architect and Town Planner<br>2. Planning a housing estate. New housing development in Oldham used as an example<br>3. Planning from the housing management point of view<br>4. 'Playground provision on Estates.' Illustrated with coloured slides showing what is being done in other countries | Film.<br><br>Mr. Terence O'Toole, Architect, Ministry of Housing & Local Government.<br>Miss M. Empson, Adviser on Housing Management to the Ministry of Housing and Local Government.<br>Mrs. M. Smith, Community Development Officer, London Council of Social Service. |
| 3rd–5th Sept. 1965 | Theydon Bois, Essex | 'Public Relations' | 1. 'Communications.' Introduction to the problem of improving communications on housing estates.<br>2. 'Public Relations in Local Government'<br>3. Discussion Groups on:<br>(a) young people helping in the activities of the association<br>(b) the different problems of associations with Community Halls, and those without;<br>(c) what do Tenants gain from an association? | Mr. Brian Groombridge, Deputy Secretary of the National Institute of Education.<br>Mr. Arthur Taffs, Public Relations Officer, Lewisham<br>Arranged by Miss Ilys Booker, formerly Organising Secretary of the A.L.H.E. |

| Date | Venue | Theme of Conference | Programme: Content | Name and Details of Speaker of Group Leaders |
|---|---|---|---|---|
| 14th–16th Oct. 1966 | Kenilworth Hotel, London | 'Conquering the Concrete Jungle – Study in a Community's Development' | 1. 'Development of Community on a Housing Estate' | Mr. Peter Wilmott, Joint Director of the Institute of Community Studies. |
| | | | 2. Discussion Groups on 'Moving In – The Expectations – The First Steps.' | Arranged by Miss Bobbie Montford, A.L.H.E. |
| | | | 3. 'Simple Methods of Self-Survey' | Miss B. W. Woollaston, sociologist on Woolwich-ERITH New Town project. |
| | | | 4. 'Amenities and the Neighbourhood' | Arranged by Graham Riches, A.L.H.E. |
| | | | 5. 'Films of Activities of Tenants' Associations' | Loaned by Poynders Gdns., Brandon and Locksley estates. |
| | | | 6. Summing up and Recommendations | Under the Chairmanship of Mr. W. R. Johannes, J.P. from Clapham Park Estate. |
| 30th June 2nd July 1967 | Knuston Hall, Irchester, Northants. | 'Looking Back – Looking Ahead' | 1. 'Looking Back' | Miss Ilys Booker, first Organising Secretary, A.L.H.E. |
| | | | 2. 'Do-It-Yourself Social Work or Paid Indigenous Local Leaders' | Mr David Jones, O.B.E. of the National Institute of Social Work Training. |
| | | | 3. 'Family Holiday Conference in the Netherlands' | Mr. G. Beun of the Dutch Folk High Schools. |
| | | | 4. 'Looking Ahead' | Mr. Graham Riches, O.S. of the A.L.H.E. |
| | | | 5. Summing Up and Recommendations | Led by Mrs. R. Arber, Chairman of the Conferences and Training sub-committee. |

# Appendix 2

Suggested material for 'Community Behaviour' content of a Community Work Course.

In an attempt to improve the understanding of field work, to develop the necessary skills to help colleagues and students to understand what the work is about, and the context in which the service is offered, the workers came to see the need for a definite, if tentative, frame of reference. This frame of reference about community and community behaviour is developed in the in-service training paper offered here as the suggested 'core' of a community work training course (see page 164 of Chapter VII).

Social case-work courses have as their core subjects human growth and behaviour and the social and psychosexual development of individuals; social group work courses have group dynamics; community work courses might well have the community process or community behaviour.

Such a core subject in a community work course would have to:

Explore some of the elements in the field-work situation as separate social units and processes (groups, institutions, internal and external relations within and between groups and institutions). Indicate the changing but recognisable patterns made by the different elements and processes. Emphasise in the community development part of the course the position of the autonomous community group within the pattern of social interaction. Show its needs, problems and the points at which service might be offered, or, where community organisation was being studied, the position of social welfare agencies.

Provide the terms of reference within which to carry on the discussion among the workers in the field, colleagues in other forms of social work, and within and between the groups and institutions themselves.

Show how thinking in this way can help to clarify the role of the worker and the agency and suggest the most appropriate methods and behaviour.

The material that follows was not specifically organised for a formal teaching situation and would have to be adapted (if seen as appropriate) not only to make it relevant to the content of other courses (case-work, group work and social administration) but to the needs and circumstances of students.

## The Nature of Community

The word *community* has been used in a number of ways—the housing estate community, the adjacent community, the wider community and the community group. The phrase 'community development' has been used to describe a particular approach and method of work. It is hoped that the context has to some extent made clear the various uses of the word *community:* it is now proposed to look more closely at the meaning.

The scientific literature itself—sociology and social psychology— does not offer the social worker any accepted definition that could make a point of departure. Nor does it offer detailed terms of reference for observation and discussion in this area of social work. But since some general, even if tentative, agreement is necessary about the content of the word *community* as used here, it is proposed to consider first the variety of emphases that exists in the definition of community as a social unit; secondly, to consider the factors that a social worker in a particular community might observe and record, in order to construct a working definition of the actual processes going on in the community which he will be attempting to affect.

The focus of attention will be on the autonomous community group as an element within a wider community.

## A Variety of Emphases

Abstract definitions of community abound, and some choice must be made among them in relation to the task to be accomplished if usage is to be consistent and relevant.

(a) *Community as an ethnic, religious, or professional category.* The concept of community is often used to designate an ethnic, religious, or similar general category within a larger social unit, as in the phrase 'the West Indian community in London' or 'the Catholic community in Liverpool' or 'the academic community in Glasgow'. By extension it is used in the same sense to designate professional or vocational groupings such as the medical, legal or artistic community in a local setting or within a whole society. This general usage emphasises one or several of the following components: shared values and interests, shared skills and techniques, shared organisational forms, shared historical background, and often a shared position in society, either in the local community or in the national society.

(b) A second usage refers to the *geographical area*, the territory shared by the residents in which they 'do and are things together', i.e. the local community, the village, the town, neighbourhoods within a city. This usage tends to emphasise the physical aspects of the community: the distance of the village from the nearest town or large city; the suburban community on the edge of a giant conurbation; the neighbourhood within a large city in relation to the city centre. There are also the physical resources: good soil, mineral deposits, the plan or layout of the streets and the division of the city into functional areas: the business areas, the manufacturing estate, the old slum areas, the new suburban estates, the recreational area in the heart of town, or the shopping area. This usage tends to see the geographical character and locality as the essential factor in the concept.

(c) A third usage tends to emphasise the community as *a social or cultural phenomenon*, and to discuss it in terms of the social interaction between persons, groups, and social institutions within a fairly homogeneous social and cultural setting.

### Elements and Processes

*Elements.* Each of the above usages is legitimate in itself and each is representative of aspects of social reality that need to be considered. No one usage is wholly exclusive of any other, and none is adequate. For our purpose, ingredients from all three definitions are essential to an adequate understanding of the problems faced in the field and of the kind of solutions chosen in attempts to resolve them. The following is a list of elements and processes which are generally considered to be necessary to any concept of community. They suggest the terms of reference necessary for the social worker.

(a) *Individuals, groups and social institutions.* A community is an established but changing pattern of association between persons, groups, and social institutions.

(b) *Age, occupation and interest groups.* A community covers a wide variety of age, occupation and interest groups.

(c) *Needs, values and resources.* Communities develop institutional forms organised in an attempt to fulfil the needs of the persons and groups of which the community is composed. This fulfilling of needs is affected by the values held and the resources available.

(d) *Traditions, processes and procedures.* The expression and recognition of need, as well as the processes by which they are fulfilled, are affected by the traditions prevalent in the community and the processes and procedures thought to be in keeping with those traditions.

(e) *Status, power, responsibility and privilege.* The association between persons, groups and social institutions within a community gives rise to a 'status system' which allocates and regulates the possession and exercise of power. It also gives rise to the right to make decisions and so allocates responsibility and privilege.

(f) *Structure and function.* This agreed relation between responsibility and privilege, which in turn regulates the status system and

the possession and exercise of power within the community, describes the structure and function of the various elements in community life and relates each to the others, so as to make a recognisable system both to the participants and the outside observer.
(g) *Location, size and age*. This recognisable system is located in a
particular place, and is affected by both its size and its age. The
community does not exist as a social form separate from the
smaller unit that it includes—for instance the neighbourhood; nor
from the larger units to which it is related—for instance the region
and the nation.

*Processes*. Obviously, the elements listed above are not separate or
isolated parts of a static social institution, but inter-related, interacting aspects of the whole. Perhaps the simplest way to suggest this
interaction is by a description of the social processes which, for the
purpose of this discussion, take place at all points and at all times
within the system.
(a) *Social interaction*. The achievement of any aim within the
system, from the simplest to the most complicated, requires that
the person, group or social institution seeking the fulfilment of
that aim must attempt in some way to modify the existing situation. Any attempt at modification makes for a continuously
changing pattern of association between persons, groups and
institutions which make up the system.
(b) *Social control*. One form of interaction of interest to us here is
social control. This occurs when one, or several, of the established
institutions in the community attempt to influence the behaviour
of persons, groups or other social instutitions to ensure that
behaviour meets the norms set down for such behaviour by the
institution attempting to exercise the control.
(c) *Social conflict*. This occurs when the various parties within a
system disagree over attempts to change the system, although
agreement may ultimately be achieved out of the conflict.
(d) *Social change*. The community situation described in this way
is therefore composed of different persons, groups and institutions
interacting and associating, attempting to fulfil needs and influence
the behaviour of others (social control), and producing differences
and difficulties (social conflict). This interaction produces social
change.

## The Essentials of Community

The elements and processes which make up the essentials of any
definition of community for the purpose of community work are
therefore:
(a) *Territorial*. The definition must include a recognition of the
geographic factor, both in terms of specific area occupied and in
relation to other territorial and social units.
(b) *Social interaction*. There are four levels of social interaction:
within the individual; between persons; within and between

217

groups, and within and between social institutions. Any adequate definition of community for the purposes of community work must emphasise this social interaction.

(c) *The cultural apparatus*. The definition must include the recognition of shared values, standards, traditions, forms of behaviour and other cultural elements.

Both the geographic and social factors must be combined to make a sufficiently cohesive whole for the participants to experience membership, and for the observer to be able to recognise the separateness of a particular social unit as a community.

Any definition must also provide the terms of reference for a discussion of community behaviour—that is, why and how things happen in a given community—and be a guide to how to set about getting relevant factual information about a particular community to aid the worker or the agency in offering the service.

*Summary*

Within the context of community work a community can be said to be a specific geographic and social area in which social interaction takes place on four levels (intra-personal, inter-personal, etc.) The community has a function and structure, related in different ways to the physical resources and the social institutions of the area. Community behaviour is characterised by conflict and co-operation, accommodation and assimilation, and other social processes, which condition the interaction of the different elements in their attempts to satisfy needs and actualise values. This interaction produces constant changes within the system, which when taken all together, are referred to as 'the community process'. This cumulative interacting system can be seen both by participants and outside observers to be a separate entity. It is related to similar social units and to the city, county, region, nation and state, and as a result of its own internal behaviour and external relationships, has a structure that distributes responsibility and privilege, allots status, and offers to and requires service from other social units inside and outside the system.

This working definition covers most of the points essential to the understanding and use of the word when discussing community development as a method of social work. This is in so far as it:

(a) Describes something of the complex set of circumstances within which the community group comes into being, exists, develops and works, and which condition its needs, the resources available to it, its methods of work, and the content of its programme. This is necessary and helpful to the worker in that it prevents his seeing the community group as an isolated social unit totally unrelated to the wider pattern of community life, and suggests the origins of some of the group's problems as well as the limitations and potentials of its work.

(b) Emphasises the dynamic and ever-changing nature of community life, and so of the community group which is a part of that process—an emphasis which is necessary and useful to the worker in recognising and using the changes that take place in community and group life. This enables him to help the group to accomplish its task.

(c) Is useful as a working definition of community in that it suggests the community as a system of 'natural events' (social interaction) through which the worker may help the group. This is helpful to the worker as it defines his role in terms of intervening in the community process and in the life of the community group which is part of that process, in order to help the group in its work.

Of course, what has been said here can only have meaning in the field-work process in relation to the *specific events* in the life of a *particular community group* as observed and interpreted by *a community worker*. But this description of the community process is sufficient to suggest that in order to intervene effectively and efficiently in the community process in the interest of the group, the worker and the agency need an approach and method of work dependent on particular knowledge, skills and techniques. This is the community development approach and method.

*The Group Process:—*

We have been discussing throughout this report a social unit we have called the community group, representing a small community in its own right, within the wider community system. For an adequate understanding of the work it is necessary to describe groups and their characteristic behaviour in more detail.

*What is a group?*

For the purposes of this discussion a group can be defined as two or more people between whom there is an established pattern of psychological and social interaction, which is recognised as an entity by its members and usually by others because of its particular type of collective behaviour.

*The kind of groups*

Groups can be primary and secondary; friendship and interest; simple and complex; formal and informal.

> *Primary and Secondary Groups.* Primary groups are those in which the association between the members is constant and intensive, as in a family. Secondary groups are those in which the association by comparison with the family is less constant and less intensive, for example a sports group, a work group, or a committee. In the primary group the relations between the members are close, personal, and comparatively lasting, and tend to satisfy a variety of basic needs, physical, psychological and social. In the secondary group the relations between members are less close, not as deeply personal, and not as stable nor as long-lasting as those in the primary group.

219

*Friendship and Interest Groups.* Secondary groups can be of several different kinds. Friendship groups are characterised by the fact that the relations between members come into being and are based on personal factors, likes and dislikes. Interest groups come into being in order to provide a means of expression and achievement to members through a particular common interest. Friendship groups are usually made up of members who share a common social background and who live in the same geographical area and attend the same school or work for the same employer. Interest or activity groups may have members from different social backgrounds or different geographical areas, drawn together in pursuit of special interest. Activity groups are most often task centred, organised around activities for a stated purpose, whereas friendship groups are often more spontaneous in their choice of activity.

*Simple and Complex.* Groups of either type vary in their complexity. A primary group may be a simple two-person family group—man and wife, or an extended family—man, wife and children, grandparents and their children, uncles or cousins. The composition will affect the variety of services the group offers its members, and so affect the experience of membership. In the same way, the secondary group may be a group of three friends meeting occasionally at the local pub, taking holidays together and going off for sporting events at more or less regular intervals, or it may be a complex secondary group within a factory which defines itself not in relation to its members' needs and the task to be accomplished, but in relation to those above (the management) and those below (the unskilled workers), and horizontally in relation to the trade union to which the group is affiliated. In a complex secondary group of this kind the organisation and structure of the group will affect both the quality and variety of experience it offers to the members, as well as the community of which it is a part.

*Formal and Informal Groups.* Groups vary from a high degree of organisation and formality to a considerable degree of informality. The formal group may have agreed procedures of making decisions and resolving conflict, and often specific membership requirements. There is sometimes an elaborate pattern of responsibility and privilege, based on length of membership, age of member, difference in skill, or responsibility assigned by majority decision. The informal group is likely to have more mobility within it, to be less highly organised and to have fewer set procedures. It will also be more spontaneous in its assessment of responsibility and privileges, and members will be free to interchange roles.

## Relations within Groups

Each of the categories of groups mentioned above can be seen to have an internal life of its own, characteristics of which the worker will, upon examination, find to include:

*Acceptance and Rejection.* In every group, one or another of the members will accept or reject one another in varying degrees. In any number of ways these feelings may be reciprocated or withheld. This acceptance or rejection may take place over just one incident or time span, or over a much longer period. Most groups that meet often and offer opportunities for intensive inter-personal relationships in one way or another find ways of handling the acceptance and rejection pattern without outside help. If the task is impeded by strong feelings, as is often the case in an interest or activity group, either the group itself will intervene by reference to 'the rules' through an official, perhaps the chairman of the committee, or by reference to an outsider—the teacher, or the club leader, or even the police.

*Conflict and Co-operation.* All the groups have to resolve conflict as part of their internal day-to-day behaviour. Conflict may arise because of the acceptance or rejection of one person by another, or because common agreement cannot be reached about what is to be done or the method to be used. In primary groups like the family, conflict is usually resolved informally without recourse to set rules or outside authority. This also applies to friendship groups and other informal secondary groups, but as secondary groups become more complex and formal they develop rules and regulations to govern choices and decisions, to resolve conflict and to guide the process of resolution. A committee might vote, refer the matter to a special sub-committee for further consideration, send the matter back to a lower committee to be reformulated, or refer it to a higher committee for advice and consent.

*Roles and Ranking.* Every group has to some extent either accepted the roles that some of its participants wish to play, or have assigned them. In the primary group like the family, the roles are assigned and accepted through contact with traditions in the larger society, often reinforced by law as in the case of marriage. In a secondary group, knowledge or skill or a special talent might give a person a special role in the group. In others the roles might be set by the group, for example, as chairman, secretary, or treasurer. As well as offering and allowing the acceptance of roles, the group evolves a ranking or stated system of its own which may be based on age, function, personality, or any other criterion, depending upon the nature and interests of the group.

*Awareness of belonging.* Groups of the kind we have been discussing here are characterised as well by various degrees of awareness of belonging. One aspect of this is the group loyalty or *esprit de corps* which is elicited from members. This sense of belonging is felt by the members and is visible to the outside observer.

Taken together, these and other characteristics of the internal behaviour of groups are called the *group process*, which refers to the changes in internal relationships between members, and which affects both the development of the group and the accomplishment of the task.

### Relations between Groups

In a community setting, no group is a completely isolated social unit. Groups of all kinds and at all stages of their development have relations with other groups, some similar in composition, some different. Relations between groups are affected by several factors, the most important of which are:

*Reason for Relationship*—as seen by each of the participating groups, to get something, to give something, to achieve status in relation to other groups, for co-operative action, or simply because one or another group is a 'natural' element in the social environment, making geographical proximity the basis for relationship.

*Differences and Similarities*—in size of membership, nature of origin, of indigenous leadership, in social attitudes and class origins, and in aims and methods of work.

*Status within the System*—the status of each group within the community system affects relationships, since it helps to decide how each group ranks the other.

*Limitations and Potentials*—the human and financial resources available to each group, its ability to achieve its aims, to remain independent, to elicit respect—these factors also affect what each group brings to its relation with other groups.

The process by which inter-group action takes place can be described in the same categories as have been used for the description of relations within the group, namely, acceptance and rejection, conflict and co-operation, roles and ranking, awareness of relationship between groups.

In a particular field-work situation the worker must be as aware of the relationships between groups as he is of the relations within the group with which he is working, since the nature and content of the relations between groups in part condition the needs of the group, the resources available and its internal behaviour, and so the performance of its task.

The relationships between groups are as much a factor in the field-work situation as relations within the group itself.

This kind of information about groups and group behaviour is necessary and useful to the worker, since the community group in any given community setting, and not the individual member or the larger social institution, is both the point of contact and the basis of operation in community development practice.

*Social Institutions*

As was pointed out in the discussion of the community process and groups and group behaviour, the community group maintains on-going relations with other social units in the community. One kind of social unit with which groups are in constant contact and which influences their behaviour is the social institution.

*Definition.* The definitions of a social institution are as varied as definitions of community.

For the purpose of this discussion, the phrase social institution is taken to mean an established complex of inter-related and organised behaviour through which social control is exercised, and by means of which accepted social values are realised.

Using this definition it is possible to speak of social institutions as being both general and specific. By 'general' we refer to social institutions as they seek to realise a more or less accepted value throughout the whole of a given society—the social institution of the family, the state, religion, education, commerce. 'Specific' refers to the institutional forms which each takes in a particular social situation, e.g. religion (the local church); education (the local school); and the state (national and local government).

Particular social institutions are the concern here, because it is the actual presence and behaviour of social institutions in any given community that affects the behaviour and work of the community group, and so the work of the field worker and the service he offers.

*Characteristics.* Most specific local social institutions can be seen to have a particular function—the school to educate, the cleansing department to collect refuse and keep the drains clear. A local institution is a particular structure with a head or a director, and with officers and staff who have been assigned responsibilities. It has particular laws, processes, procedures and traditions, a developed hierarchy with a distribution of privileges and responsibilities, a building, offices, a particular programme of service (to the public or to other institutions), specific hours during which the service is given, and specific conditions attached to the giving of the service.

*Behaviour.* Each of these characteristics contributes to the establishing of a particular pattern of institutional behaviour which is of interest here on several counts:

(a) Because social institutions tend to define social problems in relation to their stated aims and objectives: juvenile delinquency, for instance, is seen mainly as an educational, medical, religious, or law enforcement problem, depending upon the institutional frame of reference used to define the problem. In consequence, the solution of the problem so defined is seen in relation to the traditional pattern of service offered by the institution.

(b) Institutions, having themselves set the conditions of service

223

partly in relation to the internal needs of the institution, tend to assume that the conditions of giving service are reasonable and appropriate, and to put the burden of proof that they are not, on the receiving party.

(c) Institutions with established ways of doing things, established relations with other, sometimes powerful institutions in the community, and with comparatively large resources at their disposal, tend to become the dominant partner in any relationship with small and less powerful units and to attempt to enforce their view of what is right and necessary.

(d) Institutions tend to develop a special language to define and discuss their service, and to use this language in internal communication, in communication with other established bodies, and in their relations with community groups and the general public.

*Relations with groups.* Of course, not every aspect of institutional behaviour is conditioned by the characteristics discussed here. Taken together, these characteristics of institutional behaviour affect the work of the community group in three ways:

(a) They tend to threaten its independence and its power of self-determination, that is, its autonomy.

(b) They tend to define too narrowly the sphere within which it should be or is allowed to operate, and so deprive it of the experience and often the resources necessary to the accomplishment of its task.

(c) Institutions in behaving in this way affect both the internal and external behaviour of the groups.

To sum up, the presence and behaviour of social institutions are relevant both to the community group and to the field worker. The relations between the community group and the relevant institutions to some extent determine the ability of the group to achieve its aims. For these reasons the worker must keep in mind both in observation and in practice:

(i)   That groups within the community are served by institutions within the community in which they exist;

(ii)  That groups give service to the social institutions within the community of which they are members;

(iii) Institutions in a community might give or might withhold status, resources, recognition or advice to any one group;

(iv)  Possible conflict between social institutions might well affect the service that a social institution was able or willing to offer to the groups with which it came into contact;

(v)   Each social institution has values, standards, traditions, processes and procedures that it feels to be 'right and proper' and which will affect the service it offers and the way in which it offers it.

The community worker will be particularly concerned to note the relations between the various social welfare bodies and how these relations affect the services offered to the community group with which he is in contact.

224

*The Community Group in an Urban Environment*

1. The autonomous community group conforms to the definition of a group as a number of people between whom there is a pattern of psychological and social interaction, which is recognised as an entity by its members and by others because of its particular collective behaviour.

2. As a group its characteristics are those of a secondary group, often with some primary group characteristics (intensive personal relations); of an interest group (with strong friendship content); of a simple group (organisation) often with complex structure (committee, interest and activity groups, sub-groups within the membership, etc.); of a formal group (organised with a constitution) often working informally, depending upon the size of the group, the stage of its development, etc.

3. As a group it has both a definite structure and a definite function:

Function—to serve the membership and community, carry on activities, raise funds, find and train leadership.

Structure—characterised by an elected committee, definite responsibilities of committee and officers, delegated responsibilities of activity volunteers, democratic procedure with elections and accountability to membership.

4. It has a recognised pattern of internal relations conditioned by all the above (the kind of group, its structure and function) and determined by the behaviour of participants and the group itself.

5. It is part of a community system, and so has external relations with other groups and social institutions as well as with the larger community itself, in order to give or receive services, to interpret its work or needs, to achieve recognition or status.

6. It is autonomous in so far as it is self-programming, deciding its objectives and methods of achieving them, finding the necessary resources from within the group and its immediate social environment. It is usually staffed and operated entirely by volunteer members of the group and is seen as independent (autonomous) by both members and outsiders.

7. As such it has special needs, not all of which can be met by the group itself, and therefore the group has to seek outside help.

8. The kind of help sought by a group gives rise to the service and decides the role of the worker offering it, as well as that of the agency sponsoring the service.

9. The problem of offering the service gives rise to the use of a particular method devised to meet the needs of this particular kind of group. The method is community development.

10. The approach and method of community development require specialist skills and techniques which differentiate it from casework, group work, and community organisation, as methods of social work.

The knowledge and understanding that can be gained from an analytical study of community is a vital part of the equipment of the community development worker. From the recognition and use of the elements we have discussed—group, institutional and community behaviour as they interact and condition field-work events—the worker and the group learn to create an environment in which the task of the group can be more easily accomplished. The understanding and use of the field-work process, conceptualised in the terms suggested here, make it possible to make sense of field-work events, and enable the worker and the agency, and later the community group itself, to plan their endeavours and to find the points at which processes and procedures need to be modified and field-work practice improved. It also becomes possible to improve communication and interpretation between field workers, colleagues, related agencies and the groups themselves, and so to provide a more ordered form of discourse for the whole enterprise.

# ANNOTATED BIBLIOGRAPHY

The author has used as basic texts ten books and three reports.

| | | |
|---|---|---|
| Anderson, Niels | *The Urban Community* | Routledge & Kegan Paul, London, 1960 |
| Biddle, William and Loureide | *The Community Development Process* | Holt, Rienhart and Winston, Inc., New York, 1956 |
| Bracey, H. E. | *Neighbours on Housing Estates and Subdivision in England and U.S.A.* | Routledge & Kegan Paul, London, 1964 |
| Friedlander, Walter A. | *Concepts and Methods of Social Work* | Prentice, Hall, Inc., New Jersey, U.S.A., 1958 |
| Jefferys, Margot | *An Anatomy of the Social Services* | Michael Joseph London, 1965 |
| Klein, Josephine | *Working with Groups* | Hutchinson University Library, London, 1966 |
| Knowles, Malcolm S. | *Informal Adult Education* | Association Press New York, 1961 |
| Mann, Peter H. | *An Approach to Urban Sociology* | Routledge & Kegan Paul, London, 1965 |
| Marsh, David (ed.) | *An Introduction to the Study of Social Administration* | |
| Rowes, Rosemary (ed.) | *Housing Management* | Sir Isaac Pitman & Sons, Ltd., London, 1959 |

The three reports are:

| | | |
|---|---|---|
| Nicholson, J. H. | 'New Communities in Britain' | National Council of Social Service, Inc. 26, Bedford Square, W.C.1. 1961 |
| | 'Training for Social Work: Third International Survey' | United Nations, Dept. of Economic and Social Affairs, New York, 1958 |
| | 'Report on Working Party on Social Workers in Local Authority, Health and Welfare Services' | Ministry of Health, H.M.S.O., London, 1959 |

TOPIC: SOCIAL WORK
*Text:* Anderson, Niels: *The Urban Community*

| Item | Whole Book | Chapter | Pages |
|---|---|---|---|
| 1. Urbanism and the Family | | XI | 263–294 |
| 2. Welfare in the Modern Community | | XVI | 403–428 |
| 3. Urbanism and Resource Control | | XVIII | 457–486 |

*Text:* Biddle, William and Loureide: *The Community Development Process*

| Item | Whole Book | Chapter | Pages |
|---|---|---|---|
| General Discussion | X | | |
| 1. An Urban Project | | III | 34–57 |
| 2. Intention and Outcome | | IV | 58–75 |
| 3. Definitions | | V | 76–87 |
| 4. The Basic Nucleus | | VI | 88–107 |

227

*Text:* Friedlander: *Concepts and Methods of Social Work*

| Item | Whole Book | Chapter | Pages |
|---|---|---|---|
| General Discussion | X | | |
| 1. Generic Principles of Social Work | | I | 7–10 |
| 2. Theory of Group Work Method | | III | 131–152 |
| 3. Social Community Organisation Methods and Processes | | IV | 201–278 |
| 4. Social Welfare, Administration and Research | | V | 283–287 |

*Text:* Jefferys, Margot: *An Anatomy of the Social Services*

| Item | Whole Book | Chapter | Pages |
|---|---|---|---|
| General Discussion | X | | |
| 1. Health and Welfare Services | | II | 49–131 |
| 2. Education, Child Care, Housing and Law Enforcement | | III | 132–211 |
| 3. Central Government Services | | IV | 212–247 |

*Text:* Marsh, David: *An Introduction to the Study of Social Administration*

| Item | Whole Book | Chapter | Pages |
|---|---|---|---|
| General Discussion | X | | |
| 1. The Growth in Development of the Social Services in the Welfare State | | I | 18–44 |
| 2. Social Provision organised on a Functional Basis | | II | 45–136 |
| 3. Social Provision to Meet Special Needs | | III | 137–208 |
| 4. Policy, Administration and Personnel | | IV | 209–239 |

*Text: Training for Social Work; Third International Survey, United Nations*

| Item | Whole Book | Chapter | Pages |
|---|---|---|---|
| General Discussion | X | | |
| 1. Current Trends in Training for Social Work | | I | 7–34 |
| 2. The Nature of Social Work | | II | 34–57 |
| 3. Community Development and Social Work | | IV | 74–101 |
| 4. The Content of Training for Social Work (Group Relations, Group Work, Community Organisation and Administration) | | XI | 227–249 |

*Text: Report of Working Party on Social Workers*

| Item | Whole Book | Chapter | Pages |
|---|---|---|---|
| General Discussion | X | | |
| 1. The Service within the terms of reference: Historical and General | | I | 186–318 |
| 2. The General Purpose Social Worker: Patterns of Future Development | | VI | 641–735 |
| 3. The Contribution of Voluntary Organisations and Workers | | XI | 1035–1037 |
| 4. Co-operation, Co-ordination and Teamwork | | XII | 1068–1107 |

TOPIC: THE URBAN COMMUNITY
*Text:* Anderson, Niels: *The Urban Community*

| Item | Whole Book | Chapter | Pages |
|---|---|---|---|
| General Discussion | X | | |
| 1. Urbanism is a Way of Life | | I | 1–23 |
| 2. The Nature of Community | | II | 24–86 |
| 3. Community Location and Space Occupancy | | V | 105–128 |
| 4. Urbanism and Population Phenomena | | VI | 129–145 |
| 5. Collective Community Behaviour | | IX | 207–224 |
| 6. How Communities Get Things Done | | XII | 295–320 |

*Text:* Biddle, William and Loureide: *The Community Development Process*

| Item | Whole Book | Chapter | Pages |
|---|---|---|---|
| | X | | |
| 1. The Larger Nucleus | | VII | 108–126 |
| 2. Microprocess in the midst of Macroprocess | | IX | 146–159 |

*Text:* Bracey, H. E.: *Neighbours on Housing Estates*

| Item | Whole Book | Chapter | Pages |
|---|---|---|---|
| General Discussion | X | | |
| 1. Families on the Move | | II | 16–27 |
| 2. Neighbour Appraisal after Occupation | | IV | 55–73 |
| 3. Neighbouring | | V | 74–92 |
| 4. Children and Teenagers | | IX | 126–145 |
| 5. Adult Social Organisation | | XI | 163–180 |

*Text:* Mann, Peter H.: *An Approach to Urban Sociology*

| Item | Whole Book | Chapter | Pages |
|---|---|---|---|
| General Discussion | X | | |
| 1. Descriptive Comparison of Rural and Urban | | II | 4–27 |
| 2. Rural-Urban Comparison: A Quantitative Approach | | III | 28–68 |
| 3. Urban Society | | IV | 69–114 |
| 4. Focus on Neighbourhood | | VI | 149–182 |

*Text:* Nicholson, J. H.: *New Communities in Britain*

| Item | Whole Book | Chapter | Pages |
|---|---|---|---|
| 1. Urban Development | | VII | 103–121 |
| 2. New Communities Compared | | VIII | 122–125 |
| 3. Community and Leadership | | IX | 146–171 |

TOPIC: HOUSING
*Text:* Anderson, Niels: *The Urban Community*

| Item | Whole Book | Chapter | Pages |
|---|---|---|---|
| 1. Urbanism and Resource Control | | XVIII | 457–486 |

*Text:* Jefferys, Margot: *An Anatomy of the Social Services*

| Item | Whole Book | Chapter | Pages |
|---|---|---|---|
| 1. Social Welfare Work by Housing Departments | | XIV | 199–211 |

*Text:* Mann, Peter H.: *An Approach to Urban Sociology*

| Item | Whole Book | Chapter | Pages |
|---|---|---|---|
| 1. The Control of Urban Development | | V | 115–148 |

*Text:* Rowes, R. J.: *Housing Management*

| Item | Whole Book | Chapter | Pages |
|---|---|---|---|
| 1. The Staff of the Housing Department | | III | 32–50 |
| 2. Rent Collection and Arrears | | VII | 95–109 |
| 3. Welfare Work in Housing Management | | VIII | 110–124 |
| 4. Supervision on Estates | | IX | 125–135 |
| 5. Maintenance and Repairs | | X | 136–158 |

*Text:* Nicholson, J. H.: *New Communities in Britain*

| Item | Whole Book | Chapter | Pages |
|---|---|---|---|
| 1. Housing Estates: In County and Out | | II | 17–33 |
| 2. New Towns—Housing | | III | 34–47 |
| 3. Expanded Towns | | VI | 82–102 |
| 4. Urban Redevelopment | | VII | 103–121 |

*Text:* Rowes, Rosemary: *Housing Management*

| Item | Whole Book | Chapter | Pages |
|---|---|---|---|
| General Discussion | X | | |
| 1. Public and Private Housing | | II | 13–31 |

TOPIC: GROUPS

*Text:* Anderson, Niels: *The Urban Community*

| Item | Whole Book | Chapter | Pages |
|---|---|---|---|
| 1. Collective Community Behaviour | | IX | 207–232 |
| 2. Groups and Class under Urbanism | | X | 233–262 |
| 3. How Committees get Things Done | | XII | 295–320 |
| 4. Leisure, By-product of Urbanism | | XIV | 347–374 |

*Text:* Bracey, H. E.: *Neighbours on Housing Estates*

| Item | Whole Book | Chapter | Pages |
|---|---|---|---|
| 1. Partying | | VI | 93–109 |
| 2. Children and Teenagers | | IX | 126–145 |
| 3. Adult Social Organisation | | XI | 162–180 |

*Text:* Friedlander, Walter A.: *Concepts and Methods of Social Work*

| Item | Whole Book | Chapter | Pages |
|---|---|---|---|
| 1. Goals and Purpose of Social Group Work | | III | 116–130 |
| 2. Theory of Social Group Work Method | | III | 131–152 |
| 3. Principles of Social Case Work Practice | | III | 152–193 |

*Text:* Klein, Josephine: *Working with Groups*

| Item | Whole Book | Chapter | Pages |
|---|---|---|---|
| General Discussion | X | | |
| 1. What happens in Groups | | II | 14–30 |
| 2. Task-related Behaviour and Decision-making | | III | 30–40 |
| 3. Task-related Behaviour and Function of members | | IV | 41–52 |
| 4. The Psychological Significance of Self-expression and Group Membership | | V | 53–63 |
| 5. The Social Significance of Self-expression | | VI | 64–79 |
| 6. Structure, Function and Morale | | II | 103–118 |

*Text:* Knowles, Malcolm S.: *Informal Adult Education*

| *Item* | *Whole Book* | *Chapter* | *Pages* |
|---|---|---|---|
| 1. Understanding Human Nature: the Psychology of Adulthood | | II | 11–28 |
| 2. Group Dynamics and the Arts of Leadership | | IV | 55–83 |

*Text:* Mann, Peter H.: *An Approach to Urban Sociology*

| *Item* | *Whole Book* | *Chapter* | *Pages* |
|---|---|---|---|
| 1. Focus on the Neighbourhood | | VI | 149–182 |
| 2. Conclusions | | VIII | 214–221 |

*Text: Report: Training for Social Work, Third International Survey, U.N.*

| *Item* | *Whole Book* | *Chapter* | *Pages* |
|---|---|---|---|
| 1. The Content of Training for Social Work: Group relations, Group Work | | XI | 227–249 |

TOPIC: THE ROLE OF THE AGENCY AND THE WORKER

*Text:* Anderson, Niels: *The Urban Community*

| *Item* | *Whole Book* | *Chapter* | *Pages* |
|---|---|---|---|
| 1. Urbanism and the Family | | XI | 263–294 |
| 2. How Communities Get Things Done | | XII | 295–320 |
| 3. Welfare in the Modern Community | | XVI | 403–428 |

*Text:* Bracey, H. E.: *Neighbours on Housing Estates*

| *Item* | *Whole Book* | *Chapter* | *Pages* |
|---|---|---|---|
| 1. Children and Teenagers | | IX | 126–145 |
| 2. Adult Social Organisation | | XI | 163–176 |

*Text:* Friedlander, Walter H.: *Concepts and Methods of Social Work*

| *Item* | *Whole Book* | *Chapter* | *Pages* |
|---|---|---|---|
| General Discussion | X | | |
| 1. The Objectives of Social Work | | I | 7–9 |
| 2. Basis of Social Case Work | | II | 16–22 |
| 3. Basic Concepts Relevant to Case Work Practice | | II | 47–78 |
| 4. Principles of Case Work | | II | 79–100 |
| 5. Goals and Purposes of Social Group Work | | III | 116–130 |
| 6. Theory of Social Group Work Method | | III | 131–152 |
| 7. Principles of Social Group Work | | III | 153–193 |
| 8. Characteristics of Community Organisation Practice | | IV | 208–218 |
| 9. The Community Organisation Worker In Social Work | | IV | 228–252 |

*Text:* Jefferys, Margot: *An Anatomy of the Social Services*

| *Item* | *Whole Book* | *Chapter* | *Pages* |
|---|---|---|---|
| General Discussion | X | | |
| 1. The Social Welfare Services and Their Staff | | I | 22–39 |
| 2. Clients—and Client-Worker Relationships | | I | 39–40 |
| 3. The Paid Worker | | XVIII | 248–270 |
| 4. The Contributions of the Voluntary Worker to Social Welfare | | XIX | 271–298 |

231

*Text:* Klein, Josephine: *Working with Groups*

| Item | Whole Book | Chapter | Pages |
|------|:---:|:---:|:---:|
| General Discussion | X | | |
| 1. Groups in their Formal and Informal Environment | | VII | 80–90 |
| 2. Structure, Function and Morale | | IX | 103–118 |
| 3. Changing ideas in Theory and Practice | | X | 118–132 |

*Text:* Knowles, Malcom S.: *Informal Adult Education*

| Item | Whole Book | Chapter | Pages |
|------|:---:|:---:|:---:|
| General Discussion | X | | |
| 1. A Problem and a Challenge | | I | 3–10 |
| 2. Informal Courses | | V | 84–122 |
| 3. Clubs, Groups, Forums and Conferences | | VI | 123–139 |

*Text:* Marsh, David: *An Introduction to the Study of Social Administration*

| Item | Whole Book | Chapter | Pages |
|------|:---:|:---:|:---:|
| 1. Policy, Administration and Personnel | | XIII | 209–239 |

*Text:* Nicholson, J. H.: *New Communities in Britain*

| Item | Whole Book | Chapter | Pages |
|------|:---:|:---:|:---:|
| 1. Community and Leadership | | IX | 146–171 |

*Text:* Rowes, R. J.: *Housing Management*

| Item | Whole Book | Chapter | Pages |
|------|:---:|:---:|:---:|
| 1. Welfare Work in Housing Management | | VIII | 110–124 |

*Text:* Training for Social Work, Third International Survey, U.N.

| Item | Whole Book | Chapter | Pages |
|------|:---:|:---:|:---:|
| General Discussion | X | | |
| 1. The Nature of Social Work | | II | 34–57 |
| 2. The Field of Social Work | | III | 58–73 |
| 3. Community Development and Social Work | | IV | 74–104 |

*Text:* Report of Working Party on Social Workers

| Item | Whole Book | Chapter | Pages |
|------|:---:|:---:|:---:|
| General Discussion | X | | |
| 1. The Existing Staffing of the Services | | II | 319–407 |
| 2. Local Authority and Welfare Services | | II | 408–557 |
| 3. The Needs of those using the Services | | IV | 558–607 |
| 4. Social Work and Health and Welfare Services | | V | 608–640 |
| 5. The General Purpose Social Worker | | VI | 641–735 |

TOPIC: SKILLS AND TECHNIQUES
*Text:* Biddle, William and Loureide: *The Community Development Process*

| Item | Whole Book | Chapter | Pages |
|------|:---:|:---:|:---:|
| General Discussion | X | | |
| 1. Intention and Outcome | | IV | 58–75 |
| 2. The Basic Nucleus | | V | 88–109 |
| 3. Relation to Social Welfare Work | | XIII | 221–230 |
| 4. Relation to Education | | XV | 243–258 |
| 5. The Encourager | | XVI | 258–280 |

*Text:* Friedlander: *Concepts and Methods of Social Work*

| Item | Whole Book | Chapter | Pages |
|---|---|---|---|
| General Discussion | X | | |
| 1. Basis of Social Case work Practice | | II | 16–22 |
| 2. Exploring a Family, Adaptation to a Stressful Situation | | II | 23–46 |
| 3. Basic Concepts Relevant to Casework Practice | | II | 47–75 |
| 4. Helping a Family through a Stressful Situation | | II | 101–115 |
| 5. Theory of Social Group Work Practice | | III | 131–152 |
| 6. Principles of Social Group Work | | III | 153–193 |
| 7. The Group Worker as a Teacher and Supervisor | | III | 194–197 |
| 8. The Day of a Community Organiser in Social Work Practice | | IV | 201–208 |
| 9. Characteristics of Community Organisation | | IV | 209–218 |
| 10. Community Organisation Methods and Process | | V | 278–281 |

*Text:* Klein, Josephine: *Working with Groups*

| Item | Whole Book | Chapter | Pages |
|---|---|---|---|
| General Discussion | X | | |
| 1. Two-group Meetings | | XI | 133–172 |
| 2. Role Playing as an Aid to Clarification | | XII | 173–181 |
| 3. Role Playing as a Training Device | | XIII | 182–192 |
| 4. Role Playing and Group Self-evaluation | | XIV | 193–233 |

*Text:* Knowles, Malcolm S.: *Informal Adult Education*

| Item | Whole Book | Chapter | Pages |
|---|---|---|---|
| General Discussion | X | | |
| 1. How to Teach Adults | | III | 29–54 |
| 2. Group Dynamics and Leadership | | IV | 55–83 |
| 3. Informal Courses | | V | 84–122 |
| 4. Clubs, Groups, Forums and Conferences | | VI | 123–139 |
| 5. Planning and Organising | | VIII | 169–197 |
| 6. Planning Good Promotion | | IX | 198–210 |
| 7. Preparing and Promotional Material | | X | 209–236 |
| 8. Evaluating Process of Adult Education | | | 237–254 |

*Text: Training for Social Work, Third International Survey, U.N.*

| Item | Whole Book | Chapter | Pages |
|---|---|---|---|
| 1. Various Skills and Methods used in Community Development | | IV | 95–98 |
| 2. Social Work Method | | IX | 196–200 |
| 3. The Case work Method | | X | 213–224 |
| 4. Social Work Theory and Method—Courses | | XII | 276–284 |
| 5. The Content of Courses | | XIV | 321–346 |

TOPIC: SOCIAL PROBLEMS AND SOCIAL CHANGE
*Text:* Anderson, Neils: *The Urban Community*

| Item | Whole Book | Chapter | Pages |
|---|---|---|---|
| General Discussion | X | | |
| 1. Urbanism as a Way of Life | | I | 1–23 |
| 2. The Village Confronted with Urbanism | | IV | 78–105 |

| | | | |
|---|---|---|---|
| 3. The Moving About of Population | | VII | 155–181 |
| 4. Urbanism and its Incongruities | | VIII | 182–206 |
| 5. Urbanism and the Family | | XI | 263–294 |
| 6. Leisure: By-Product of Urbanism | | XIV | 347–374 |
| 7. Social Change and Conformity under Urbanism | | XVII | 429–456 |

*Text:* Biddle, William and Loureide: *The Community Development Process*

| Item | Whole Book | Chapter | Pages |
|---|---|---|---|
| General Discussion | X | | |
| 1. Introduction—a New Hope | | I | 1–4 |
| 2. The Larger Nucleus | | VII | 108–126 |
| 3. The Rural Scene | | X | 160–174 |
| 4. The Metropolitan Scene | | XI | 308–320 |

*Text:* Bracey, H. E.: *Neighbours on Housing Estates*

| Item | Whole Book | Chapter | Pages |
|---|---|---|---|
| General Discussion | X | | |
| 1. Families on the Move | | II | 16–27 |
| 2. Choice of Neighbourhood | | III | 28–54 |
| 3. Neighbourhood Appraisal after Occupation | | IV | 55–73 |

*Text:* Mann, Peter H.: *An Approach to Urban Sociology*

| Item | Whole Book | Chapter | Pages |
|---|---|---|---|
| General Discussion | X | | |
| 1. An Introduction to the Problem | | I | 1–4 |
| | | II | 4–27 |
| 2. Rural-urban A Quantitative Approach | | III | 28–67 |
| 3. Urban Society | | IV | 69–114 |
| 4. The Control of the Urban Environment | | V | 115–148 |

*Text:* Marsh, David: *An Introduction to the Study of Social Administration*

| Item | Whole Book | Chapter | Pages |
|---|---|---|---|
| General Discussion | X | | |
| 1. The Growth and Development of the Social Services and the Welfare State | | II | 18–44 |
| 2. Social Service for the Maintenance of Income | | III | 47–69 |
| 3. Social Policy and the Physical Environment | | VI | 104–119 |
| 4. Policy, Administration and Personnel | | XIII | 209–239 |

*Text:* Nicholson, J. H.: *New Towns in Britain*

| Item | Whole Book | Chapter | Pages |
|---|---|---|---|
| General Discussion | X | | |
| 1. The Scope of the Report | | I | 7–9 |
| 2. Recommendations | | X | 172–179 |

*Text:* Rowes, R.: *Housing Management*

| Item | Whole Book | Chapter | Pages |
|---|---|---|---|
| General Discussion | X | | |
| 1. Historical Background | | I | 1–12 |
| 2. Lettings | | VI | 80–94 |

| | | | |
|---|---|---|---|
| 3. | Rent Collection and Arrears | VII | 94–109 |
| 4. | Welfare Work in Housing Management | VIII | 110–124 |

*Text: Report of Working Party on Social Workers*

| *Item* | *Whole Book* | *Chapter* | *Pages* |
|---|---|---|---|
| General Discussion | X | | |
| 1. The services within Terms of Reference: Historical and General | | I | 186–318 |

# SELECTED BIBLIOGRAPHY

1. Anderson, F. and Burke, B. *Some Observations on a Non-directive Approach to Community Self Study* (International Review of Community Development, No. 4, 1959).
2. Anderson, Niels. *The Urban Community—A World Perspective* (International Library of Sociology and Social Reconstruction, Routledge and Kegan Paul, 1960).
3. Anderson, W. A. *Fringe Families and Their Social Participation* (Bulletin 909, Cornell Agricultural Experiment Station, Ithaca, New York, 1955).
4. Bailey, J. C., Seaman A. Knapp. Schoolmaster of American Agriculture, New York (Cambridge University Press, 1948).
5. Baker, W. B. *Community Development in Canada: A Memorandum on Potential Contributions to the Developing Countries* (Community Development No. 12, 1963).
6. Batten, T. R. *Training for Community Development; a Critical Study of Method* (London: Oxford University Press, 1962).
7. Beck, B. M. *School Social Work: an Instrument of Education* (Social Work, Vol. 4, No. 4, Oct. 1959).
8. Benne, K. D. *Ideas and Communities* (Community Development No. 5, 1960).
9. Bergwin, P. and Morris, D. *Group Process for Adult Education* (Community Services in Adult Education, Indiana, 1951).
10. Beveridge, Lord. *Voluntary Action: A Report on Methods of Social Advance* (London: George Allen and Unwin, 1948).
11. Biddle, W. W. and Biddle, L. J. *The Community Development Process: The Rediscovery of Local Initiative* (New York: Holt, Rinehart and Winston, Inc., 1965).
12. Biestek, F. P. and S. J. *The Casework Relationship* (Chicago, Illinois: Loyola University Press, 1957).
13. Bracey, H. E. *Neighbours on New Estates and Subdivisions in England and U.S.A.* (International Library of Sociology and Social Reconstruction, Routledge and Kegan Paul, 1964).
14. Brennan, T. *An Experiment in the Use of Adult Classes in Social Research* (Fundamental and Adult Education, Vol. V, No. 4, 1953).
15. Buell, B. *Community Planning for Health and Welfare Services* (Community Development No. 4, 1959).
16. —, and Associates, *Community Planning for Human Services* (New York: Columbia University Press, 1952).
17. Caring Community, The (Published by the National Council of Social Service; Ref. No. 709, London, 66).
18. Cartwright, D. and Zander, A. *Group Dynamics: Research and Theory* (White Plains, New York: Row, Paterson and Co., 1956).
19. Chatterjee, B. *Urban Community Development in India* (a paper submitted to the Seminar on Urbanization in India, University of California, Berkeley, 1960).
20. Clarke R. T. (ed.) *Working for Communities* (National Council of Social Service, 26 Bedford Square, London, W.C.1, 1963).
236

21. Clinard, M. B. *Evaluation and Research in Urban Community Development* (Community Development No. 12, 1963).

22. Club Management—a Handbook for Guidance of Club Officers; (National Council of Social Service, 26 Bedford Square, London, W.C.1, Ref. No. 361/1, 1956).

23. Cohen, J. *Social Work and the Culture of Poverty* (Social Work, Vol. 9, 1964).

24. Collison, P. *Social Research and Community Centre Leadership in Urban Areas* (Community Development No. 3, 1959).

25. —, and Cooney, E. *Leadership in Community Associations* (Community Development No. 6, 1960).

26. Communities and Social Change (National Council of Social Service, 26 Bedford Square, London, W.C.1, 1962).

27. Communities and Social Change, Introductory Survey (National Council of Social Service, 26 Bedford Square, London, W.C.1, 1963).

28. Communities and Social Change, Implements for Social Welfare (National Council of Social Service, 26 Bedford Square, London, W.C.1, 1962).

29. Community Development in Urban Areas (Department of Economic and Social Affairs, United Nations No. 61, IV. 6).

30. Community Development (H.M.S.O. 1958).

31. Community Organisation, 1959 (Papers Presented at the 86th Annual Forum of the National Conference of Social Welfare, Columbia University Press, New York, 1959).

32. Community Organisation, an Introduction (National Council of Social Service, 26 Bedford Square, London, W.C.1, 1962).

33. Community Organisation, Work in Progress (National Council of Social Service, 26 Bedford Square, London, W.C.1, 1963).

34. Councils and Their Houses (H.M.S.O. 1959).

35. Cousens, F. R. *Indigenous Leadership: A Study of Perception and Participation in Two Lower Class Neighbourhood Organisations* (Community Development Nos. 13 and 14, 1965).

36. Creative Living, II. The Community Association (National Council of Social Service, 26 Bedford Square, London, W.C.1, No. 674, 1964).

37. Cullingworth, J. B. *Housing Need and Planning Policy* (London: Routledge & Kegan Paul, 1960).

38. —. *The Swindon Social Survey: A Second Report on the Social Implications of Overspill* (The Sociological Review, Vol. 9, No. 2, New Series, University College of North Staffordshire, Keele, 1961).

39. David, P. *The Human Dimension in Public Housing* (Social Work, Vol, Vol. 9, No. 1, 1964).

40. Dictionary of Sociology (Ed. Fairchild) (Philosophical Library New York, 1944).

41. Dillick, Sydney. *Community Organisation for Neighbourhood Development—Past and Present* (New York: William Morrow, 1953).

42. Durham, A. *Some Principles of Community Development* (Community Development No. 11, 1963).

R

43. Du Sautoy, P. *The Organisation of a Community Development Programme* (London: Oxford University Press, 1962).
44. Eaton, J. W. *Community Development Ideologies* (Community Development No. 11, 1963).
45. Elliot, G. L. *How to help Groups make Decisions* (New York: Association Press, 1959).
46. Families Living at High Density (Ministry of Housing and Local Government, Sociological Research Section, Ref. 5955 H.M., London).
47. Festinger, L., Schachter, S., and Back, K. *Social Pressures in Informal Groups* (London, Tavistock Publications, 1959).
48. First Hundred Families, The (H.M.S.O., 1965).
49. Foster, G. M. *Traditional Cultures: and the Impact of Technological Change* (New York: Harper and Bros., 1962).
50. Friedlander, W. A. (ed.) *Concepts and Methods of Social Work* (Englewood Cliffs, New Jersey: Prentice Hall Inc., 1958).
51. Gardiner, R. K., Judd, H. O. *The Development of Social Administration, 3, Community Development and Fundamental Education* (London: Oxford University Press, 1959).
52. Hamilton, Gordon, *Theory and Practice of Social Casework* (New York: Columbia University Press, 1947).
53. Handasyde, E. *City Community* (National Council of Social Service, 26 Bedford Square, London, 1949).
54. Harper, E. B., Dunham, A. (ed.) *Community Organisation in Action* (New York: Association Press, 1963).
55. Heasman, K. *Christians and Social Work* (S.C.M. Press, 1965).
56. Heffernan, W. J. *Political Activity and Social Work Executives* (Social Work, Vol. 9, No. 2, 1964).
57. Heron, A. *Solving New Problems, Preparation for Retirement* (National Council of Social Service, 26 Bedford Square, London, W.C.1, 1961).
58. Hillman, Arthur. *Community Organisation and Planning* (New York: Macmillan Co., 1950).
59. Industrialisation and Social Work (A bibliography prepared by the United States Information Service, American Embassy, Bonn, 1956).
60. Industrialisation and Social Work—Some Aspects of the British Experience (British National Conference of Social Work, 1956).
61. Infield, H. *A Prototype of Sociological Experiment—The Modern Co-operative Community* (International Archives of Sociology of Co-operation, Vol. 1, No. 1, 1957).
62. —. *Observation on the Nature of Co-operative Theory* (International Archives of Sociology of Co-operation, No. 4, 1958).
63. International Exchange of Experience in Housing and Community Development—Outline of U.S. Experience (U.S. Housing and Home Agency, 1950).
64. Jacobs, J. *The Death and Life of Great American Cities* (London: Jonathan Cape, 1962).
65. Jeffreys, Margot. *An Anatomy of the Social Services* (London: Michael Joseph, 1965).

66. Jennings, H. *The Redevelopment of an Old Area in an English City* (Community Development No. 2, 1958).

67. Johnson, Arlien. *Community Organisations* (The Social Work Year Book 1945. New York: Russell Sage Foundation, 1956).

68. Kaufman, H. G. and Cole, L. W. *Sociological and Social Psychological Research for Community Development* (Community Development No. 4, 1959).

69. Klein, Josephine. Working with Groups (London: Hutchinson University Library, 1966).

70. Konopka, Gisela. Group Work in the Institution (New York: Whiteside Inc. and William Morrow, 1954).

71. Knowles, M. S., Overstreet, H. A. *Informal Adult Education* (New York: Association Press, 1951).

72. Kuenstler, P., Ramzi, M. T., Tinbergen, J. *World, Nations and Groups in Development* (The Hague: Monton and Co., 1963).

73. Lapiere, R. T. *A Theory of Social Control* (New York: McGraw-Hill, 1954).

74. Lassell, Margaret. *Wellington Road* (London: Routledge and Kegan Paul, 1962).

75. Lippitt, R. *Some Recent Advances in Understanding Group Life* (Fundamental and Adult Education, Vol. VIII, No. 4, 1956).

76. —. *Training in Community Relations* (New York: Harper and Bros., 1959).

77. Lomas, G. M. (ed.) *Social Aspects of Urban Redevelopment* (National Council of Social Service, London, Ref. No. 714).

78. Lowry, R. P. *The Myth and Reality of Grass-Roots Democracy* (Community Development No. 11, 1963).

79. Luchterhand, E. *Factory and Community: Three Case Studies* (Duke of Edinburgh Study Conference IV, 1956).

80. Lyfield, W. G., and Schmidt, W. H. *Trends in Community Development: Some Results of a Survey* (Community Development No. 4, 1959).

81. Living in Council Houses—Report of a Conference. (The Society of Housing Managers, 1960).

82. McDowell, J. *Community Centers in an Industrialized Society* (Community Development No. 1, 1958).

83. Madge, Charles. *Society in the Mind: Elements of Social Eidos* (London: Faber and Faber, 1964).

84. Mairet, P. *Pioneer of Sociology* (The Life and Letters of Patrick Geddes), (London: Lund Humphries, 1957).

85. Mann, Peter H. *An Approach to Urban Sociology* (International Library of Sociology and Social Reconstruction, Routledge and Kegan Paul, 1965).

86. Marsh, David G. *An Introduction to the Study of Social Administration* (Routledge and Kegan Paul, 1965).

87. Matthews, M. S. *Guide to Community Action: A Sourcebook for Citizen Volunteers* (New York: Harper and Bros., 1954).

88. Mayo, Elton, *The Social Problems of an Industrial Civilization* (Boston: Harvard University, 1945).

89. Mead, Margaret. *Cultural Patterns and Technical Change* (Paris: U.N.E.S.C.O., 1954).

90. Meier, R. L. *Science and Economic Development: New Patterns of Living* (New York: Massachusetts Institute of Technology Press, John Wiley and Sons, Inc., 1956). (London: Chapman and Hall).

91. Meister, A. (ed.) *Community Development, Training Local Leaders, No. 3.* (International Federation of Settlements and Neighbourhood Centres, 1959).

92. *Field Problems in Community Development, No. 12* (International Review of Community Development, 1963).

93. Mezirow, J. D. *Community Development as an Educational Process* (Community Development, No. 5, 1960).

94. Mial, C. and Mial, D. *Community Development, U.S.A.* (Community Development No. 5, 1960).

95. Mobilization for Youth, Master Annotated Bibliography of the Papers of (Mobilization for Youth Inc., New York; 9, 1965).

96. Molloy, P. N. *Training Local Leaders in Community Associations* (Community Development No. 3, 1959).

97. Morgan, Arthur E. *The Community of the Future and the Future of Community* (Community Services Inc., Yellow Springs, Ohio; 1957).

98. Morris, Cherry (ed.) *Social Case-Work* (London: Faber and Faber, 1955).

99. Morris, R. N. and Mogey, John. *The Sociology of Housing: Studies at Barinsfield* (International Library of Sociology and Social Reconstruction, Routledge and Kegan Paul, 1965).

100. Mumford, Lewis. *The City in History* (London: Secker and Warburg, 1961).

101. Murdock, G. P. *Social Structure* (New York: Macmillan Co., 1949).

102. Murray, C. E., Bowens, M. G., Hogrefe, R. (ed.) *Group Work in Community Life* (New York: Association Press, 1954).

103. Neighbourhood and Community (Liverpool University Press, 1954).

104. Nicholson, J. H. *New Communities in Britain, Achievements and Problems* (National Council of Social Service, 26 Bedford Square, London, W.C.1. Ref. 586, 1961).

105. Nisbet, R. A. *Moral Values and Community* (Community Development No. 5, 1960).

106. —. *The Quest for Community* (New York: Oxford University Press, 1953).

107. Ottaway, A. K. C. *Education and Society: An Introduction to the Sociology of Education* (International Library of Sociology and Social Reconstruction, Routledge and Kegan Paul, 1962).

108. Ponsiden, J. A. *Community Development as a Process* (Community Development No. 6, 1960).

109. —, J. A. (ed.) *Social Welfare Policy: Contributions to Methodology* (The Hague: Monton and Co., 1963).

110. Rein, M. *Organisation for Social Change* (Social Work, Vol. 9, No. 2, 1964).

111. Responsibility in the Welfare State
(The Birmingham Council of Christian Churches, 1961).
112. Riesman, D. *Flight and Search in the New Suburbs* (Community Development No. 4, 1959).
113. Rogers, M. L. *Autonomous Groups and Community Development in the U.S.A.* (Community Development No. 4, 1959).
114. Ross, M. G. *Case Histories in Community Organization* (New York: Harper and Bros., 1958).
115. —. *Community Organization: Theory and Principles* (New York: Harper and Bros., 1955).
116. —. *Community Participation* (Community Development No. 5, 1960).
117. Rothman, J. *An Analysis of Goals and Roles in Community Organization Practice* (Social Work, Vol. 9, No. 2, April, 1964).
118. Rowies, R. J., Wrigley, J. (ed.) *Housing Management* (London: Isaac Pitman & Sons, 1959).
119. Sainsbury, E. E. (ed.) *Field Work in Social Administration Courses* (National Institute of Social Work Training, Ref. 719, 1966).
120. Sanderson, D. and Polson, R. *Rural Community Organisation* (New York: John Wiley and Sons, 1939; London: Chapman & Hall).
121. Schweinitz, E. de, and Schweinitz, K. de. *Interviewing in Social Services, II, Human Relations in the Social Services* (London: National Council of Social Service, No. 636, September, 1962).
122. Self Help in Social Welfare (Proceedings of the 7th International Conference of Social Work, The South-East Asia Regional Office, International Conference of Social Work, Bombay, India, 1955).
123. Serra, B. M. *The Integration of Social Research and Field Action in a Programme of Community Education* (U.N.E.S.C.O. Fundamental and Adult Education, Vol. III, No. 4, October, 1956).
124. Shamin, I. *The Role of Lay Leaders in Community Development Work* (Community Development No. 3, 1959).
125. Sherif, Muzafer. *An Outline of Social Psychology* (New York: Harper and Bros., 1948).
126. Simon, H. A. *Administrative Behaviour* (New York: Macmillan Co., 1953).
127. Syhne, W. Ann. *Evaluation of Results in Social Work* (Social Work, Vol. 8, No. 4, October, 1963).
128. Slamson, S. R. *Creative Group Education* (Association Press, 1945).
129. Slum Clearance Urban Redevelopment and Low Rent Housing (The relationship between). (U.S. Housing and Home Finance Agency, Washington, 1950).
130. Social Research and Community Development in European Problem Areas—Report of European Seminar on (Palermo, Sicily, 1958. Ref. U.N./TAA/SEM/1958/REP2 REVI Geneva, 1958).
131. Social Workers in the Local Authority, Health and Welfare Services, Report of the Working Party on (H.M.S.O., 1959).
132. Spencer, J. *Stress and Release in an Urban Estate: A Study of Action Research* (London: Tavistock Publications, 1964).

133. Spicer, Edward H. *Human Problems in Technological Change—A Casebook* (New York: Russell Sage Foundation, 1952).
134. Sprott, W. J. H. *Sociology* (London: Hutchinson University Library, 1959).
135. Smith, M. A. *The Social Workers—'Work in Community'* (B.B.C., 1965).
136. *Ten Years of Community Development in London* (Community Development No. 6, 1960).
137. Solomon, D. *An Approach to Training for Community Development* (Community Development No. 3, 1959).
138. Taylor, C. C. *A Critical Analysis of India's Development Programme* (The Projects Administration, Government of India, Ref. 1/1 CPA/56, Delhi).
139. —, and Ensminger, D. *Role and Status Relationships in Program Administration* (Community Development No. 12, 1963).
140. Terrisse, A. *Open Forum: The Human Aspect of Fundamental Education* (Fundamental and Adult Education, Vol. V, No. 4, October 53, U.N.E.S.C.O).
141. Tonnies, Ferdinand. *Community and Association* (Routledge and Kegan Paul, 1955).
142. Torrance and Mason. *The Indigenous Leader in Changing Attitudes and Behaviour* (International Journal of Sociometry, Beacon House Inc., Vol. 1, No. 1, 1956).
143. Training for Social Work: An International Survey (Department of Social Affairs, No. 1950, IV, 11. Lake Success, N.Y., 1950).
144. Training for Social Work: Third International Survey (Department of Economic and Social Affairs, Sales No. 59, IV, U.N., N.Y., 1958).
145. Training for Social Work: Fourth International Survey (Department of Economic and Social Affairs, Sales No. 65, IV 3, U.N., New York).
146. Trecker, H. B. *Group Process in Administration* (New York: Woman's Press, 1950).
147. —, (ed.) *Group Work Foundations and Frontiers* (New York: William Morrow & Co., 1955).
148. —. *New Understandings of Administration* (New York: Association Press, 1961).
149. —. *Social Group Work Principles and Practice* (New York: Whiteside Inc., 1948).
150. Troubled Metropolis, The (Report of the Fifth Annual Winter Weekend Conference, The Canadian Institute of Public Affairs, Toronto, 1959).
151. Vapnarsky, C. A. *An Approach to the Sociology of Housing* (Community Development Nos. 13 and 14, 1965).
152. Varon, E. *Communication: Client, Community and Agency* (Social Work, Vol. 9, No. 2, 1964).
153. Vercker, C. and Mays, J. B. *Urban Redevelopment and Social Change* (Liverpool University Press, 1961).
154. Wade, Alan D. *Social Work and Political Action* (Social Work, Vol. 8, No. 4, 1963).

155. Warren, R. L. *Social Research and Community Policy* (Community Development No. 4, 1959).
156. Wickwar, Hardy and Margaret. *The Social Services: An Historical Survey* (London: The Bodley Head, 1949).
157. Wilson, Roger. *Difficult Housing Estates* (Tavistock Publications, 1963).
158. Wirth, Louis. *Community Life and Social Policy* (The University of Chicago Press, 1956).
159. Woodroofe, K. *From Charity to Social Work: In England and the United States* (London: Routledge and Kegan Paul Ltd., 1962).
160. Worthington, G. *Older Persons as Community Service Volunteers* (Social Work, Vol. 8, No. 4, 63).
161. Zealey, Ph. *Training Local Leaders for Community Development* (Community Development No. 3, 1959).

# INDEX

Abbey Community Centre,
  Westminster, x, 32
Accounts, keeping of, 22
Adult education, social work on,
  159–60
Annual general meetings, 54, 69:
  planning and organisation, 29
Association of London Housing
  Estates, xiii, 8–9, 26–7, 32–4,
  54, 57, 70, 92, 117, 119–21,
  139, 142, 153, 154; Annual
  Report 1966/67, 197–206;
  club-room courses, 34–8;
  conference on work with old
  people, 38–44; division of
  work, 33; Executive
  Committee and sub-
  committees, 33, 34; groups in
  affiliation, 4; publications, 5;
  services, 4–5; voluntary funds,
  xiii
Autonomous groups in wider
  community, 152–3; 'on
  Estate' and 'off Estate'
  groups, 153, 157–8
Autonomy, 1, 16–17, 174;
  'unattached' groups, 17

Beatrice Webb House, conference
  at, 27–9
Bristol Social Project, 162
British Red Cross, xii

Case conference and training
  record, illustration of, 124–6
Case studies and illustrations:
  communication, 98–101;
  community process, 179–82;
  encouraging co-operation,
  85–9; establishing priorities,
  74–7; evaluation, 106–9;
  examples of helping a group,
  71–89; finding and using
  resources, 83–5; identifying
  social welfare need, 71–4;
  interpretation, 101–4;
  recording, 117–26;

representative community
  group, 53–71; self-evaluation,
  80–3; working out a crisis,
  77–80
Change of environment, 13
Club-rooms, x, xi, 2, 131
Club-room courses, 34–8;
  committee procedure and
  officers' duties, 35–8; follow-
  up, 38; recruitment, 34–5;
  typical programme, 35
Committees, 2–3, 17–25, 54, 57,
  69; and public relations, 23;
  communication within, 98–9;
  criticism of, 17–18; division
  of labour, 23–4;
  encouragement for, 96;
  handling money, 22; learning
  procedure, 20, 35–8;
  operation of, 18; problems
  for autonomous groups, 21;
  responsibilities, 21;
  sub-committee problems,
  126–8; use of authority, 20
Communication, 98–101, 176;
  between association and
  statutory body, 99–101; with
  association, 99; within
  committee, 98–9
Community: definitions of, 9–10,
  215–16; essentials of, 217–18;
  nature of, 215
Community Associations, ix–xii,
  1, 5, 7–8, 14
Community Centres, x
Community development: and
  other methods of social work,
  178–82; as method of social
  work, 168–83; categories of
  community process, 178–9;
  comparison with community
  organisation, 182–3;
  continuing need for work,
  184–6; definitions of, 11–12,
  169; examples of community
  process, 179–82; helping
  process, 170–3; various uses

Community development—*cont.*
of phrase, 168–9; workers'
role, 173–6, 183; working
description, 176–8
Community groups, *see* Groups
Community organisation and
community development,
182–3; approach and method,
183; nature of the concern,
182; objectives of the two
methods, 182–3; worker's
role, 183
Community participation,
training for, 158–60
Comparative studies, 157–60:
adult education, 159–60;
community groups not on
estates, 157–8; New Towns,
160; overseas experience,
160
Community work course,
suggested material for
'community behaviour'
content, 214–26
Conditions of field-work practice,
129–50: difficulties of
sponsoring agencies, 145–9;
difficulties of workers, 143–5;
factors affecting development,
129–35; stages of
development, 135–43; values
and standards, 149–50
Conferences, 27–9, 113, 207–13:
on work with old people,
38–44
Constitutions for community
groups, 2, 54, 69: model, 25,
187–96
Consultative service, need for, 3–4
Continuity record, illustration of,
122–4
Co-operation, encouragement of,
85–9
Crisis within a community group,
77–80

Definitions, 9–12
Deteriorating neighbourhoods,
work in, 44–8

Development of groups, 129–43:
age of estate, 130; amenities,
130–1; club-rooms, 131;
factors affecting, 129–35;
leadership, 132–4; location of
estate, 129–30; meeting
places, 131; size of estate,
130; social origins and
attitudes of groups, 131–2;
stages of development,
135–43; wider context, 134–5
Development of service, 7–9,
13–52: beginnings of field-
work, 13–16; beginnings of
self-service, 32–44;
deteriorating neighbourhoods,
44–8; immigrant groups,
48–52; inter-group work,
26–32; needs of groups,
16–20; phases, 7–9; problems
and difficulties of groups,
20–5; settling-in problems,
13–14
Difficulties of field-workers, 143–5:
acceptance, 143–4; doing too
much, 143; rejection, 144–5
Difficulties of sponsoring agencies,
145–9: administration, 146–7;
interpretation, 147–9;
responsibility without control,
149
Downham estate, ix

Education Act 1944, x
Estates: age, 130; amenities,
130–1; different interest
groups, 153–4; location,
129–30; size, 130
Evaluation, 106–11, 113, 172, 176:
field-worker's role, 110–11;
illustrations, 106–9;
objectives, 109–10; process,
110

Field-work, 4–5: basic policy,
15–16; beginning, 13–16; case
studies, 53–89; conditions of
practice, 129–50; content of
situation, 11; elements, 10–11;

examples of helping a group, 71–89; examples of practice, 53–89; fundamentals of process, 98–111; process in community development, 10–12; role of workers, 6, 90–128, 136–9, 173–6, 183; skills and techniques, 90–128, 176; workers' difficulties, 143–5

Financial problems of groups, 21–2: accounting for money spent, 22; use of funds, 22

Finsbury, community group in, x

Flats, 4: living in, xii; settling into, 13

Formation of groups, 135–7

Focus, selection of, 93–5

Fundamentals of field-work process, 98–111: communication, 98–101; evaluation, 106–11; interpretation, 101–6

Greater London Council, Housing Committee, xiii

Groups, 1–4: autonomy, 1, 16–17, 174; committees, 2–3, 17–25, 54, 57, 69; constitution, 2, 25, 54, 69, 187–96; definition of, 10; development of, 129–43; difficulties and problems, 3, 20–5; formation, 135–7; importance of, 184; need for consultative service, 3–4; needs of, 3–4, 16–20; numbers, 4; self-service by, 32–44; size 4; social origins and attitudes, 131–2

Harold Hill estate, ix

Helping process, 170–3: observation and enquiry, 170–1; formulation of problem, 171; suggestions for modification, 171–2; evaluation, 172; re-planning, 172–3

Housing Act 1936, x

Identity: 'unattached' autonomous groups, 17; work of committees, 17–19

Immigrant groups, work with, 48–52: advisers from West Indies, 49, 52; autonomous groups, 50–1; indigenous leaders, 51; racial tension, 49; social integration, 51; Standing Conference of West Indian Leaders, 50; West Indian groups, 44, 45, 48–50; West Indian leadership, 49–50

Immigration Act, 52

Indigenous leaders, 51, 132–3, 158: working outside immediate locality, 154–5

Individuality, 19

Information giving, 90–1, 176

Inner London Education Authority, xiii

In-service training, 155, 167, 168

Integration with wider community, 135, 139–43: phases of working service, 139–43; 'observation', 139–40; preliminary contact, 140; initial advice, 141; intensive service, 141–2; specialised service, 142; gradual withdrawal, 142–3

Inter-group work, 26–32: inter-estate discussions, 29–31; week-end conferences, 27–9

Interpretation, 101–6, 147–9, 176: content, 104–5; definition, 101; differences in objectives and frames of reference, 106; events and situations, 104; illustrations, 101–4; levels, 105; processes and procedures, 104; recurring factors, 106; social attitudes, 105

Leadership, 132–4: indirect leaders, 134; indigenous leaders, 132–3; sociopathic leaders, 133–4

Lewisham, community group, x

London Council of Social Service, x–xiii, 5, 8–9, 14, 26–7, 32, 33, 44, 146, 163: Community Centres (now Community Development) Department, ix, xiii, 32, 44; voluntary funds, xiii; work in deteriorating neighbourhood, 44–8; work with immigrant groups, 48–52

London County Council (L.C.C.), ix–x, xii–xiii, 33; grants from, ix, x, xiii

Mental health, community care for, 156–7: team work, 156

Ministry of Education, and community centres, x

Narrative recording, 115: analysis, 120; check sheet, 118–19; comments, 120–2; observation and awareness, 121–2; plans, 121; questions, 121; single-visit illustration, 117–22; summary sheet, 119–20

National Federation of Community Associations, ix, 33

Needs of groups, 3–4, 16–20: autonomy, 1, 16–17; identity, 17–19; individuality, 19; need for acceptance and support, 20

New Towns, 160

North Kensington, community centre in, x

Old people, work with, 28–9, 38–44: co-operation with Local Authority workers, 39–41; failure to complete weekly visiting schedule, 39–41; lone workers, 39, 41–3; reasons for work, 43; resentment of intrusion, 39–40; rise and fall of programmes, 39, 42

Overseas work, study of, 160

Oxford House, 39

Oxhey estate, ix

'Paisley Common': study of representative community group, 53–71; and wider community, 70; chronological account of field-work, 58–69; constitution and committees, 54, 57, 69; contacts with other bodies, 54, 55, 70; development, 70; finance, 54; leadership, 69; parking problem, 56–7; pattern of participation, 56, 69; personalities, 55–6; problems, 56–8, 70; programme of social activities, 54–8, 69; reason for existence, 70–1; standard of behaviour, 57; tenants' associations, 53–8; youth work, 57

Physical Training and Recreation Act 1937, x

Placement opportunities, 167, 168

Priorities, establishment of, 74–7

Problem families, services to, 151–2

Problems and difficulties of groups, 3, 20–5: channels of communication, 23; committee work, 20–1; division of labour, 23–4; establishment of procedures, 25; finance, 21–2; involving residents, 24–5; public relations, 23

Professional training, 161–8

Programmes, development of, 135, 137–8, 154

Public relations, 23

Recording, 111–28, 176: aid to efficiency, 113; anecdotal, 115; awareness, 111–13, 121–2; basis of evaluation, 113; basis for planning, 113; building professional body of knowledge, 114; case

conference and training record, 124–6; continuity, 114; continuity record, 122–4; controlled comment, 114; different kinds, 114–15; episodic, 115; essay, 115; focus for conferences, 113; illustrations, 117–26; imaginative planning, 114; influence on policy, 113; meaningful questioning, 114; narrative, 115, 117–22; objectivity, 114; observation, 111–12, 121–2; principles, 114; public interpretation, 114; purpose, 111–13; single-visit, 117–22; suggested system, 116; usefulness to worker and agency, 115
Rehousing problems, 13–14, 129–30
Residents' meetings, 18
Resources: available, 92; finding and using, 83–5

St. Helier estate, ix
St. Paul's Cray estate, ix
Self-evaluation, 80–3
Services to groups, 4–7: approach and method, 7; contact with groups, 5; development of, 7–9; role of agency, 6–7; role of worker, 4–6; summary, 5
Settling-in problems, 13–14
Skills and techniques of field-workers, 90–128, 176: acting as go-between, 92–5; encouragement and support, 95–8; fundamentals of field-work process, 98–111; giving information, 90–1; level of intellectual and emotional awareness, 92; passing on skills, 91–2; recording, 111–28; resources available, 92; role of the worker, 90–8; selection of forms, 93–5

'Social clubs', 1, 14–15
Social origins and attitudes of groups, 131–2
Social welfare need, identification of, 71–4
Sociopathic leaders, 133–4
Sources of information for report, 12
Stages of group development, 135–43: starting point, 135; exploration, 135, 136; formation, 135–7; development of programmes, 135, 137–8; established associations, 135, 138–9; integration with wider community, 135, 139–43; worker's role, 136–9
Standing Conference of Housing Estate Community Groups, xii, 32
Sub-committees: and voluntary agencies, 126–8; problems of, 128
Supervision in community work, 167–8

Tenants' associations, x–xii, 1, 14, 53–8
Tenants' club-rooms or common rooms, x, xi, 131: management and finances, xi, 2
Theoretical study, 160–1
Townswomen's Guild, xii
Training, 161–8: case-work orientation, 161–2; current attitudes, 161–3; for community participation, 158; in-service training, 155, 167, 168; new perspectives, 161–3; placement opportunities, 167, 168; specimen suggested course, 164–7; statutory and voluntary bodies' staff and, 155; supervision, 167–8; voluntary youth leaders, 30

Values and standards, 149–50

Visiting, 91: and recording, 114–26

Voluntary bodies, 126–8: and sub-committees, 126–7

Wansfell Adult Education College, conferences at, xii, 27, 29, 32

Week-end conferences, 27–9, 207–13

West Indian groups and leadership, 44, 45, 48–51

Westminster: Abbey Community Centre, x; community group, x

Wider community: autonomous groups in, 152–3; integration with, 139–43; relations with, 155

Worker's role in community development, 173–6: avoidance of exploitation, 175–6; characteristic of role, 174; confidentiality, 175; establishment of role, 173; methods of participation, 174–6; non-judgmental behaviour, 175–6; promoting participation and agreement, 174; responsibilities, 175–6; skills and techniques, 176; strengthening autonomy, 174

Youth work on estates, 27–32, 57: difficulties, 28–31; failures, 31–2; nature and content, 28; training of voluntary leaders, 30; voluntary leaders from outside, 30–1

Y.W.C.A., 30